THEY WORE

garnet & black

THEY WORE

garnet &
black

Inside Carolina's Quest for Gridiron Glory

by Don Barton

Spur Publishers Columbia, South Carolina

A publication of Spur Publishers,
Box 8055, Columbia, S.C. 29202

ISBN 0-9615503-0-9
Cover and book design by Lewis Brierley

THEY WORE

garnet & black

Carolina's Head Football Coaches –

Billy Laval
1928-34

Don McCallister
1935-37

Rex Enright
1938-42, 1946-55

Warren Giese
1956-60

Marvin Bass
1961-65

Paul Dietzel
1966-74

1928 to 1984

J. P. Moran
1943

William (Doc) Newton
1944

Johnnie McMillan
1945

Jim Carlen
1975-81

Richard Bell
1982

Joe Morrison
1983-

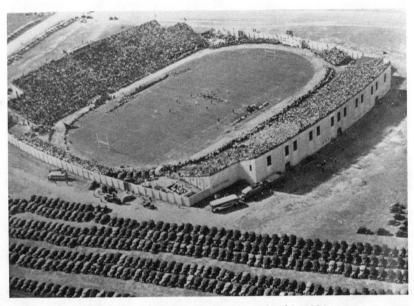

The original Carolina Stadium, completed in 1934.

Williams-Brice Stadium was enlarged to seat over 74,000 in 1982.

Preface

"If we sometime feel discouraged at the prospect for successful athletics in the College, yet must we plod forward, awaiting the time when the tide of our fortunes comes to the flood. Patience, dear cynic, patience."

The above paragraph appeared in the "Athletics" section of the 1898 University of South Carolina yearbook, *The Garnet and Black*. It might have been just as appropriate in many other Carolina annuals through the decades that followed. Particularly in the decades of the 1930's through the 1970's, Carolina's efforts toward building a football program of national prominence have ranged from ambitious to fanatical. Even as far back as 1915, overzealous alumni took it upon themselves to recruit football players, notably from Pennsylvania, without bothering with such details as eligibility or enrollment in school.

Still, hope has sprung eternal in the breasts of true Gamecock followers, who have never ceased to believe that better days are in the offing. An alumnus once quipped, "I would be ten years older, but my parents were Carolina fans, and they were always saying, 'Wait'll next year!'"

There were always enough bright spots through the years to encourage the faithful, most of them occurring from the 1930's forward. Prior to that, the majority of Gamecock football victories came at the expense of other South Carolina schools, including Newberry, Erskine, Wofford, Presbyterian, and Charleston. The Gamecocks were below the break-even mark against arch rival Clemson, 9-18-1, and even smaller Furman, 9-10-0.

Through 1930, the Gamecocks were 2-8-0 against Georgia, 2-13-3 against North Carolina, and 1-4-0 in games with Georgia Tech.

In the 33 seasons leading up to 1930, Carolina's football teams had labored under 15 different head coaches, with Sol Metzger, who served the five years from 1920 throught 1924, holding the longevity record. Metzger's 26 wins, 18 losses, and two ties gave him one of the school's better records, percentagewise, but 12 of those victories were over members of what was known as the South Carolina "Little Four," composed of Erskine, Newberry, Presbyterian, and Wofford.

Branch Bocock succeeded Metzger in 1925, coming out of his career as a fullback at Georgetown University with the distinction of being the only Protestant to have captained the team at that school. Bocock had two winning seasons, 7-3-0 and 6-4-0, including eight wins over intra-state opponents, but he resigned in the spring of 1927, and an aspiring lawyer, Harry Lightsey, agreed to take the job for one year. Lightsey had turned out great teams at Columbia High School, but he had no intentions of making coaching his career.

Meanwhile, Carolina trustees couldn't help but notice that Furman had beaten the Gamecocks five straight times, 1923 through 1927, outscoring them 78 to 10 in the process. A young coach named Billy Laval, who hadn't played football as a student at Furman, was the mastermind behind the success of the Purple Hurricane, as the team was known.

Following the philosophy, "If you can't beat 'em, join 'em," Carolina hired Laval, and he came to Columbia amidst great fanfare and optimism. When Laval's Gamecocks won their first five games of 1928, including a 6-0 win over a powerful University of Chicago team, Carolina alumni were convinced that "next year" was here.

A devastating 32-0 loss to Clemson brought them back down to earth in a hurry, and a scoreless tie with The Citadel in the next game did nothing to re-kindle the fire.

Laval established a new longevity record of seven years for Carolina football coaches and had 39 victories, 26 defeats, and two ties to show for it. The Gamecocks upgraded their schedules during this era, playing Duke, Virginia, Maryland, Georgia Tech, Louisiana State, Auburn, Villanova, Temple, Tennessee, and Florida.

In spite of reaching what appeared to be a new plateau, the University trustees didn't feel that Laval was the answer, replacing him in 1935 with Don McCallister, who had produced winning high school teams in Toledo, Ohio.

Three losing seasons later McCallister was out, and Rex Enright began an 18-year tenure, including three years in the Navy, that ended with his giving up coaching to become full-time athletic director after the 1955 season. Enright upgraded the schedule still further and was the architect of several of the biggest wins in Carolina's history. His 1953 team, which ended the season at 7-3-0, was the first in the school's history to be listed in the national rankings by the Associated Press.

Enright's overall record was 64-69-7, but his eight wins, against six losses in the Big Thursday series with Clemson earned him a special place in the hearts of Gamecock fans.

When Enright moved up, Warren Giese, an assistant to Jim Tatum at Maryland, began a five-year tenure. In the second game of his first season, 1956, Giese brought Carolina its first victory over Duke since 1931, so the Board of Trustees placed him on academic status, tantamount to a lifetime contract.

Giese's record, 28-21-1, was creditable, but his fifth season at Carolina produced only three wins; he had dropped four of five games to Clemson; and it was ruled that his program was heading downhill.

With one swift stroke, the Board moved Giese up to athletic director and brought one of his former assistants, Marvin Bass, back from the Georgia Tech staff to become head man in Columbia.

In his five years, Bass never had a winner, finishing 17-29-4, but his last Carolina season, 1965, produced a tie with Duke for the Atlantic Coast Conference title. He also had a 3-2 mark against Clemson, but his stint at USC ended during 1966 spring practice, when he accepted the head coaching position with Montreal of the new Continental League.

Never have Carolina hopes soared as high as they did following the announcement that Paul Dietzel, Army coach who had produced a national championship team at Louisiana State in 1958, would be the new head coach here. Dietzel lasted for nine seasons, compiling a 42-53-1 record, but he did win the Atlantic Coast Conference title in 1969, taking Carolina to its first bowl game since the inaugural Gator Bowl (after the 1945 season). The Gamecocks appeared in the Peach Bowl against West Virginia, coached by Dietzel's ultimate successor, Jim Carlen.

A new criterion for a successful season was now a bowl invitation, as the number of post-season contests swelled. Surely, Carolina teams in previous years, particularly 1953, 1956, and 1958, would have gone to bowls under circumstances that existed in the 1980's.

In the second game of 1974, Dietzel announced his resignation from the head coaching position, to be effective at the end of the season. He had lifted the program to a new level, particularly in leading the building of facilities necessary to build a winning football team. Under his guidance athletic dormitories and dining facilities were built (The Roost), and the football stadium was enlarged to seat around 56,000.

Carlen, who had been successful at West Virginia and Texas Tech, followed Dietzel to the coach's chair and was hailed as the "real thing," when his first Carolina team won seven games, including a 56-20 rout of Clemson, and went to the Tangerine Bowl (losing to Miami, O.). Carlen's 1979 squad gave the school its first eight-win season in modern times and went to the Hall of Fame Bowl. Gamecock fever hit a new high in 1980 when Carlen's prize recruit, running back George Rogers, won the Heisman Trophy, and the team went to the Gator Bowl (losing to Pittsburgh).

Such success, which brought record crowds to Williams-Brice Stadium, would seem to have solidified Carlen's position at Carolina, but, following a 6-6 season in 1981, he was suddenly fired.

The first move at replacing Carlen was the hiring of Bob Marcum, who had held the same position at Kansas, as athletic director. His first assignment was to find a new head football coach, and he found him, Richard Bell, on the staff that Carlen had left behind.

Despite facing a made-to-order bowl schedule, Bell's first (and only) Gamecock team could manage only four wins, along with committing the unforgivable sin of losing to Furman. When he refused to follow Marcum's orders to fire four assistant coaches, Bell was dismissed and, after a law suit, was paid for the four remaining years on his contract.

Marcum's choice to follow Bell was Joe Morrison, ex-New York Giants star who had built fine teams at Tennessee-Chattanooga and the University of New Mexico. Morrison's 1983 team had a losing season but created fan enthusiasm and optimism with their style of play. In 1984 he catapulted USC fans up to Cloud Nine by winning ten of eleven regular-season games and taking the team to the Gator Bowl (losing to Oklahoma State). The final rankings of 11th by Associated Press and 13th by United Press International were the best ever for Carolina.

Carolina fans called Morrison's accomplishments "Black Magic," based on the all-black attire worn by the Gamecock coach on the sidelines. Another product of the successful year was the term "Fire Ants," applied to the defensive unit, because of the manner in which they swarmed around the ball. Such was the excitement over this apex in Carolina football that a special book, devoted entirely to the 1984 season, was written by Tom Price, USC Sports Information Director, and entitled, "The '84 Gamecocks: Fire Ants and Black Magic."

Typically, Carolina fans accepted the 1984 record as something that would become the norm for teams of the future, as trustees began to discuss further enlargement of Williams-Brice Stadium, which had been expanded to accommodate around 74,000 in 1982. Gamecock supporters filled the stadium for most of the home games in 1984, with 67,200 that witnessed the Kansas State game representing the season's smallest turnout.

Even before the magic year of '84, Carolina fans had long been established as among the most loyal in the nation. For years bowl committees had searched hard for excuses to invite the Gamecocks, because of their large following.

Nowhere was this support more evident than in contributions to the Gamecock Club, the athletic booster organization, which began its real growth during the Dietzel years. After Dietzel's first year the club raised $218,127, and the sum reached $757,144 in his last season as head coach, 1974.

Carlen's first year saw the amount reach $801,586, and six years later, following three bowl teams and a Heisman Trophy winner, Gamecock Club members gave $1,928,127. Contributions increased to $2,362,580 in Bell's only year, to $2,742,670 in the highly-successful football year of 1984, and to over $4 million, as the 1985 season neared.

Along with booming attendance, this placed Carolina among the elite nationally, as far as athletic revenues go.

This book traces Carolina's efforts toward football respectability, from the early 1930's through 1984, as seen through the eyes of various players. Although the subjects were outstanding players in their own right, they were not chosen necessarily as *THE BEST*. They are representative of different teams and serve as excellent spokemen for football at Carolina during the years in which they played.

This is in no way an attempt to document Carolina football, season by season, but it recalls significant games, players, and coaches, as witnessed through the eyes of the players involved in this book. It also provides in-depth views of these players, their individual careers at Carolina, and what has happened to them since they left the University.

One common trait seems to permeate the players featured here, and that is a strong continued interest in and loyalty to the University, their coaches, and their teammates. Another common denominator is the pride which they express in the teams that they represent, even though some fell short in the won-lost column. It was a pride in striving and playing the game, knowing that, regardless of the outcome, they had given it their best shot. Often that was more than adequate . . . . on other occasions it wasn't.

However, they and their teammates kept alive over five decades an enthusiasm and desire among Carolina fans to succeed to the ultimate degree. That ultimate was 1984, during which the Gamecocks were ranked as high as No. 2 in the nation in both wire service polls, losing only one game during the regular season.

Football underwent many changes between 1934 and 1984, and the Carolina campus has grown into one of the nation's premier educational centers. As for the men represented in this book, no matter when they played, it can be said, without qualification, that they wore the Garnet and Black in a manner that should inspire future Gamecocks for decades to come.

1932-33-34

TOM **craig**

31

END

In a career that overlapped that of the immortal "Gaffney Ghost," Earl Clary, Tom Craig helped move Carolina football to a higher level of competition. Years later this was determined to be almost a medical miracle.

1 TOM CRAIG

When Tom Craig was 66 years old he learned for the first time that he had been an invalid all his life.

You'd never convince those who saw him play "60-minute" football as an end for the University of South Carolina in the early thirties. Or those who competed against his record-setting performances for the Carolina track team, or knew him as a center for the winningest basketball team in the school's history.

Tom still isn't convinced, although he has the word of competent physicians, who performed open-heart surgery on him in 1979 and made the astonishing discovery. His wife, Betty, whose father (The Rev. M.M. Whiteside) was superintendent of the South Carolina Baptist Hospital in Columbia from 1918 to 1957, recalled:

"They couldn't understand how Tom could have played sports at all. They said he had an atrium septum defect—a hole in the wall between the two atrium chambers of his heart—and that it had been there since birth. One doctor said that he should have been dead by the age of thirty-five!"

Fortunately for Tom Craig and Carolina's athletic program, he never suspected what was going on inside his heart. Athletically, there's never been a stronger one beating through the rigors of competition on old Melton Field, the Davis Field track, or in the Carolina fieldhouse.

And it carried him with vigor through active careers in the Navy, coaching, YMCA work, and, for the most part, commercial real estate.

A half-century ago Carolina's football ambitions centered around the mythical South Carolina "state championship" and the unofficial leadership of the Southern Conference, a loosely-knit league with no requirements for playing other members in football and, thus, no definite champ. For example, Carolina had a claim to the title in 1933, winning all three of its games against conference competition, Clemson, Virginia Tech, and North Carolina State. Don't look for any evidence of this in the trophy room.

The "state championship" was a matter between Carolina, Clemson, and Furman, who were competing somewhat on even terms, while it was practically unheard-of for those schools to lose to any others within the state in that era. Individual accomplishment was limited to the all-state team, to which Tom was named in 1932 and 1933, and the all-conference, which was dominated by the North Carolina "big four." Tom made the All-Southern second team in 1933 behind Tom Rogers of Duke.

Not that Carolina officials were oblivious to winning in sports competition, as evidenced by their hiring of Billy Laval as head football coach in 1928. Laval, who had never played a lick himself, had been successful at Furman, and the fact that his teams had beaten Carolina five straight times no doubt figured in the choice.

Laval recruited Craig out of tiny Six Mile High School, which experimented with football for the first time during Tom's senior year. Still Craig's physical attributes, 6-1 and 190 pounds, and his proficiency in basketball attracted the attention of coaches at Carolina and Clemson.

Craig recalled, "I had my bag packed and was ready to go to Clemson, and I got word that same day that, if I came to South Carolina and made the team, I'd get a full scholarship. Clemson had offered me a job, and that was all."

Craig already had older brothers at Clemson (Johnson) and Carolina (Ed), but neither was an influence in his college choice.

Once at Carolina Tom spent a freshman year under the tutelage of A.W. (Rock) Norman, who later coached at Clemson, before joining a group of "red shirts" for the 1931 season.

"The reason they redshirted me was that I had shown potential to grow some," Craig explained. And Tom did, ultimately to 6-3 and 210 pounds.

During Craig's three varsity years, Carolina lost only two games to intra-state rivals, beating Clemson twice and registering a win, loss, and tie against Dizzy McLeod's Furman teams. It was also during this era that the Gamecocks began to reach outward to take on some of the national powers of the day. It must be pointed out that in the 1920's and 1930's the big names in college football included Colgate, Villanova, Temple, Duquesne, Fordham, and, yes, the University of Chicago, which Laval's team upset, 6-0, in his second game as Carolina coach.

Tom didn't get into the action in a 1932 opening win over Sewanee, also a respectable team of the day, but he was a star in the 7-6 win over Villanova in Philadelphia on October 1.

"That was considered a big upset," Craig said, "and I scored our touchdown on a pass from Grayson Wolf (quarterback). I started that game and all the rest of the games during my college career."

Craig's first "Big Thursday" game was an unqualified success, as the Gamecocks won, 14-0, and Craig was on the receiving end of an 18-yard pass from Earl Clary at the Clemson nine-yard line to set up the second touchdown.

Tom's brother, Johnson, was at right tackle for the Tigers in that game.

Craig: "I didn't have any particular feeling about the Carolina-Clemson game, except that my brother was playing on the other team. We had a lot of fun out of that, but we didn't have any direct contact, because he was playing on one side of the line, and I was on the other. For years after we finished school we went to the Carolina-Clemson game together. He'd go to his side of the field, and I'd go to mine then, after the game, we'd get in the car and drive home together."

At that point of Craig's sophomore season the Gamecocks were four and one, but nine days after the Clemson game they faced a powerful Tulane team in New Orleans. The Green Wave had been to the Rose Bowl the previous season, losing to Southern California, and had an All-America halfback named Don Zimmerman, whom Craig described as the best runner he faced during his college career.

Craig: "Tulane scored the only touchdown of the game (won 6-0) on a long run by Zimmerman—about 50 yards. It was off tackle and a perfect play. Everybody blocked whom they were supposed to, and I don't think anybody touched him."

However, one of the most memorable games in Carolina football history concluded the 1932 season, as the Gamecocks moved into Birmingham to meet undefeated Auburn, the favorite to receive the Rose Bowl bid to meet West Coast champion Southern Cal.

Craig: "We were able to control the ball on Auburn with our running game. I think they scored the first two touchdowns, but we came back on them, and the game ended in a twenty-twenty tie. That cost them the bid to the Rose Bowl. Clary had a real good game against them, and so did our fullback, Pot (Allen) Brown."

That enabled the Gamecocks to finish the season on the plus side, winning five, losing four, and tying two. The state of the college game was illustrated by the lack of scoring, Carolina registering only 93 points, and their opponents just 63 in 11 games.

As Craig mentioned, "Passing really wasn't a factor in the offenses. No special passing downs, just when we thought it would be the best play to call." For instance, in the Carolina-Clemson game of that year the Gamecocks attempted only five passes, completing two, while the Tigers, although losing, tried but seven, connecting on one.

Craig described Laval's offense as "a modified punt formation, which is a short punt formation, not a whole lot different from the single wing."

Prior to Tom's enrollment at Carolina, Laval had used an imaginative "Crazy Quilt" formation that he devised, featuring the center over the ball, the guards dropping back a yard deeper than the center and facing outward, while the tackles and ends faced inward. The team would shift, sending the halfback up to end, and the end back to the wing, where he could get the assignment of blocking the defensive tackle. The backfield lined up in the single wing, the box, or some closely related set-up.

Craig: "The Crazy Quilt was outlawed before I started playing. Laval was the one that forced the change in the rule to require linemen to remain set for a second before the ball is snapped. In the Crazy Quilt the linemen would move just before the snap, getting an advantage in blocking.

"Billy Laval was a good coach, and he had the admiration of the players to the greatest extent. He had some good assistants, but maybe he didn't use them like he should have . . . like they do now.

"Billy got personally involved in the coaching—line, backfield, everything. I would classify him as a tough disciplinarian, but he did most of it on the field. If you didn't measure up, then you did extra work on the field, like running laps, or doing it over and over until you got it right.

"He was very straight-laced. You could count on him—anything he told you, you could put it down and live by it. A straightforward fellow."

Although Laval's coaching record was a respectable 39 wins, 26 losses, and six ties, he was not retained as head coach following the 1934 campaign, Craig's senior season. Why?

Craig: "I can't answer that, except that we've had a lot of

Tom Craig in a Carolina uniform of the early 1930's.

other coaches to leave the same way. It was just one of those things. A coach doesn't win as many games as the community thinks they ought to . . .;"

In Craig's opinion Laval was a competent coach, "about even on offense and defense. He was a good diagnostician, particularly in drawing up a defense for a game you were going to play.

"We didn't switch defenses, once a game started. We mostly used a six-two-two-one or a six-three-two defense, depending upon the opponent. Occasionally we played a seven-man line. Whether or not the opponent was a passing team really didn't figure in the type of defense that was chosen, because passing was not a major factor."

The effectiveness of the Laval defenses is confirmed by the statistic that, in 30 games played during Craig's three-year career, only nine opponents scored more than one touchdown, and 11 of them were held scoreless.

Offensively, Earl Clary was the Gamecocks' offensive weapon in 1931, 1932, and 1933, and he is always in the argument when Carolina fans express opinions on who was the school's all-time greatest back. His nickname, "The Gaffney Ghost," was obviously inspired by his similarities to Red Grange, Illinois' "Gallopin' Ghost" of 1922, 1923, and 1924.

Craig: "Earl was a highly-sought-after player in high school and I had heard quite a bit about him. He had a hard charge. He wasn't particularly quick or fast, but he could shock you so hard, he was just difficult to tackle. He was able to break tackles, because he knew how to throw his weight and meet the shock. I've seen him break many tackles, and leave 'em lyin' right where they were.

"If I had to compare him to another runner it would be Jim Brown (all-time great for the Cleveland Browns). Jim was faster, but he was a shocker, too. Left 'em in their tracks. Earl would rate right up there with any of the modern day runners.

"Earl was noted for his offensive play, but he was one of the finest defensive backs that anybody could have behind them. I played end, and he played right behind me, and he was a topnotch man to have back there. All I had to do was strip the interference, and he was there to make the tackle. Earl was a quiet, honest boy— good integrity and pretty much a model athlete.

"He would be a super player today, with all the training and equipment they now have. Weights and everything. All we did was practice and run. Practice and run. Some boys would work in heavy duty labor jobs in the summer, but nobody lifted weights."

Any modern-day players who feel they have to absorb a lot of punishment won't get too much sympathy from Craig, who says, "The helmets were terrible. The worst part was that you could hardly block a man without getting your cheekbone into it. The headgear fit tightly around the face, and the only shock space was in the top. On the side there was no protection at all."

There were no athletic dormitories, such as Carolina's present "Roost," with its dining room, study rooms, etc.

Craig: "We had a tenement that we all stayed in, and we had our meals at a boarding house off the campus. But they were good meals."

At the time Carolina had an enrollment of around 2,000, and the athletic budget was modest, even in comparison to other Southern schools, such as Duke, North Carolina, Georgia, Tennessee, Auburn, and so forth.

Craig: "Bowl games were never even discussed. (Only the Rose and Orange Bowls existed.) And there wasn't any thought of getting to play in the National Football League."

So, it was playing for fun, glory, and an education, without the promise of big bucks in the pro leagues after college. A crowd of 7,000 was considered good for a normal Carolina home game, so multiply that by two or three dollars per ticket, and it's obvious that there wasn't much room for frills for Craig and his teammates, who rode many a hot bus or train to Charlotte, New Orleans, Philadelphia, Birmingham, Greenville, and Raleigh.

Craig: "Our home games were mostly played on Melton Field (now site of the Russell House, student activities building), with the Clemson game and a few others played in a wooden stadium at the State Fairgrounds. A typical crowd at the Fairgrounds would be from seven to ten thousand people."

The beginning of what ultimately became Williams-Brice Stadium was dedicated at the second game of Craig's senior season, 1934. The City of Columbia, taking advantage of a new government public works program initiated by the Franklin D. Roosevelt administration, built a football stadium of Bluff Road, opposite the Fairgrounds and named it, "Columbia Municipal Stadium." Several years later it was turned over to the University and was known as "Carolina Stadium" until the name was changed in tribute to a bequest from the estate of Mrs. Martha Williams Brice, providing for expansion of the seating capacity to 56,140. Originally the stadium had around 18,000 permanent seats, later undergoing expansion programs in 1949 (33,000) and 1959 (43,000).

The dedicatory game was successful, as the Gamecocks defeated VMI, 22-6, and this sent the team toward a final record of five wins and four losses in, what turned out to be, Laval's final season as coach.

There was good news and bad news for Craig and the other seniors on the team. The "good" was their only win over Furman (2-0), while the "bad" was the only loss to Clemson (0-19).

Craig's more pleasant memories were of his junior season, when the Gamecocks finished 6-3-1 beat Clemson, and ended with a major upset over Auburn in Birmingham. The game was billed as "the battle for revenge," as Auburn still ached from losing the Rose Bowl bid because of a tie with Carolina the previous year. It turned out to be a showcase for Earl Clary, whose first game in a Carolina uniform had seen him lead a 7-0 upset over Wallace Wade's first Duke team.

However, word was that Clary was "under the weather" during the week of the Auburn game, still suffering attacks of appendicitis. It was reported that Laval suggested to Clary that it might be a morale booster for the team; if he would just start the game, then come out after the kickoff. Clary started and never came out.

Craig: "I don't recall hearing that Earl was sick, but he looked full speed to me during that game. It was one of the best he ever played.

In a 16-14 victory over the Plainsmen, Clary tackled Auburn star Allan Rogers in the end zone for a safety and scored two touchdowns in a personal performance that was described by the Associated Press as "an amazing exhibition of drive and speed." Earlier Atlanta Journal sports editor Ed Danforth had described Clary, "as hard to catch as a straw hat blown by the wind."

Later the Gaffney star was named to the All-Southern team and gained high honorable mention on the Associated Press All-America squad, and he was a charter member of the Carolina and state of South Carolina athletic halls of fame.

As of 1933, the "old" Southern Conference split, with some of the teams, including Georgia Tech, Alabama, Tulane, Tennessee, Auburn, and Vanderbilt, helping to create the Southeastern Conference, while Carolina, Clemson, Duke, North Carolina, N.C. State, and others formed the core of a "new" Southern Conference. In its first year Carolina won all three of its conference games, over Clemson, Virginia Tech, and N.C. State, having just as much of a claim to the "championship" as any other team, although some records list Duke as the titleholder of that season.

Thus, Tom Craig could well be the only athlete in his school's history to play on conference championship teams in both football and basketball. Craig was the back-up center to Dana Henderson on the basketball team that won the first Southern Conference tournament, beating Duke, 33-21, in the finals and finishing the 1932-33 season with a record of 18 wins against only two losses.

"We were tops in the nation," commented Craig, referring to a post-season victory for Eastern supremacy over Pittsburgh in the Carolina fieldhouse. The team, featuring the Tompkins brothers, Bennie and Freddie, won 33 straight games over a two-season span, establishing a record that was intact as of 1985.

Although by no means a self-promoter, Craig's record speaks loudly for him as one of the top three-sport performers ever to represent the University.

He participated in a number of events for the track team, including shot put, discus, javelin, high jump, and both high and

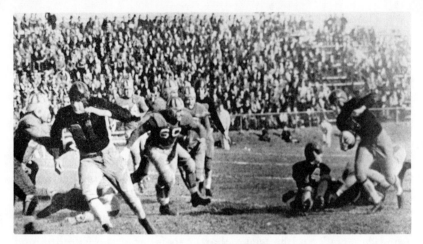

Supplying the lead block for Earl Clary is Tom Craig (31).

low hurdles. In one dual meet, against Wofford, he won all six of those events.

The South Carolina state meet at Presbyterian College in Clinton was the most important happening of the year in track.

A two-foot tall silver trophy was displayed by Craig, as he recalled an interesting story behind it: "At the 1933 state meet I placed first in the shot, discus, and high jump, and placed in the javelin, but they gave the trophy for the outstanding performer to another fellow who only won the four-forty. The Columbia newspaper didn't like it, so they bought me this trophy!"

In 1934 Craig saved the newspaper some money by winning the top award at the meet, and, at the same time, becoming the middle man in a most unusual chain of events. The older Craig brother, Johnson, had set records in the shot put and discus at the Clinton meet, and Tom established new marks in both. A few years later younger brother, Larry, surpassed Tom's accomplishments in the events while performing for Carolina!

Record-searchers would be hard-put to find Gamecock athletes who were involved in greater all-around success than Tom Craig. The football teams for which he played won 16, lost 11, and tied three, including two shutouts against Clemson and major upsets over Villanova and Auburn, while the basketball teams won 50 and lost only 12. And he walked away with a large number of first places and records in track.

Filed-away in his memory bank are associations with team-mates with whom he shared the bitter and the sweet. There was Hal Mauney, who later became president of Southern Railway, described by Craig as "ahead of any quarterback we played against that year (1934). Hal was a good ball-handler, good passer, good punter, and he had real good speed." (Mauney was elected to the USC Hall-of-Fame in 1971.)

Craig can still see the crisp blocks of Fred Hambright (another Hall-of-Fame member), as he cleared the way for Clary and fullback Allie McDougall. And there are special memories of the young freshmen who enrolled with him in 1930, such as Clary, Freeman Huskey (tackle), Roy Stroud (center), Bob Robbins (fullback), Nelson Fortson (guard), and Dean Fowble (guard).

Could Tom Craig make it on current Gamecock football squads?

Craig: "I'd have a hard time trying to make any of these teams, because of the size of the players and everything. I was big in my day—six-three and two hundred ten. If I could, I'd like to make it at the same place, as an end."

Just as he succeeded on the athletic fields, excelling in versatility, Craig was accomplished in four post-college careers—coaching, administrator, military, and business.

His career as a coach followed his graduation and lasted but one year, as he coached football, baseball, basketball, and track, along with teaching five subjects, at Brookland-Cayce High School at Cayce, near Columbia. The school had a real bargain at $125 a month!

Three years as athletic director for the Columbia YMCA followed, terminated by his induction into the United States Navy, where he served for three years (1943-46) and attained the rank of Lieutenant Commander.

Following the war years he started his own commercial real estate business by purchasing property for a parking lot, across from the old Columbia High School. This was the beginning of a highly-successful Tom Craig Company, for years one of the more prominent ones in the Columbia area.

Among Craig's civic accomplishments was election to the Columbia City Council in 1958, when he led the voting and carried 20 of the 21 precincts. He served on the Council for four years, choosing not to offer for re-election at that point.

Along with his other endeavors, Craig enjoyed a private career

Tom Craig and his wife, Betty, in 1985.

as husband and father, having two daughters, a son, and seven grandchildren.

Craig reached into his wallet and produced a Gamecock Club membership card that told of 40 straight years of loyalty. There weren't many Carolina home games over that span that kicked off without Tom in the stadium. He had known most of the Carolina head football coaches, including Rex Enright, Paul Dietzel, and Marvin Bass, with whom he played handball regularly during the early 1960's.

His appraisal of Carolina's athletic ambitions is quite objective.

Craig: "Our progress really began under Dietzel, when they started building facilities equal to the other schools. Before that there was the desire, but we just didn't have everything necessary, as far as drawing the good players. I think we're pretty close now.

"There are still some schools a little deeper in their programs, like Georgia, Alabama, L.S.U., Auburn, and Tennessee. But now we have (Joe) Morrison and everything that goes with it—stadium seating capacity, community support, and so forth, is extraordinary now.

We should be able to compete with the major schools in the Southeast."

Even with problems of a defective heart that somehow provided the strong beat for a super-active athletic, military, and business career, Tom Craig still had the physical appearance of a gladiator, as his years numbered in the seventies. He stands tall as representative of an era when football at Carolina was nowhere near the top of the ladder, but Craig and his colleagues played with dedication and distinction to move the program a rung or two higher than it had been before they took their first walk across The Horseshoe, downed their first boardinghouse meal, or donned their first garnet jersey.

Author's Note: Tom Craig died in Columbia on September 16, 1985, at the age of 74.

LARRY **craig**

70

END

Although he didn't even play high school football, Larry Craig became one of the finest ends ever to wear a Gamecock uniform. He also became Carolina's first National Football League star and a Green Bay Packers hall-of-famer.

2 LARRY CRAIG

arry Craig devoted 15 years of his life to playing the game of football, which took him on a journey from Carolina Stadium through the big cities of the National Football League, where he played alongside and against legends of the game. Yet in spirit he never departed from the undulating hills and farmlands of the South Carolina Piedmont.

Thirty-five years ago Craig said "no" to college and professional coaching enticements, so that he could return to where his heart had been all the time. And now he looks out over his 722 acres, instead of the Green Bay Packers playing field. He hears the lowing of beef cattle, rather than the roar of stadium crowds.

Not that he didn't go all-out in his gridiron career, because he played his positions with sufficient ardor and skill to become all-pro and the only end to be chosen (as of 1985) for the University of South Carolina Athletic Hall of Fame.

Nobody—not even Larry—had that possibility in mind when he enrolled at Carolina in 1935. You see, he was a farm boy who went to high school at Six Mile, South Carolina, a tiny crossroads about ten miles north of Clemson. The school's only competitive sport was basketball, and Larry Craig followed in the footsteps of older brothers and played the roundball game back when a center jump occurred after every basket.

Brother Johnson· had attended Clemson, where he lettered in three sports, and brother Tom earned football basketball, and track letters at Carolina in 1932, 1933, and 1934.

To borrow a rural expression, giving Larry a football scholarship was like "buying a pig in a poke," but that's what Billy Laval's staff at Carolina did.

Craig: "Big reason I wound up at Carolina is that Tom was already established over there—had done real well in athletics—and Johnson, up at Clemson, had made his name in sports. Wally (another brother, who lettered in 1938) and myself went to Carolina with no background at all in football. We were big country boys and could move pretty good, so I guess they figured enough of Tom and Johnson would rub off on us to, at least, make a stab at it."

When he enrolled at Carolina in 1935 Larry was a wiry six feet, one inch, 185 pounds of bone and muscle, hardened by heavy-duty farm chores, as much as by his scholastic sports activities. While Larry was in the transitional stage from high school to college, the University had hired Don McAllister, who had been a big winner as a high school coach in Toledo, Ohio, to succeed Billy Laval as head coach.

Folklore had it that Larry was walking across the campus one day and was spotted by McAllister, who asked him where he had played football. And the reply was, "I've never played, but I'd like to try."

That makes a good story for a player who turned out to be what many consider the finest ever to come out of Carolina, considering his ultimate professional accomplishments. But the truth of the matter is that A.W. (Rock) Norman, who had coached Tom Craig as a freshman and watched him perform for three varsity years, already knew what diamonds-in-the-rough the Craig boys were and had anticipated Larry's trying his hand at football.

Larry found himself surrounded by a lot of freshman teammates who didn't have Southern accents, as McAllister brought with him several of his graduating seniors from Toledo. Vincent Kelly (guard), Ralph Dearth (quarterback), and Frank Urban (center) were three that came to mind, and others followed. After playing on the freshman team under Norman, giving Larry his first real football instruction, the group was ready to move up to play for McCallister, whose first Gamecock team had won three and lost seven. That included a 44-0 loss to Clemson.

Craig was not overly impressed with McAllister's program, as he reminisced on a cold January morning in 1985.

Craig: "He came down with great expectations, but it didn't pan out so great. If I gave you an honest opinion—now, you don't have to write this—I didn't particularly care for McAllister's coaching . . . his ability to handle the boys. I felt like he was strictly high schoolish in most everything he did. He just didn't live up to expectations—I'll put it that way."

Asked if he meant that McAllister's approach was more adaptable to high school than college, Craig replied, "Well that would be my opinion. That wouldn't hurt. His record would determine that, wouldn't it?

"He taught basic football. Single wing formation, some passing. Didn't bring anything new in there. We had a pretty good passer in Ed Clary (cousin of Earl Clary), and Jack Derrenbacher was a good fullback. I don't recall that he was too big on trick plays and that 'off-brand' football, as I call it. Chances are that he had the Flying Trapeze play, but I don't recall it."

Reference to the Flying Trapeze play was in response to a question, as the write-up of the 1935 Carolina-Clemson game described its use by the Gamecocks. The play sent Don Tomlin running wide, and Clary, sweeping even wider to the rear. Clary took a lateral from Tomlin and, in turn, wheeled around and lofted a lateral almost the width of the field to Bob Johnson, who fired a long pass to an intended receiver. It was an uproductive effort on this occasion, as Clemson defensive back Net Berry waited patiently, picked-off the pass and ran it back all the way to the Gamecock 20-yard line.

Back to McAllister, Craig continued, "He tried to be a stern person. Had an organized practice, and he did a lot of individual work with the boys. He tried awful hard, but the step from high school to college was probably something he hadn't thought too much about. I guess he came to Carolina with the same thoughts, feelings, and ability to put it to the boys that he had with high school boys."

Two years later Larry had the opportunity to play for another head coach, Rex Enright, who had been an assistant to Harry Mehre at Georgia for several years. Enright had played for Knute Rockne at Notre Dame, and he brought the famous Notre Dame shift with him.

Craig: "It was a different football world when Enright came and brought all of his staff out of Georgia. Rex came in with the ability to handle the boys and coach college football at that level, right off the bat. They went to work and changed things around a good bit.

"In nineteen thirty-six and thirty-seven the morale wasn't very good. The big thing was lack of respect for the coaching staff. That's another big reason for the poor showing by the McAllister organization. It was just altogether a different set-up when Rex Enright came."

The accomplishments of the 1936 and 1937 Gamecock teams can by summarized in a few sentences. You could say that they won the "Florida state championship" in 1936, because they defeated both Florida (7-0) and Miami (6-3). Florida State was an all-girls school in those years.

The major achievement of 1937 was a 13-13 tie with North Carolina, but six of the ten victories of the two-year period were over the likes of Erskine, Presbyterian, The Citadel, Davidson, and Emory and Henry.

By comparison Enright's first season, which ended with six wins, four losses, and a tie, was a phenomenal success.

Craig: "We had a lot of 'ifs.' We'd have had a hang of a season, with just a little luck. We played Fordham (0-13) in the Polo Grounds (New York City), and we had a pass dropped that would have been a sure touchdown. It would have made a big difference."

Teams on the 1938 Carolina schedule might be unimpressive, if you go by the strength of those teams in 1985. However, a look back into the 1930 records shows Villanova with a 7-2 mark in 1932, 7-2-1 in 1933, a ranking of No. 6 in the final 1937 AP poll, and an 8-0-1 finish in 1938. Duquesne defeated Mississippi State in the 1937 Orange Bowl, Catholic University downed Mississippi in the '36 Orange Bowl, while Fordham was the nation's third-ranked team in 1937, and lost only one game during the 1938 season.

The Gamecocks defeated Duquesne (7-0) and Catholic U. (7-0), and tied with Villanova (6-6). Outside of the loss to Fordham, Carolina suffered one-point defeats at the hands of Georgia (7-6), and Wake Forest (20-19), and a 34-12 setback to a Clemson team that finished 7-1-1.

Craig recalls, "When we played Fordham they still had two of the famous Seven Blocks of Granite. (Fordhan's line, which included the immortal Vince Lombardi and didn't give-up a touchdown in 1936.) Alex Wojciechowicz was at center, and Harry Jacunski was at end. Harry came up to Green Bay and played on the team with me, and Alex played for Detroit and had a great career."

Another accomplishment of no minor portions for Carolina fans was the first victory over Furman (27-6) since 1934. The Gamecocks had only 84 points scored on them in 11 games, which spoke well for the defense against such an imposing array of opponents. Five teams were held scoreless, while three were held to single touchdowns.

Craig: "It would have to indicate that defense was the strength of that team—we had a hang of a good defense. We had some outstanding linemen—Stan Nowak, Pop Howell, Irving

Granoff, Big Durham, John Burns at center. Joe Hatkevich. And we had good backs, like the Henson boys, Pinhead and J.B., and Al Grygo. Ed Clary played quarterback, and Big Durham was a good passer. Dewitt Arrowsmith, too.

"Grygo was a hang of a good back. He was a shifty runner. Wasn't a great big guy, but he was good enough to come up to the pro league and play for the Chicago Bears, and make a hang of a good showing up there. He was as good as most backs in the country, I'll put it that way. He wasn't all that fast, but he had the ability to move—his moves were good. He could pick the holes. Often good running backs don't have to be speed demons—you see that nowadays. They have the ability to pick the open spaces, and Al had that ability.

"Ed Clary could have gone to the pros—he was drafted, but he didn't want to play pro ball. I think he would have made it.

"Alex Urban (center) was a good ball player, too. He was another one who came up to the pros, with Green Bay, and did fairly well."

Although the Gamecocks were beaten by Clemson, 34-12, their supporters were sufficiently impressed and showed their appreciation by presenting Enright and his family a silver pitcher and goblets.

Craig: "Our senior year, we felt like we could play with Clemson on even terms. However, we fell a little short. That team felt that we could play with most anybody, and the record we had proved it.

"My biggest asset was being a little rugged, blocking and defense. Not a good pass catcher. I was too tight. We were a good running team but had a pretty balanced attack. Clary and Durham could throw the football pretty good, and we did enough (passing) to keep the defenses honest. Running was always the big thing in the Notre Dame system."

Did Knute Rockne's propensity for making inspiring pep talks to his squad rub-off on Enright?

Craig: "It had its effect on everybody that played under Rockne. But as far as Enright going to the dressing room and making speeches, like we heard about Rockne, he didn't do that. Neither did (Curly) Lambeau (Craig's coach at Green Bay), who was on the same Notre Dame team with Enright. They were not the type to think they could pour it out and change all the complexion of your feeling during the game. Enright and Lambeau were much alike in

Larry Craig in a 1938 Gamecock uniform.

their coaching. Their abilities to coach and win. Lambeau had one of the best records in the pros, and he did most of it with Notre Dame football.

"Enright could have been just as good in the pros, and Lambeau could have coached college football. Enright and Lambeau were friends, that's how I ended up at Green Bay. During my senior year, coach Enright asked Lambeau to come down and take a look at me. And I was drafted in the eighth round by Green Bay."

Almost in one year, Larry Craig had blossomed into a bonafide football player, blending his natural speed and strength (now up to

200 pounds) with football skills that were honed by the Enright staff, which included Ted Petoskey, former All-America end at Michigan. Of course, he made the South Carolina All-State team, which didn't create a lot of excitement in the NFL, but he was also chosen for the All-Southern Conference first team, the second Gamecock to be so honored since the new league was created in 1933.

Larry followed in his older brother's (Tom) footsteps by playing three sports at the University, surpassing his state records in the shot put and discus, and earning a berth on the basketball team.

When Enright called Lambeau and advised him to make a Packer out of Larry Craig, he initiated one of the bright careers of the NFL.

Craig: "I negotiated the contract in the athletic office (USC). Green Bay sent line coach Richard Smith, and we sat in coach Enright's office. That contract called for $175 a ball game. That was a typical rookie contract, unless you came out of one of those big schools, with All-America honors. The Big Ten sent a lot of boys to the pros, because they got so much publicity.

"This was the same year (1939) that Sid Luckman (all-time passing great from Columbia University) went to the (Chicago) Bears. I guess they already had it mapped out what they were gonna try to do with me. They put me at defensive end and, on offense, at blocking back. I weighed two hundred and five, and that was adequate size in those days for blocking back and end. I would rate my speed second in the league. Among the backs, everybody. I was blessed with good speed. Don Hutson (all-time great pass receiver who played for Alabama) was the fastest. He could beat me by one step in the hundred-yard sprint. I'm sure that I was next to the fastest in the league."

What Craig's presence and abilities allowed Lambeau to do was move Hutson to safety on defense, thereby moving him farther away from crushing blocks by big linemen and the responsibility of breaking-up interference and meeting power backs head-on. Hutson could then move back to end on offense, where he could dazzle the football world with his pass-catching wizardry, while Larry shifted to blocking back.

Craig: "Hutson was the greatest pass catcher there has ever been, I guess. There has never been a football player with any better hands and ability to get open than Don. He had nine-seven speed, and I think he would play even better today than he played in those years (1935-45). The throwers today have the edge. Back then the patterns were different. Back then, down and out was about the only pattern you had. It's much different now. We were mostly a running team."

To say that Larry's debut in professional football was successful would border on understatement, because he was a starter at the outset and rapidly impressed teams around the league. In the November 16, 1939 issue of *The New York Times*, sports columnist John Kieran penned an article entitled, "The Country Boys from Green Bay," which included these paragraphs:

"Oh, well," said Curly (Lambeau), with a wave of his hand, "everybody knows most of our boys. Arnie Herber and Don Hutson and—but say, we have one youngster who's quite a boy. He's Larry Craig, an end. He played at South Carolina.

"Ah, South Carolina! Rex Enright coaches down there."

"Sure!" said Curly, "You know Rex? We were together at Notre Dame. Well, this boy Craig—we use him as a blocking back on the offense and put him at end on the defense. He's a whale at tearing in there and busting up a play. Furthermore, when we put him at end on defense we drop back Don Hutson. Don has been around longer and knows better how to defend against forward passing."

That column was written as the Packers neared the end of a 9-2 season, which was concluded with a 27-0 victory over the New York Giants in the championship game.

Craig: "Our winners share was eight hundred dollars, and in nineteen forty-four we won the championship again and got about fifteen hundred."

Compare that to the $64,000 in playoff money received by each member of the San Francisco Forty-Niner 1985 Super Bowl champions. That's the amount that went to a modern-day ex-Gamecock, Max Runager, for punting the football a few times.

On the subject of salaries Craig pointed out that the "good boys" were earning from $12,000 to $15,000 a year, with a few super stars, such as Hutson, getting above that. "The year I got up there we had two all-pro guards making forty-eight hundred a year."

Green Bay's big rival was the Chicago Bears, coached by George Halas and one of the more successful franchises in the league. In 1944 Al Grygo was signed by the Bears, placing him on the same field with Craig once more, but this time on the other side of the line of scrimmage.

Craig: "Al was a hundred and seventy pound boy, and I weighed two twenty, and he was supposed to block me on certain plays. Putting a hundred and seventy pounder on someone who weighed as much as I did was asking an awful lot. Grygo was a good friend of mine, and he got me by the arm and said, 'Look, you've already gotten your letter. So, take it a little easy on me!' Then, we'd go out together after the game to eat!"

One of the last people to visit Grygo in a Columbia hospital before he died was his old teammate, opponent, and friend, Larry Craig.

In 1949, after 11 seasons of running head-on into the increasingly large behemoths of the NFL, Craig decided to say goodbye to Sunday afternoons in big city stadiums, treks along the rails and airlanes that crisscross America, and weekdays on a far-away practice field that had been a temporary destination in a journey which began almost two decades before in Six Mile. He would return to the soil of his native state, but, this time, to land that he had been "putting aside" near Ninety-Six in Greenwood County, where his brother, Johnson, served with the Soil Conservation Department.

Craig: "I never really had any ambitions to coach, although I had a few opportunities. Coach Enright asked me to join his staff, and I had an opportunity to go to the Redskins as their defensive coach under Ray Flaherty. But I had spent so much time up there, and I had been a farm boy all my life. I started buying land in nineteen forty, and added a little bit along the way. Johnson knew every farm in the county, and he located this land. He has a farm next to me, and we started out together. When I got through playing ball we split it up. I have about seven hundred and twenty acres, and Johnson, six hundred and twenty.

"When you play twelve years, age begins to tell on you. I played two games every Sunday—going both ways—and I had played an awful lot of rough football. Every move on defense I made was bumpin' heads with some big tackle or guard, and, then on offense, the blocking back had a key assignment on every play—blocking ends and tackles.

"So, I guess I had more contact in that time than anybody who played football. I averaged about fifty five minutes a ball game the whole time I was there. And I never had to leave a game injured.

"Yes, I lost some teeth. The Bear boys took care of a couple for me. Why in the world they waited so long to cover up their faces, I don't know!"

Larry Craig left Green Bay with two less teeth than when he arrived, but he also left the memory of one of the greater performers ever to display the familiar "G." Many have worn that insignia with distinction—Don Hutson, Cecil Isbell, Tobin Rote, Paul Hornung,

As a blocking back for the Green Bay Packers, Larry Craig (54) sends a Washington Redskin defender (35) into the wide open spaces.

Bart Starr, Jerry Kramer, Max McGee, Jim Taylor, and others who have contributed to the Packers' 11 championships. Add Larry Craig to those names that compose the Green Bay Hall of Fame, for which he was an early choice.

Craig's admirers among opposing teams were numerous, and they were strong in their support of Larry when he was named to the South Carolina Hall of Fame in 1975. (He was named to the USC Hall of Fame in 1976.)

Bobby Layne, Detroit Lions quarterback: "I would have to consider him one of the five best defensive ends in my fifteen years of professional football. I got to know Larry personally, especially on the field, because we met on quite a few occasions!"

Sammy Baugh, Washington Redskins passing great: "I have been asked by many people to name someone who gave me the most trouble when I was attempting to pass. I always say Larry Craig, because we were never able to handle him consistently. We tried to keep our best blocker on him, but he still rushed me harder than anyone I ever played against."

Art Rooney, President of the Pittsburgh Steelers: "He is considered by some to be one of the top three premier defensive ends, ranking behind Gino Marchetti and Willie Davis."

George Halas, Chicago Bears head coach: ". . . his reputation as a hard-hitting back on offense, and as a terrific end on defense was unexcelled."

Quite a reputation among the immortals of the world's most glamorous and prestigious sports league, for an individual who chose to give it up for the quiet life of a cattle farmer. In spite of his unqualified success in the NFL, Larry feels that he fits more comfortably in the surroundings in which he decided to live out his life. There he found someone to share that life—Helen Connelly of Ninety-Six—whom he married in 1947. The Craig's only child is a daughter.

The world of honors has been generous to Larry Craig— including several All-Pro selections—but he summarizes his experiences more in terms of personal gratitude.

Craig: "Well, all those honors are great, but the real highlight was being able to make the college team without any experience in high school, then going to Green Bay and being able to make their team and play the first year I was there."

As for his Alma Mater, Craig states, "I feel their successes and defeats as much as anybody. However, I don't get down to too many of the games. I met (Jim) Carlen and (Paul) Dietzel. I haven't met this (Joe) Morrison boy yet. But he looks like he's got his head on his shoulders just right."

Craig chuckled, when asked if there is anything about his life that he would change, replying, "I would have liked to finish Carolina about six years ago . . . those dollars you see the boys (pro contracts) making. But I feel pretty good about everything that happened, from the time I got to Carolina—to Green Bay."

It turned out to be the best of two worlds for Larry Craig, a farm boy who, almost by happenstance, was able to spend his youth in an exciting wonderland of college and professional football, then, at his own pace, come back down to earth to do what he felt all along that the good Lord wanted him to do.

1940·41·42

LOU **sossamon**

CENTER

The star of Lou Sossamon rose in two of Carolina's greatest upsets, a victory over Clemson in 1941 and a tie with Tennessee in 1942. Four decades later he was still a part of the team, as a member of the University Board of Trustees.

3 LOU SOSSAMON

When Louis Sossamon was a second grade pupil in Gaffney, a small textile town in the South Carolina Piedmont, about the only thing he knew about football was that Earl Clary had the place in a frenzy. On Friday afternoons in the autumn the whole town dropped everything to gather at the football field and watch their super star work his ball-carrying magic. Before Louis played his first high school B-squad game in 1936, Clary had long since completed a brilliant career at the University of South Carolina. Rides on special trains from Gaffney to Columbia to see the "Gaffney Ghost" play were already faded memories for Sossamon.

However, football fever had become a continuing epidemic in Gaffney, and every able-bodied boy aspired to be another Earl Clary or, at least, a reasonable facsimile. Sossamon was one who succeeded in playing the game with the proficiency worthy of his former hero, although he reached that level at a much different position—center.

Over half a century after he first watched "the Ghost" haunt opposing teams, Sossamon looked back over a productive life that allowed him to become one of Carolina's most distinguised football players and student leaders, and follow a business career that made him owner of his hometown tri-weekly newspaper, *The Gaffney Ledger*. Military service and three years of professional football were sandwiched in between.

Those years, if anything, have seen Sossamon's interest in the University and its football teams increase, especially since he began following them in 1982 from his vantage point as a member of the school's Board of Trustees.

At the age of 63, Sossamon's physical appearance suggested that he might still be willing to meet a running back head-on or move back to protect the passer. It's a challenge he won't have to meet, of course, but his track record through the years indicates that he wouldn't back off.

Sossamon seemed to enjoy reminiscing—and who wouldn't?

Sossamon: "My early football days were enhanced by a fellow named Henry Brabham, who still lives in Gaffney. He coached what we called the B team. There were not too many on the team, but we had a lot of fun."

The Gaffney varsity had a lot of fun, too, in the two years that Sossamon played center, winning big against teams, not only from nearby, but from Birmingham, Knoxville, and Winston-Salem.

Sossamon: "In our final game (1938), on Thanksgiving Day, we beat Spartanburg seven to nothing. A teammate of mine named Harold Middlebrooks (later played at Carolina) and I had an invitation to go to Washington with a couple after the game. So, we rode all night to Washington, and the next morning we went to the Congressional library, and we picked up a copy of the *Greenville News*. We saw that Gaffney had accepted an invitation to play in the Little Tobacco Bowl in Richmond against Fork Union Military Academy. It was my first bowl game, but we got beat seven to nothing.

"That year Harold (Middlebrooks), Billy Lavendar, Charles Millwood, and I—four of us from Gaffney—went to play in the Shrine Bowl in Charlotte. It was the second Shrine Bowl, and, incidentally, Gus Hempley, who later played on the team with me at Carolina, had kicked the ball to start the first Shrine Bowl the year before.

"In the Shrine Bowl we played against four boys from Asheville, North Carolina, and all of them came to the University. Fred Lytle, Herb Coman, Bobo Carter, and Elmore Carter. In the second half of the Shrine game I broke my shoulder and had my arm in a sling for several weeks.

"Mother and Daddy had to come to Columbia for a church meeting in February, and I rode with them. I meandered over to the athletic office at the University, walked in, and spoke to Coach Enright.

"He said, 'How would you like to have a scholarship to the University?' I had never had any contact from South Carolina—at that time they didn't do a lot of recruiting like they do now. I had a feeler from Coach Howard at Clemson, but I don't recall anybody recruiting me heavily.

"Funny thing about it, when I met Coach Enright in person I just liked him so much as a man, and I said, 'Yes sir, I'd like to have a scholarship.' And I entered school at that time for the second semester.

"I really don't know what he based the scholarship on. I never even talked to anybody but the head coach. I guess it was the Shrine Bowl."

Although he followed Earl Clary's career as a Gamecock very closely, Sossamon didn't necessarily have a burning desire to follow in his tracks. His attraction to Carolina was independent of that influence.

Sossamon: "I never was interested in Clemson, because I didn't like the R.O.T.C. program and the boys shaving their heads too much. My brother had been at the University—Frank. He came on a football scholarship, then was injured and didn't complete his sophomore year under (Don) McAllister. He didn't particularly like McAllister, and he went to Charleston and started working at the drydock.

"I was very thankful that I did have a scholarship, which consisted of two dollars a week spending money, board, books, tuition, laundry, and free passes to the theater. Back then we could stop by the Toddle House, spend ten cents, and get a piece of chocolate pie.

"It was one of the lucky things that happened to me. And the many people I've met at the University since then had just been great."

Louis cut his teeth, along with about 17 others, on the freshman team, coached by Ted Petoskey. One game that stuck in Sossamon's memory took place in Athens, Georgia.

Sossamon: "It was right funny, we went to Georgia, I can remember, we had about eighteen boys. It looked as if they had about eighty on the sidelines! It was a hot day between the hedges, and every time we'd look up, they'd be sending-in fresh players."

One of those "about eighty" Bulldogs was Frankie Sinkwich, an All-America back who won the Heisman Trophy in 1942. Sossamon played against Sinkwich three times in varsity games—1939, 1940, and 1941—then was a teammate of his in professional football with the New York Yankees of the All-American Football Conference after World War II. Sossamon, like many others, found more success playing *WITH* Sinkwich than *AGAINST* him.

Sossamon: "His asset was that he was so quick starting. I can remember when I went to pro ball, and we used the single wing my first year, and I had to snap the ball to people like Sinkwich, Ace Parker (all-American at Duke in 1936), and Buddy Young (Illinois great), and lead 'em. And it was a tough job to lead those people just right with a soft pass when they're taking off around right or left. I remember one game Parker went off one way, and I snapped the ball the other way. I don't know who was wrong!"

That stray pass was a rarity, if not unique, in the Sossamon playing experience, because, as he recalled, "I always had great pride in snapping the ball. During my career in college I don't think I ever made a bad snap. Coach Enright would have me out snapping the ball to Glen Rice (halfback and punter) thirty minutes before we ever started practice. I got to where I could snap the ball without looking."

When Sossamon enrolled at Carolina in 1939 the fuse of World War II had already been lit, and before the year was over the German army invaded Poland, while Albert Einstein was writing a secret letter to President Franklin D. Roosevelt on the feasibility of the atomic bomb. Football was being overshadowed by news of Europe in turmoil, but Sossamon and his 17 freshman teammates were preparing themselves as thoroughly as possible for their forthcoming varsity wars.

Sossamon: "We used to scrimmage the varsity on Melton Field, and if we didn't do well, we had to stay out there and scrimmage some more. We had a boy named Moon (Charles) McCullough from Macon, Georgia—a tackle—and he had one eye and a glass eye. One day he lost his eye in a scrimmage, and we had to stay out there with the lights on Melton Field—all of us crawlin' around—tryin' to find his glass eye."

Before Sossamon played his first varsity game against the University of Georgia in the 1940 season-opener, the Nazis had entered Paris, Dunkerque had been evacuated, and Italy had entered the spreading conflict. This led to the passage of the Selective Service Act by Congress, and soon, many young American males would be receiving greetings from their local draft boards. This would be the last season before 1945 that would be little affected by "The War."

The Gamecocks, in their third season under Enright, faced a tough first half of their schedule, losing to Georgia, Duquesne, Clemson, and Penn State. The ultimate record was three wins and six losses, bringing back very few pleasant memories for Sossamon, although he cracked the starting lineup at the outset and remained there throughout his college playing days.

Although the Gamecocks lost, 21-13, to Frank Howard's first Clemson team, which finished 6-2-1, the gap seemed to be closing between the two bitter rivals. One feature of the "Big Thursday" encounter was the introduction by Enright of the punt return reverse. Early in the third period the Tigers punted to Dewitt Arrowsmith at the Gamecock 25, and he headed for the west sideline with the Tigers in hot pursuit. Meanwhile Al Grygo sprinted in from the opposite direction, took the ball from Arrowsmith and, behind a wall of blockers, streaked up the east sideline, moving 75 yards for a touchdown. This maneuver was used by a number of schools in succeeding years, before punting specialists who lofted the ball into the clouds practically eliminated the punt return as a weapon.

This was one of several innovations by Enright, who gained a lifelong admirer in Louis Sossamon, who was a pall bearer at his former coach's funeral in April of 1960.

Sossamon: "When I first met Coach Enright he was a warm, friendly man I thought I'd like to be associated with. When you first meet somebody, and you can size 'em up in a little while, sometimes you're wrong. This time I was absolutely right about Coach Enright. He was a man with a big heart. He tried to be fair with all the boys, and yet he was business-like on the field. I don't think I've ever heard Coach Enright use any foul language on the field. I think the boys really appreciated that. I know I did.

"He was a warm person, sincere, considerate, and concerned. If you were hurt, or needed clothes, or something was wrong in your family, he was one of the first ones to come see you and talk to you about it. One of the boys, for example, was in a little bit of financial trouble, and I was in the coaches' office when Coach Enright called him in. I happened to overhear the conversation. He told the boy he'd make sure he got home right away to see his family.

"The biggest handicap he (Enright) had was financing and lack of assistant coaches. How many do they have now? We had Ted Toomey, Sterling Dupre, Frank Johnson, and Ted Petoskey. Coach Enright even coached basketball one year.

"The only one we had scouting was a fellow named Tatum Gressette. I'll tell him today he's one of the primary reasons we beat Clemson in nineteen forty-one. He scouted Clemson every game they played, and then he'd come back to the old fieldhouse, and we'd go in and have a meeting. He'd tell us the name, number, and weight of every individual on that team, what they could do, and where they were going to do it on the field. (Gressette was the first director of the BAM (Buck-A-Month) club, the original Carolina athletic booster organization.)

"Of course, Coach Enright looked over the overall program, best he could, but he was primarily involved in the offense. We used the Notre Dame box, which he had played. It was the forerunner of

Lou Sossamon tosses San Francisco ball carrier John Straykalski for a loss, as he wore the uniform of the New York Yankees. (New York Times Photo)

the T. The only difference was that you shifted out of the T to right or left. The T-formation is so much quicker and faster now than what we used. You don't have the risk of snapping the ball and dropping it. You might compare it (Notre Dame box) to Dallas' line. When they come out the quarterback gives a count, and the line will jump up and go back down. Anything you can do to distract the defense and get their minds to thinking on something else . . . And they might have put the stronger linebacker on the right, then you'd shift to the left. When you came out of the huddle you had the prerogative of shifting either way—to get away from the strong point in the defense.

"I would say that our most effective play was the tailback taking the ball off tackle, or faking off tackle and going outside. You'd have a blocking back and fullback, and also the wingback blocking for you. And a guard pulling out sometimes.

"As far as discipline on the team goes, I believed in Coach Enright so much, I never was concerned. I felt that most of the players on our team were in real good condition—it never was a problem. He asked us to observe training rules, as far as getting to bed on time, particularly the Thursday and Friday before a game.

"He was a quiet fellow, but Coach Enright could get his message across without getting excited. On some of the games, I recall, he'd talk to us in a low tone, then he'd get just a little excited about things himself. And, before it was over with, we'd want to knock the doors down getting out of there. He was, 'You fellows have a job to do. Get out there and do it'."

It required very little thought for Sossamon to identify his most satisfying season. It was 1941 in a breeze. The Gamecocks finished with four wins, against four losses and a tie, but the performance of the team was far better than such a record would indicate.

At Chapel Hill the Gamecocks opened the season with a 13-7 win over North Carolina, their first over the Tar Heels since 1927. However, the teams had not played each other on a regular basis. A new star arose for Carolina, as Stan Stasica, a sophomore from Enright's hometown of Rockford, Illinois, scored the winning touchdown (13-7) on a brilliant 65-yard run.

That performance proved to be typical of Stasica, who was named to the Associated Press All-Southern team at the end of the season. It was Stasica's only season at Carolina, as he was inducted into the army prior to 1942, and he enrolled at the University of Illinois after the war.

Sossamon had an opportunity to observe a number of running backs at close range, having played against and with Sinkwich, with Ace Parker, against pro great Elroy (Crazylegs) Hirsch, and with 1949 All-American at North Carolina, Charlie Justice, at Bainbridge Naval Base while he was in the service. None of those Hall-of-Fame members impressed him any more than Stasica and Furman's Dewey Proctor, against whom he played in college, and to whom he later snapped the ball at Bainbridge.

Sossamon: "Stasica was the same type runner as Justice. If we'd had him in 1942, we would have had a much better season.

"One of the finest backs I have ever played with or against was Dewey Proctor at Furman. Dewey was a horse. Dewey was a real powerful runner and very difficult to bring down. Sinkwich was an explosive runner, but he didn't have the power that Proctor had."

Another back on the 1941 Gamecock team also drew praise from Sossamon, who commented, "Al Grygo was the same type runner as Crazylegs Hirsch." Hirsch was a great back for Wisconsin, then became the premier pass receiver in the NFL for the Los Angeles Rams, primarily for what he could do *AFTER* he caught the ball.

Grygo and Stasica in the same backfield gave Carolina opponents a lot to think about, but that opposition included potent teams such as Georgia, Clemson, and Penn State. Georgia, which eventually went to the Orange Bowl and defeated Texas Christian, hosted Carolina in the second game, and it turned out to be the only one-sided loss of the year for the Gamecocks, 34-6.

Sossamon: "It was in that game that Sinkwich broke his jaw. I think Steve Novak, who was playing right end for us, went in and probably caught Sinkwich with an elbow. He had to have his jaw wired, but he played the rest of the season."

The pièce dé resistance of 1941 was an 18-14 victory that knocked Clemson from the ranks of the unbeaten and was one of only two losses for the Tigers that year. It was his performance in that game that played a major role in gaining All-Southern Conference honors for Sossamon, as well as Stasica.

In this game it was Stasica's passing and Grygo's running that put 18 first-half points on the board for Carolina, as the defense bottled-up the Tigers' powerful single wing offense. One of the defensive stars for Carolina was end Gus Hempley, who had already been inducted into the army at nearby Fort Jackson but could play, because he had not yet officially withdrawn from school.

It was reported that, following the game, Hempley celebrated into the wee hours with some of his teammates, making a shambles of the military curfew. The following day he reported to his commanding officer to explain the violation, and, after receiving a description of the "company punishment" he would receive, Hempley saluted, and, as he turned to walk away, couldn't help but notice a slightly tarnished Clemson ring on the officer's finger!

Carolina's ranks were becoming depleted, as the draft and injuries took their toll. Fullback Ken Roskie suffered a broken arm in a 3-0 loss to Kansas State in a game that involved a two-day train ride to Manhattan, Kansas, for the Carolina team. It was also the only game during Sossamon's college career that involved a field goal.

In fact, extra points presented an often insurmountable challenge to the Gamecocks, who could have used a few in a 6-6 tie with Wake Forest and a 7-6 loss to Miami that year. For the record, Carolina scored 16 touchdowns in 1941 and was able to convert only four point-after attempts.

Sossamon: "I even tried kicking extra points onetime, and Coach Enright said he'd just let me center the ball from then on. We'd always try to score touchdowns—I don't ever remember us trying a field goal in my three varsity years at the University. You find better kickers today, because they specialize in it. And field goals became prevalent with the emergence of the soccer-style kickers."

Carolina's Southern Conference record for 1941 was four victories and a tie, which meant that they were narrowly edged for the league title by Duke, which had a ranking of No. 2 in the final Associated Press poll. The Blue Devils played Oregon State in the Rose Bowl, which was moved to Durham, because of the outbreak of the war with Japan and ensuing fears of an attack on the nation's west coast.

The 1942 season found Carolina's football roster drained by the armed forces, and, in the football brochure, the coaching staff was listed as follows:

Head football coach: Rex Enright
Backfield coach: Rex Enright
Line coach: Frank Johnson
End coach: Frank Johnson

Sossamon was one of only five "surviving" seniors, along with end John Leitner, tackle Harold Middlebrooks, center James Funderburk, and fullback Ken Roskie. Most of the squad would be saying "farewell" to civilian life during or after the season, but some would figure in post-war Gamecock lineups, including tackles Neil Allen and Dom Fusci, guard Doyle Norman, center Bruce Tate, end Bob O'Harra, and quarterback Earl Dunham.

Ironically, what turned out to be a disastrous season, record-wise (1-7-1) was introduced with a crowning achievement—a scorless tie with a Tennessee team that would go through the season unbeaten, win the Southeastern Conference championship, and defeat Tulsa in the Sugar Bowl. Sossamon had an outstanding game that would propel him toward a second team berth on the Associated Press All-America selections.

Sossamon: "I remember vaguely that Tennessee had a strong running game and that Bobby Cifers was their backfield star. We used a seven-man line most of the time, but I had the prerogative of playing head-on center or dropping back out, whatever I thought was the best thing to do. Most of the time we'd use a six-two

Lou Sossamon wearing Garnet and Black.

In 1985 Lou Sossamon was still going full speed, as publisher of the Gaffney Ledger and as a member of the USC Board of Trustees.

defense—sometimes a five-three—but against Tennessee we went with a six-two or a seven-man line. Tennessee was a power team, and we were geared to stop running attacks. (Carolina held the Volunteers to 87 yards rushing.)

"Against Tennessee I played mostly head-on. Most of the plays were off tackle or to the outside. But, playing head-on, what I was trying to do was get my tip from the blocking back and also the guards. The guards were pulling, and, I'd try to shoot the gap and cut in behind the interference."

Obviously, Sossamon was successful in what he was doing, but he preferred to talk about contributions made by teammates.

Sossamon: "Glen Rice did a terrific job of punting—he was a great punter—got his punts off fast and kicked them very high. In a closely contested game it's (punting) a weapon. We were having trouble moving the ball (Carolina gained only 40 yards rushing), but we were able to hold them. We stopped 'em when it counted.

Incidentally, Glen wore contact lenses when he played, and that was unheard of back then."

An account of the game in *The State* newspaper said, "Louis Sossamon, Carolina's great center from Gaffney, was one of Carolina's defensive bulwarks, but he had able support from every player who strutted the Garnet and White uniform and flaunted it under the Tennessee nostrils."

Sossamon considered it one of the three best games he played at Carolina, along with the 1941 victories over North Carolina and Clemson.

On December 11 the Associated Press announced its All-America team, which included Sossamon, behind first team choice Joe Domnanovich of Alabama, against whom Sossamon had played during the season.

Discussing the reasons for his selection, Sossamon commented, "I look back and I can pretty well hit it on the button. It was good publicity by Frank Wardlaw (journalism professor and director of the USC News Service). He put out a lot of material to sports writers around the country. And that year we went down and played Alabama, and I had a pretty good game, and the boy down there made All-America center. Publicity. Any athlete needs it to make honors. And I think that my playing better than forty-five minutes a game was a factor.

"I also enjoyed blocking so much. I don't say that I was the greatest blocker. But I contributed there, because I had a great desire to get the job done with the man I was facing. The center didn't have many decisions to make on offense. If someone lined-up in front of you, you had to block that man. If not, you had to go for one of the linebackers, to help one of the guards, depending on which way the play was going.

"We really didn't give much thought to pass protection. We just had straight blocking, working more on running plays, punting, and kickoffs."

As an indication of the confidence shown in their passing game, even with an obvious opportunity to defeat Tennessee with a single score, the Gamecocks only attempted seven passes. And three of those were caught by Tennessee!

Sossamon: "Passing wasn't considered that much more of a weapon than the running game. If you attempted ten and completed five, that was considered a good passing game."

Drawn from memories that had faded over four decades were

those who wore the Garnet alongside him, as the United States intensified its crusade to crush the Axis powers—Germany, Italy, and Japan.

Sossamon: "The fellow I had more respect for and still do is Earl Dunham. Earl was a real student in college (Phi Beta Kappa), as well as a student of football. I believed in what he was doing—calling signals. Earl was just a fine, outstanding boy.

"Bill Milner, John Leitner were gung-ho football players. They'd get in the trenches with anybody. Harvey (Blouin) was a great football player, but he went into the service. Dutch Elston was a leader in forty-one, no question about that. I talked to Dutch on the telephone two days ago. He's retired (in California). He was in education there, and he coached O.J. Simpson (great running back for Southern California and in the NFL) in junior college.

"Grygo—Twinkletoes—was an inspirational type boy, and you felt once he got his hands on the ball, he could score for you. He was a fantastic teammate."

Louis left Carolina with another teammate of sorts, marrying his campus girl friend, Kathryn Edgerton of Orangeburg. Kathryn's father was Dr. N.B. Edgerton, who was head coach at Carolina from 1912 to 1915, compiling a record of 19 wins, 13 losses, and three ties, not bad in comparison to other coaching marks at the University. Dr. Edgerton later went into active medical practice and became Chief of Staff at Columbia Hospital.

Sossamon confessed to being an average student, adding quickly that his wife was elected to Phi Beta Kappa. Qualities of leadership, however, were most conspicuous in Sossamon to his fellow students, as he was elected captain of the 1942 football team, president of the student body during his senior year, and president of the Sigma Alpha Epsilon social fraternity.

After serving in the Navy from 1943 to 1945, during which time he played on the powerful Bainbridge Naval Base team for two seasons, Sossamon entered civilian life again.

Sossamon: "I was stationed at Pearl Harbor and returned to San Francisco to be discharged. There I signed a contract to play with the New York Yankees, which were owned by Dan Topping and Dale Webb. I spent three years, from nineteen forty-six to nineteen forty-eight, with the Yankees. My contract the first year was for ten thousand dollars, and I received an eight hundred dollar bonus, because I averaged forty-five minutes a game.

"My first year I would play two-ways (offense and defense) in the first quarter, another team would come in for the second quarter, and I'd play defense in the second quarter. They started platooning the next year.

"We played Cleveland for the championship in nineteen forty-seven and nineteen forty-eight. They beat us both times, ten to seven in Cleveland and seven to nothing in New York. I received eight hundred dollars for the championship game, and we had about sixty-three thousand people in the stands.

"I got word at the beginning of the nineteen forty-nine season that they (Yankees) no longer needed me. I did play two games that year, and one of my teammates was Tom Landry (later coach of the Dallas Cowboys) at defensive halfback."

Thus, Sossamon had rubbed elbows with some of the all-time greats of college and professional football, before he returned to Gaffney to become ad manager for his father's newspaper. While playing a couple of service games at Pearl Harbor, Louis had even had Stan Musical (Hall-of-Fame outfielder for the St. Louis Cardinals) as a waterboy.

In 1969 Sossamon purchased the newspaper from his father and became President and Publisher, positions he still held in 1985.

During his years of absence from South Carolina, Sossamon's interest in his old school never waned, and once back home they didn't line-up very often in Carolina Stadium without Sossamon looking on. In 1982 that interest became official, as he was elected by the State Legislature to the University Board of Trustees.

Sossamon: "The University had given a lot to me, and I felt I could give the University something in return. (He serves on the Intercollegiate Activities Committee, which had jurisdiction over the athletic program). I'm pleased with the progress we have made and the caliber of people we have at the University. The (football) coaching staff—Joe Morrison and his assistants—is the finest in the United States.

"They have discipline and dedication. I heard that when Joe Morrison first came here he had a meeting with the players, and some of them had their hats on and their feet up on the furniture. He told them, 'Now, fellows, my mother taught me that when I was in the house to take my hat off.' All the hats came off. 'She also told me not to put my feet on the furniture.' The feet came off the furniture.

55

"Another thing, the boys believe in him. He'd like to see all his boys graduate. And they have an English tutoring class of ten boys. He went in and told them, 'You boys are here to learn English. If you cut this class, you're cutting practice. And, if you cut practice, you don't play.' They all attended and did well.

"Serving on the Board has given me insight, as to how silly we can be as individuals. It's like sitting in the stands, and someone is being critical. And somebody turns to him and asks, 'What year did you play?' 'I didn't play.' You sit on the outside, and it's easy to be critical, until you know all the facts."

Confidence in the educational aspects of Carolina was demonstrated by the Sossamons when they enrolled their two daughters and son at the University, where they all received degrees. The son (Louis Cody Sossamon, Jr.) now assists his father at the newspaper.

Although Lou Sossamon and his Carolina teammates were not distinguised by won-lost standards, they plowed new ground and lifted horizons for Gamecock football during a troubled time, when the only winning of importance had to do with the life-and-death struggle that was taking place in the villages of Europe and on islands with odd names in the Pacific Ocean.

Amidst all this Carolinians, began to observe a wider world, stretching beyond state borders, and when the war was over and America could become enthralled with collegiate sports once more, they looked to a broadening circle of rivals. The teams of the Sossamon era had established a competitiveness on an interstate level, challenging the likes of Georgia, Penn State, Alabama, and Tennessee.

They had broken domination by North Carolina and Clemson and played on even terms with a Tennessee team that ranked seventh best in the nation (AP).

Personally, Sossamon achieved the highest individual honor yet achieved by a Carolina player (2nd team AP All-America), and was the second Gamecock to be selected to play in a post-season all-star game, the 1942 Blue-Gray game in Montgomery, Alabama. (Back Ed Clary played in the 1938 Blue-Gray game.) He was the first from the University to be named to the All-Southern team twice (1941 and 1942).

In 1968 Sossamon was among the second group to be inducted into the University's Athletic Hall of Fame, and it was most appropriate that the coach he admired, Rex Enright, was inducted (posthumously) on the same evening. Sossamon is also a member of the South Carolina (State) Athletic Hall of Fame.

Over four decades had passed since he last suited-out in the garnet jersey with the white shoulders and a big number 50 on the back, but in 1985, in many ways, Louis Sossamon was still very much a member of the team.

BRYANT **meeks**

46

CENTER

Coach Rex Enright once called Bryant Meeks the best athlete with whom he had ever been associated. In his semi-retirement, Meeks recalls his ex-coach as one of the great influences on his interesting and productive life.

4 BRYANT MEEKS

bryant Meeks is a living testimony to three influences that have helped him become a highly successful individual, as a businessman, husband, father, and civic servant.

There's the YMCA program in his hometown of Macon, Ga., which Meeks credits with getting him on the right track in his early youth. And the college football scholarship, without which he would likely never have received a higher education. Then, Rex Enright, who was Bryant's head football coach at the University of South Carolina for only one year, but to whom he credits a very positive impact on his life.

If you are around Meeks for more than a few seconds, you'll also receive a glowing endorsement for Sarasota, Florida, where he now spends about half his time playing golf and racketball, and the rest of his "working day" in the investment and real estate business.

Meek's Gamecock connection spanned his junior and senior years in college, in which he was a good student and campus leader, along with playing center on the football team well enough to earn a second team berth on the 1946 Associated Press All-America team.

Carolina's football program was moving from war to peace during the days in which Meeks performed so magnificently on offense and defense, combining good speed with the grace of a basketball player and the strength of a shot putter. Twenty-six years after his final game in Carolina Stadium he was remembered with sufficient esteem to earn induction into the school's athletic hall of fame, the 11th football player to be so honored.

You could call Carolina's success as a team while Meeks was in school just average, with a 2-4-3 record in 1945 and 5-3-0 in 1946. Still the '45 team became Carolina's first to be invited to a postseason game, meeting Wake Forest in the Gator Bowl at Jacksonville.

Hence, at the age of 59, Meeks looked back over achievements that were by no means predictable when his family moved from Jacksonville, Fla., to Macon in 1936 to open a tiny restaurant with two tables and five stools.

Meeks: "Pretty soon after that my parents were divorced, and Mother ran the restaurant, which continued to expand. I joined the YMCA, and that probably kept me from being a 'dead end' kid. That's the reason I've always been so dedicated to the Y; because of its principles.

"The war started when I was a sophomore at Lanier High School. I wanted to go out for football but had to work in the restaurant, and I almost left home over it. I told Mother to let me play football and basketball, or I'd leave home. And she did.

"As a junior I went out for the B team, and toward the end of the season I was one of the boys they moved up to the varsity. I played center, and I had pretty good size. When I was a senior the center from the previous year was still on the team, and I didn't play first string until the fifth game. I finally beat-out that fellow.

"Our team just had an average season, but we did beat Tech High of Atlanta. And certainly nobody contacted me about a college football scholarship. I also threw the shot put for the track team and played center on the basketball team, and one night an assistant football coach for the University of Georgia came to our basketball game. He asked me if I had any offers of a football scholarship, and I said, 'No sir.' Then he asked me if I'd be interested in trying out.

"Chances of my going to college were very thin, so I went up to Athens and tried out. We did wind sprints and all kinds of drills, coordination tests, and so forth. I was always reasonably fast for a lineman, weighing a hundred eight-five to a hundred ninety, and I was almost six-three.

"In nineteen forty-three freshmen were eligible at Georgia, which had beaten UCLA in the Rose Bowl the previous season. Then everybody went into the service—it's a wonder Coach (Wally) Butts didn't have a stroke. We were all either seventeen-year-olds— like me—or four-Fs. Quite a comedown from coaching a Rose Bowl champion and then a group of ragamuffins.

"We had a reasonably good team, and I lived through it. I was the starting center for every game and enjoyed Coach Butts, although he was the meanest guy you ever saw. Butts was a terror, believe me! But being able to play as a freshman was a great opportunity for me, and my scholarship was room, books, tuition, meals, and fifteen dollars a month.

"We did lose our game to Georgia Tech, with Franklin Broyles and all those great players."

However, for Meeks, becoming a rising sophomore had its disadvantages, such as moving into the draft age for the United States Army.

Meeks: "I took the Air Force exam but failed it; but a friend asked me if I wanted to go to Atlanta with him to take the exam for the Naval Air Force. I figured I had nothing to lose—I was discouraged and didn't want to be drafted. Anyhow, I passed this time and went into the navy on March first, nineteen forty-four. I was assigned to Mercer, where I stayed for sixteen months, and it was there that I started dating Jackie Griffis, the girl I'd marry one day. We had been in grade school together in Macon.

"It was then that I was given a choice of going to Naval Preflight or midshipman's school and get a commission. I elected school and was transferred to the University of South Carolina Naval R.O.T.C. program. It turned out to be a blessing in disguise—in many respects."

When he referred to blessings, Bryant was thinking in terms of himself, but it also turned out to be one of the finest recruiting moves in Carolina's football history—totally unsolicited.

Meeks: "One of the first things I did was to go over to see the coaches, because I knew I'd be there during the fall. So I went out for football."

Enright, who had begun coaching Carolina in 1938, was in the Navy, having been replaced in 1943 by J.P. Moran and in 1944 by Doc Newton. Now, it was Johnny McMillan's turn for a one-year regime as head coach.

McMillan, a native of Fitzgerald, Ga., had played for Enright in 1938, and had turned out highly successful teams at Sumter High School, from which he came to Carolina as an assistant to Newton in 1944.

Meeks: "McMillan was a very, very serious man, but I liked him a lot. Many people thought he just didn't have any personality, but I believe it was that he was just so intent on what he was doing, he didn't have time to smile and do other things. He was certainly dedicated to football. In retrospect, I can't remember how I really felt about his football knowledge. I know specifically how I feel about Coach Enright—he had a very significant influence on my life when he came back the next year.

One of the assistant coaches on the 1945 Carolina staff had a closer association with Meeks, and he was Lt. Bob Hayden, who had been an all-East quarterback at Harvard and whom Meeks described as "really a quality man."

Meeks: "Later he tempted me—in June of nineteen forty-six—when I got out of the Navy. Haley said, 'How would you like to go to Harvard,' and I told him that I'd never even thought about it. That's an awful long way from home.

"He told me that he'd give me a job with his paper company after I finished (Harvard). I often wonder what would have happened, if I had taken his advice."

That Gamecock squad was a mixture of Naval R.O.T.C. cadets, and those ineligible for the draft because of age or other reasons. College rules of the day still limited substitutions, so players had to go both ways—offense and defense—and substitutions were usually made because of injury, rather than for rest or special talents.

Meeks: "We had a real good spirit on that team but really didn't have much experience. I played six consecutive sixty-minute games, and it almost killed me. At the end of the sixth game I weighed 175 pounds. Something happened during that season that changed my whole attitude toward football. That's when we went down to play Alabama in Montgomery. They beat us by some horrible score. (It was 55-0 by an Alabama team that finished the season ranked No. 2 in the Associated Press ratings.) I've never been hit like I was hit in that game, and I always thought I was in pretty good shape. I had charley horses and bruises from it, and I made up my mind that I was really not in condition and that I would never get tired in a football game again. I got so tired that day, it was a wonder I was not hurt seriously.

"Later I used to preach, when I was coaching, that the times when you get hurt are when you're lying on the ground and can't protect yourself, or when you're tired and you're loafing.

"But this Carolina team was another ragamuffin team, but we had a lot of closeness. We were just a group of individuals who showed up and played football, because we enjoyed it. Of course, I had wanted to coach ever since I was in high school, because my high school coach, Tom McWhorter, had such an influence on me by making me behave myself that I made up my mind that's what I wanted to do."

Carolina used the Notre Dame box offense, which McMillan learned in his playing days under Enright, but he had precious little time to mold a team for the opening game against Duke, which had beaten Alabama in the Sugar Bowl the previous season and was on its way to a third straight Southern Conference championship. The game was a mismatch, with the Blue Devils prevailing, 60-0.

Meeks: "The thing I remember about the Duke game is that someone hit me from the blind side and knocked me into the high jump pit. I never will forget flying through the air and thinking, 'How could this happen to me?' From then on I was very careful about being hit from the blind side'"

One of the stars for Duke was Bill Milner, a guard who had played for Carolina in 1941 and 1942 but was in the Navy program at Duke and finished his college football career there. Milner was later an outstanding lineman for the Chicago Bears.

The Gamecocks picked-up a couple of wins against Presbyterian and Camp Blanding before the Alabama debacle, which led into the Big Thursday game against Clemson. With World War II finally over, a record crowd of 25,000 overflowed Carolina Stadium for the game, in which Clemson was heavily favored. The Tigers were 3-1 entering the game and would finish the season at 6-3-1.

However, this day was ruled by the Carolina defense, which intercepted six Clemson passes, held the Tigers to 178 yards rushing, and benefited from 100 yards in penalties against their opponent.

That deadlock became habit-forming, because the Gamecocks travelled to Miami, Fla., for a 13-13 tie with Miami, then moved to Charlotte for a stand-off with Wake Forest by the identical score. The regular season ended with a 19-13 loss to Maryland at College Park, and Carolina players began making their plans for Christmas holidays.

Surprisingly, the newly-founded Gator Bowl in Jacksonville, Fla., determined that it would be worthwhile to invite Carolina and Wake Forest to play-off their tie on New Year's Day of 1946. The presence of Rex Enright, who was stationed at Jacksonville, was no small factor in that judgement.

Meeks: "Some of us were kinda shocked. I had already made plans to go home to Macon and work, because I needed the money, but we voted to accept the Gator Bowl invitation. Then the University decided they couldn't give us any spending money, so a group of us got together and went to see the president of the University (Admiral Norman M. Smith) in his office. It was almost like a union meeting. I made the mistake of calling him (Admiral Smith) 'Mister,' because I forgot that he was an admiral, and he seemed a little shocked. The essence of the meeting was that we wouldn't accept the invitation to the Gator Bowl, unless the University could give us spending money to replace money we could earn. We had figured out how much we'd earn during the holidays, and it came to about a hundred and fifty dollars. So, at that meeting the University decided to give the players a hundred and fifty dollars, and we were happy as all get-out!

"It took a lot of nerve on our part to do that. Today, nobody would even think about it."

Although Carolina held a 7-6 halftime lead, Wake Forest won that inaugural Gator Bowl game, 26-14, before a crowd of 7,362.

Meeks: "The Gator Bowl was no big, blown-out affair. Seems that I recall one dinner, a few radio interviews, and some newspaper coverage. We only practiced about a week for the game, so we weren't in the best physical condition. I was the team captain, and I won the coin toss. In fact, I still have the silver dollar in my safe deposit box.

"Speaking of coin tosses, one day Coach Enright told me that anytime I had the opportunity to call the toss, 'Call tails,' he said. Studies had been done at Duke University on probability, and eighty per cent of the time it was tails. In my lifetime I've always done that—playing golf, or whatever. And most of the time it has been tails!"

When Enright returned to coach the Gamecocks in 1946 Meeks was the only returning starter from the previous season, and it couldn't have been a more valuable association from Bryant's standpoint.

Meeks: "Coach Enright had a very big influence on my coaching life. Every week we'd meet on Monday, and he'd say, 'This is basically what they do,' He'd have all their (opponents) plays analyzed and the percentages. Like, in this situation, ninety per cent of the time they're gonna do this, and so forth. Teaching me what to call, because I did call the signals. He would lay-out the defense and go into the reasoning for the defense—why you want to play this— the strength of this defense—the weakness. I can remember a lot of things he said.

"I thought he had a great football mind, but this man also had a significant influence on me as a person. I liked his manner—the way he treated people. He didn't yell and scream—as Butts did—and

Bryant Meeks, as he appeared in his career as star center for Carolina.

as other coaches do. Each coach has his own personality.

"I'd run through a brick wall for a fellow like Rex Enright, because he treated me as a human being.

"I learned a lot about organization from Coach Enright—the importance of working together toward common objectives. These are lessons that have been very valuable to me during my whole lifetime. I was dedicated to him one hundred per cent.

"At that time he had the Notre Dame mystique about him—that might have been part of it. But I remember his saying, 'They run this play in this situation—look out for this and look out for that.' He had a defensive game plan that was well-organized.

"With our personnel I think we did a pretty good job. A little bit more formal approach to the game, similar to the analytical approach of today that's done with computers for the Dallas Cowboys. I would say his strength was defense, as opposed to offense. I can't remember us being a wide open, strong offensive team."

Calling offensive plays for the Gamecocks that season was Earl Dunham, whom Meeks described as "one of the smartest people I've ever known," adding, "Coach Enright had a lot of respect for him."

Always in the back of Meeks' head was that his goal was to coach some day, and he cataloged everything that he felt would be of value in such a career.

Meeks: "Awhile back a friend asked me if I had anything left over from the Steelers (Meeks played for Pittsburgh following his graduation from Carolina). The only thing I had was a playbook I did. In those days very few teams had a playbook, because they were so afraid of it getting into the hands of opponents. I committed to memory all the assignments of all the players and wrote 'em down in my 1947 calendar. I still have it—it's a treasure. The single wing, as devised by Dr. Jock Sutherland (Pittsburgh Steelers coach)."

Besides his association with Enright, Meeks had other memories of the 1946 season, which saw college football return to somewhat a normal state, except for the average age of the players. Returning veterans dotted the rosters, and Carolina had its share, with Dunham, tackle Dom Fusci, guard Max Walker, guard Doyle Norman, tackle Jake Land, end Bob O'Harra, halfback Jim Hunnicut, quarterback Bo Hagan, halfback Bobby Giles, center Bruce Tate, and others.

Football was more of a family affair during this era than anytime in history, as many of the service veterans had acquired wives along the way.

Meeks: "I got married on Sunday, September 1, 1946 and came from Macon to Columbia in a 1933 Chevrolet. This was our honeymoon—we stayed in Hotel Columbia—somebody gave me the expenses, but I don't remember who. The next day Jackie went for a job interview, and I went to football practice. I might be the only fellow in the world to spend his honeymoon on the football field!"

The 1946 season had some good and bad memories for Bryant, but the record of 5-3 included a 26-14 victory over Clemson. One of the losses was a close 14-6 decision to an Alabama team that had defeated Southern California, 34-14, in January's Rose Bowl.

Meeks: "Alabama had an All-America center named Vaughn Mancha, and he had only one eye or, at least, impaired vision in one eye. Red Wilson (end) hit him on a punt return and crumpled him— on the blind side. Red was a freshman, and he came back to the huddle and said, 'Look, Bryant, look! They're hauling off that All-American so and so. It was a perfectly legal block, but Red really put the screws to him. (Wilson was from Meeks' hometown of Macon.)

"Years later a friend of mine here in Sarasota—George Lambert—and I were talking about that. He got to play in that game because Mancha got hurt."

The most thrilling win of that year was over Maryland, 21-17, on a scoring pass from Hagan to Whitey Jones with only 17 seconds left.

Meeks: "That's the game in which I broke my nose. I have bad memories of that game. I don't remember who the fellow was, but he hit me in the nose with his elbow and broke it. I bled like a stuck hog, but I played the rest of the game and was really upset.

"Later in the season when I got a telegram from Pittsburgh about playing professional football, I had a personal quandry as to whether I should come back and play and get my masters degree, or go to Pittsburgh and get on with my life. (Meeks still had one year of eligibility remaining.) I thought about the fellow who hit me in the nose, and it almost prompted me to come back just to play against him again. I wanted to get back at him so bad, I didn't know what to do."

The decision was to turn pro, and it resulted in Meeks' first trip by air—to Pittsburgh. Later, in Minnesota, Meeks would earn his pilot's license and log over 900 hours of flight time.

Meeks: "Al Grygo (former backfield star at USC and the Chicago Bears, who was an assistant coach at Carolina) was very helpful to me in my negotiations with Pittsburgh. I ended up making six thousand each season, and that was a lot more money than a lot of pro linemen were making. I heard that some of the Redskins linemen were making as little as fifteen hundred to eighteen hundred a year.

"Pittsburgh used the single wing, so I had to learn to snap the ball end over end for Sutherland. He wanted it to come into the thigh of the receiver standing straight up with the laces facing the front. That's the way it had to be. I must have snapped the ball three or four hundred times a day the first season. And I got pretty good at it.

"My first season we were the first Pittsburgh team to be involved in the championship playoffs until they reached the Super Bowl years. We were tied with the Philadelphia Eagles for the Eastern Division championship and lost to them in a playoff game.

"I played mostly on defense, although in college I always thought I was better offensively than defensively. I always enjoyed blocking, because I had good coordination and good speed."

After his senior season Meeks had received a bushel of honors, including selection as second team center on the Associated Press All-America, All-Southern Conference, and recipient of the Jacobs Blocking Trophy as best in the category among college players in the state of South Carolina. He was also voted Carolina's best athlete by the students and received the Jack Dempsey Adams Hat award.

What meant even more to Bryant was an accompanying quote from Enright, describing him as "the finest athlete I've ever known."

Meeks: "I was always proud of that, because he had known a lot of good athletes." (Enright played on the team with the legendary Four Horsemen at Notre Dame.)

Meeks was also a student leader, being selected to Blue Key National Honorary Fraternity, serving as president, an office he also held in Sigma Nu social fraternity.

As to the honors he received in college, Meeks comments: "Those things never crossed my mind—they really didn't. I've always tried to do the best that I can do at whatever I'm doing. I wasn't playing for notoriety, but just doing the best I could. I've been criticized many times in my lifetime for being too conscientious—but that's the way I am.

"I really thought I had a better season in forty-five than forty-six. A lot of that stuff is publicity, and often it's before the fact, rather than after the fact."

In 1985 Meeks was still in playing form, as he enjoyed semi-retirement in Sarasota, Florida.

One opponent from Meeks' NFL experience left an indelible impression on him.

Meeks: "In the forty-eight season, playing against the Philadelphia Eagles, a fellow named Frank Kilroy—now the General Manager of the New England Patriots—and I'd probably hit him in the head, if I'd see him today on the street—or a back alley—but I'd get a big piece of lumber to do it. He was a huge man. He hit me in the mouth with his elbow on a kickoff return, and I lost five teeth—with one lick. Fractured all of my gum and all of that bone. I had tackled Steve Van Buren right before the half, and his knee hit me in the head. I was still a little dizzy, as we kicked off in the second

half. I completely blanked out. I don't even remember this fellow
Kilroy hitting me, but I did walk off the field under my own power.

"Very few people in those days wore face masks. I didn't practice for three weeks. But the next week when I went over there
(practice field) fifteen or twenty face masks showed up on head gear.
Of course, it's standard equipment now. Fortunately, I always had a
high pain tolerance, so it didn't bother me.

"At Pittsburgh I weighed only a hundred and ninety pounds—
the smallest center in the NFL—so they didn't think I could block
anybody. After I lost those teeth in nineteen forty-eight I couldn't
open my mouth except to drink through a straw for fourteen days,
and I lost down to a hundred and seventy-five pounds."

"After that season I came down to Florida, where my wife's
folks had moved. Bill Bruckland, who coached the Sarasota High
School team, and I had been roommates at Georgia, and he offered
me the job as line coach, so I took it. The next year Bill left, and I
became head coach. I enjoyed my four years of coaching and still
have my former players come to see me and call me coach. I like
that."

During the next 30 years of his life Meeks compiled a highly
successful record as a businessman, starting out in 1955 with a
petroleum subsidiary of Allied Chemical Corporation. His career
took him to Lake Worth, Fla., and then to Minneapolis, Minn.,
where he spent seven years as vice president and general manager
of Home Gas Company, which employed 230 people, served 30,000
customers, and had annual revenue in excess of $6 million.

This led to his appointment as General Manager, Marketing,
of Allied's Union Texas Petroleum Division in Houston, Tex., with
225,000 customers and 1,300 employees.

Having learned a wealth of sophisticated management techniques, Meeks was enticed by United Inns of Memphis, Tenn., to
become Vice President for Business Development. This New York
Stock Exchange company operated 35 Holiday Inns, 17 full service
car washes, and a furniture manufacturing company.

Meeks: "This was the greatest thing that ever happened to
me. I learned how to put deals together, leverage, finance . . . and
how to be patient."

Always in the back of Bryant's mind, however, was the beauty
of the Sarasota area, and the enjoyable life styles of that still pro-
gressive Florida west coast community.

Consequently, when the opportunity to go into business for
himself surfaced there, Meeks couldn't resist, and he became Presi-

dent and half-owner of MAB, Inc., which owned a wholesale plumbing supply company, a wholesale tire business, a lumber and building materials business, and a barbecue restaurant.

On the side he served as a consultant to United Inns on two Holiday Inns in West Germany, and as President of a fish and fruit processing company, which exported to the United States, in Colombia, South America.

This intense business life provided financial security for Meeks and his family, so in 1980 he divested himself of some of his interests in order to follow a more relaxed schedule. Now his role as a realtor and business consultant allows him to play golf twice a week and racketball four times.

Hailing back to his experience with the YMCA as a youth in Macon, Meeks became deeply involved with the Y in Sarasota, serving as President and leading a re-organization movement that transformed it from a floundering program to one of great facilities and vitality.

Although Bryant and Jackie counted mostly blessings during the first 38 years of their marriage, tragedy came in 1976, when their son, Michael, died as the result of an automobile accident that occured just six days after his wedding. The Bryants have a daughter, Trudy Faye, and a son, Randall Alton, a political science major at American University in Washington.

Through its football history, if the University of South Carolina can lay claim to a tradition of greatness at any single position, it would likely be center/linebacker. As far back as the early 1900's Ed Girardeau and Ed Smith played the position with distinction, followed by Bill Boyd and Julian Beall in the twenties, and Louis Sossamon of the early forties. The decades that followed World War II produced Harry Jabbusch, Larry Smith, Leon Cunningham, who wore the Garnet and Black in the fifties, plus the two-platoon stars of the sixties and seventies, and James Seawright, who roamed the Gamecock defense in th early eighties. Four of the 18 football players who had been installed in the Carolina Athletic Hall of Fame, as of 1984, were centers—Sossamon, Meeks, Smith, and Cunningham.

None played the position with greater determination, intensity, and skill than Bryant Adams Meeks, who was a Gamecock only because of the fortunes of war. Yet few contributed as much to the school in so short a time but left with a greater appreciation for his experience there.

1943-46-47

ERNIE **lawhorne**

During Ernie Lawhorne's 12 seasons as a player and assistant coach at Carolina, the Gamecocks experienced only one losing season. Now Lawhorne is a prototype Carolina supporter.

HALFBACK

5 ERNIE LAWHORNE

t a university with a long history of avoiding its own alumni on coaching staffs, Ernie Lawhorne is a rare bird. In a 12-year varsity football career as player and assistant coach, Lawhorne was involved with teams that compiled a record of 67 victories against 44 losses and a tie, experiencing only one losing season. Not bad for a school that had a cumulative record barely above the .500 mark through the 1984 season.

However, Lawhorne comes across as just happy to be around when some good things happened, rather than attempting to claim any of the credit. He was privileged to share the experience of some of Carolina's greatest victories before leaving the world of college football for the less turbulent and more rewarding (monetarily) life of an insurance agent with Boyle-Vaughan Associates in Columbia.

As a tailback for Lanier High School in Macon, Ga. in 1941, Lawhorne caught the eye of few college recruiters. Carolina's Rex Enright had already established a foothold in Macon by recruiting several athletes, including Earl Dunham for football and Dick Anderson, who ended-up playing basketball after an injury that ended his gridiron days.

Lanier used the Notre Dame shift, Enright's offense at Carolina, which gave its players an advantage in adapting to the Gamecock system.

Lawhorne: "It was very similar to the single wing, except you lined-up behind center and shifted to one side or the other, according to the play. But you ended up in about the same thing as the single wing.

"The first time I met anyone from Carolina was in Augusta. We played Richmond Academy and I had one of those go-to-hell nights where it looked like everything fell right, and I looked like an All-American. And Coach Enright came in the dressing room afterward and asked me if I'd be interested in going to South Carolina. At that time all I could think of was Auburn—I wanted to be a veterinarian. Later I went over to Auburn and worked out and broke my ankle in the workout, and unbeknowing to me, I had a scholarship, had I just held them to it, but I didn't know that. So I went back to Macon and got over the ankle injury, and coach Enright called me and asked me to come up. Back in those days everybody worked out. I think there were five or six of us from Macon that came up, and they took four of us on scholarship."

Lawhorne added that Pat Thrash, Jim Hunnicutt, and Charlie Gaines were the other three. With the advent of World War II a Naval R.O.T.C. unit was established at Carolina and most of the football players, including Lawhorne, were enrolled in the program.

Among the members of the 1942 Carolina freshman team were Thrash, an end, Bobby Giles, a back, and Bettis Herlong, who completed his college career as a tailback at Duke after the war. Red Ozburn, a tackle, and Jack Couch, a back, and Phil Alexander, a tackle, were other 1942 freshmen who were Lawhorne's teammates on post-war teams.

The 1942 Carolina freshmen won all four games they played, but with the military draft in full force, who would be available for the 1943 varsity was uncertain. In fact, Enright was a naval officer when football season arrived, and J.P. Moran, an officer in the Naval R.O.T.C. unit at Carolina was appointed football coach. His assistants were notably some of the more mature players on the team.

The Gamecocks, because of the availability of R.O.T.C. personnel, were in better shape that many of the college teams, particularly those without military units. Carolina played an abbreviated seven-game schedule, including five teams located in South Carolina and two in North Carolina. They defeated Newberry, Presbyterian, Clemson, Charleston Coast Guard, and Wake Forest, while losing only to the 176th Infantry (Fort Jackson) and North Carolina.

Along with Lawhorne, there were several players on the '43 squad who would figure prominently in post-war Carolina football, including Thrash, Dom Fusci, Neil Allen, and Al Faress.

Lawthorne: "I remember the Clemson game very well, because Butch Butler (Clemson tailback), whom we thought was in the service and hadn't played up until that time, played that day. I understand that he was still in school, so he was eligible, so they brought him back out of the service.

"We won the game (33-6) against Clemson, but they were handicapped at that time, because they didn't have any Naval R.O.T.C. unit or anything to hold 'em in school."

Lawhorne's punting played a significant role in the game, especially in the first half, when the Gamecocks failed to score, and the Tigers converted a fumbled punt recovery at the Gamecock nine into the only touchdown of the half. A Lawhorne punt was a factor in getting the Gamecocks on track in the third quarter.

Lawhorne: "We practiced a quick kick during the week, and I didn't know he (Moran) was gonna call a quick kick, but Butler had just quick kicked, and we were in a hole. On second or third down we got the call from the bench to quick kick, and I never had done it in college under pressure, but, anyhow, I kicked it, and the wind caught it, they let it hit, and it rolled a mile. I think it ended-up about a 62-yard kick."

Two plays later the Tigers fumbled to set-up Carolina's first score in a 33-6 romp in which Clemson gained one yard rushing, none passing, and made one first down, on a penalty.

Fusci, one of Lawhorne's 1943 teammates, was a stocky Brooklynite who wanted to get all of the fun he could out of football, and he tells this as a true story:

With changes in military assignments players were shipping in and out of the Carolina football reservoir with regularity, and Moran never had the identical squad from one week to the next. In the third quarter of the Clemson game, with the score tied, a strange face appeared in the huddle beside Fusci.

"Who are you," Fusci asked, "and what position do you play?" The boy told Fusci his name and that he played tackle.

"Well, I play tackle, too," Fusci whispered, "so why didn't you tell me you're supposed to replace me?"

"I thought you might get mad," the youngster explained. The Gamecocks broke from their huddle, while Fusci tried to think of a way to get off the field before the ball was snapped, saving his team a penalty for having too many players. As the team lined up, Fusci eyed the nearby Clemson sideline and sprinted for it, as Tiger coaches shouted to the defense to watch the man in motion.

Clemson's defenders shifted in the direction of the "man in motion," and, as Fusci tumbled into the Clemson bench area, the ball was snapped. Phil Cantore, Gamecock back, scooped up a loose pitchout toward the opposite side of the field, and sprinted down the sideline on a 70-yard touchdown run that put South Carolina ahead to stay.

After the fifth game of the season Lawhorne was inducted into the Navy, in which he served until early 1946, when he returned for the spring semester at Carolina. Another Navy returnee was Enright, who was busily assembling the best possible squad to resume his efforts toward building a competitive football program.

The Gamecocks opened the season with Newberry, winning by only 21-0, despite freshman quarterback Bo Hagan's 55-yard touchdown run on the first offensive play. Alabama, featuring All-America passing wizard Harry Gilmer, who had high school players all over the nation jumping into the air to throw the ball to imitate his style, was Carolina's second opponent. Coached by Frank Thomas, who was Enright's fellow Notre Dame alumnus, the Crimson Tide had beaten Southern Cal in the Rose Bowl in January and was rated as a national contender this season.

Lawhorne: "On the night before the game (in Columbia) Enright and Thomas, who were very close friends, went to see Columbia high play Savannah on old Melton Field. One team used the "sleeper play" and scored. Thomas turned to Enright and said, 'You know, that ol' play seems to work nearly every time.'

"The next day, in the first half, we sent two players in, and three came out, except that Earl Dunham stayed in bonds right at the sideline. In those days a player could get outside of the official. So, the ball was snapped, and Earl was all by himself down the sideline, and Bo hit him with a pass that gave us a 6-0 lead at halftime."

Alabama rallied in the second half behind Gilmer's passing and won the game, 14-6, but Carolina was encouraged that they could play that close a game with a national power.

Lawhorne had the unique experience of having the nation's Secretary of State practically in his lap during the Clemson game of that year. Hundreds of counterfeit tickets for the Big Thursday game had been sold before the sham was discovered, and a major gate-crashing occurred when holders of all types of tickets massed outside Carolina Stadium as gametime neared.

By kickoff the actual playing field was the only space in the stadium not occupied by humanity, and officials had to halt play several times to move spectators off the field. Secretary of State James F. Byrnes, a South Carolinian, was seated almost at ground level and couldn't see over the heads of those around the field, so he joined the milling throng on the sidelines.

Lawhorne recalls, "When I came out of the game, I was kneeling beside Mr. Byrnes. He was almost in my lap!" Carolina won the game, 26-14.

Entering the final three games of that year Carolina had the makings of an outstanding record, standing at 4-1, as they faced Clark Shaughnessy's Maryland team at College Park. With time running out Carolina trailed, 17-14, and was confronted with a fourth-down situation in Gamecock territory.

Lawhorne: "Coach Enright sent me in, told us to get in punt formation, and told me, 'If you feel you can hit Red (Wilson) over the middle, do it.' Red was open, and I threw to him for a first down. Bo (Hagan) completed a pass to somebody else, then, with only 17 seconds left, hit Whitey Jones in the end zone to win the game (21-17)."

"Up until then we were a good football team, but we struggled in the final two games (Duke and Wake Forest), because of injuries. I was really a defensive back, but even I had to play quarterback some in the last two games, because Bo and Droopy Atwell were out with injuries."

Thus, the first post-war season ended at 5-3, and there was nothing in the first three games of 1947 to convince the Gamecocks that they were moving up the football ladder.

After beating Newberry in the opener the Gamecocks found themselves trailing Jim Tatum's powerful Maryland team, 19-0, at halftime. The Terps used a split-T offense, powered by Lu Gambino, a great running back.

Lawhorne: "At halftime Coach Enright told our two linebackers to line up on the inside shoulders of the guards, and use a certain key on a given back. We used that defense the rest of the game, and Maryland didn't score again. We had put that defense on the board a few times, but we never had played it. It became known as the 'Carolina defense.' Its weakness was deep, because we only had two guys deep. But Maryland wasn't throwing the ball much. They believed they could run over anybody, which they usually did."

Carolina's offensive rally fell short in a 19-13 loss, and the Terps moved on to the Gator Bowl, where they tied with Georgia, 20-20.

The following week found the Gamecocks in Memphis, Tenn. to meet Mississippi, which featured quarterback Charlie Connerly, later an NFL star, and All-America end Barney Poole, who had played for great Army teams during the war.

Steve Wadiak, one of Carolina's all-time greats, picks up yardage against Georgia Tech.

Bishop Strickland is brought down after a good gain against Clemson.

Lawhorne: "It started raining during warm-ups, and Coach Enright told us back in the locker room, 'The Lord has blessed us today. They'll never throw the ball in this weather.'

"So we bunched up on the line of scrimmage, and, on the first play, Connerly drops back and hits that guy for fifty-four yards right down the middle. And I've never seen it rain that hard.

"Right after that we were threatening to score, but somebody missed a block on the tackle, and he came right through and grabbed the hand-off from our quarterback. Our halfback went on through and didn't realize what had happened. That guy scored on the play, and that started us down right there."

Mississippi won the game, 33-0, to place the Gamecocks at 1-2, but they wouldn't taste defeat the remainder of the season, finishing with a 6-2-1 mark. One of the victories, 26-8 over Furman, featured two punt returns for touchdowns by Lawhorne.

Lawhorne: "Any journeyman in America could have done that. It was a reverse punt return, using two safetymen, and we used to practice it a lot. We would set-up a wall, and once you'd get inside that wall you were free."

Carolina gave-up its last points of the season in a 21-19 win over Clemson, as they won shutouts over Miami, The Citadel, and Wake Forest, while battling to a scoreless tie with a fine Duke team. Lawhorne: "Miami had a great back named Harry Gault, who also did their punting. Early in the game he got off a punt that must have gone sixty-five or seventy yards, but, going down the field, he got hit so hard that the top of his helmet broke off. It was when they first started using those plastic helmets. They had to take him out of the ball game, and he didn't play anymore that night, and I think that had a lot to do with us winning the ball game (8-0). I remember Bobby O'Harra (end) got a safety on a blocked punt.

"In the Duke game we had the ball down on our goal line, and Red Harrison went into the line on fourth down. We thought he had scored, although they pushed him back; but when we looked at the film it looked like he scored."

As a player Lawhorne experienced 16 victories against only seven loses and a tie, with three wins over Clemson. Ernie was more than a football player, however, participating in enough other activities to earn election to Blue Key national honorary fraternity. And his athletic achievements included baseball (second base) and track (javelin). He was married to Isabel Gooding of Columbia prior to his senior season, later starting a family that included a son and three daughters.

Lawhorne departed from the University with a degree, a job with the South Carolina State Parks administration, and an almost reverent appreciation for his head football coach.

Lawhorne: "You know, I came to the University from an orphanage, and when I left the orphanage this was my home—and Enright, to me, was a father. He was the same fellow whether you won or lost. He always tried to reason, to see why this happened or why that happened. "A number of the schools we were playing were out of our league, as far as money being put into our programs and the facilities they had. But I never heard Coach Enright complain about it. He felt that by playing these bigger teams it would move us up—and I think it did.

"Coach Enright was a definite move up for Carolina. With equal facilities and with his coaching ability, he would have done well in any era of football. He was a very intelligent man; a graduate of the Notre Dame Law School and much more than a football coach."

Lawhorne pointed out that Enright was a good psychologist and also had a sense of humor.

Lawhorne: "After the Mississippi game (0-33 in 1947) in which Enright thought a lot of us really didn't give a hundred per cent, we were riding back on the train from Memphis, and Enright said he wanted a meeting with all the players and coaches. We met in one of the cars, and he just put it on the line. He said, 'Fellows, if you're gonna try to act like a bunch of pros, we'll handle it like pros.'

"Back in those days the players got so many tickets for this and so many for that. So Enright said, 'The first team will get four tickets, the second team will get two tickets, and the third team will get one ticket.'

"And that's the way it was from then on, and we did real well, so it must have worked. (Carolina won five and tied one during the remainder of the season.)

"I also had the privilege of playing with both Steve Wadiak and Bishop Strickland. Wadiak was a freshman in forty-eight, and Strickland was a sophomore. I got my shoulder hurt at the first part of that season and couldn't play anymore, so I started coaching freshmen. Wadiak was still there when I joined the Carolina staff in fifty-one.

"Steve was the fastest guy on the take-off I've ever seen in football. We used to run the old hand-off play, where you just went straight ahead, and he could be past the linebacker before he could get set.

"Wadiak was also an exceptional defensive player—probably better defensive player than offense. He did play both ways some. He was a vicious tackler and had exceptional jumping ability—just a knack for the ball. He was probably the best all-around football player I've ever been associated with. He had great defensive ability and great offensive ability.

"He had more speed than Alex Hawkins and could do things that you don't coach. Alex played with less ability but did a lot with it. Overall, Steve had a little more natural ability and a lot more speed.

"His running mate—Bishop Strickland—was just a great complement to Wadiak, because he was such a powerful runner and hit with such explosiveness. Bishop had great speed also. A lot of people don't realize the speed he had. Bishop was about five-eleven and played at about two-ten, so he was really a ball that went through there. He was a punishing type runner. You tackle him two or three times, and you were thinking of home and mother.

"Bishop was an exceptional blocker. He could get to a man's knees real quick. When you had Wadiak, you didn't have to put the guy on the ground. If you could just brush him, Wadiak could get around him.

"I thought that tandem of halfbacks was about as good as we've had at Carolina."

As of 1984, Wadiak was second in career rushing yardage at Carolina, with 2,878, while Strickland ranked 8th, with 1,865.

Lawhorne recalled one of the big names in collegiate football history that was almost a teammate of his. Charlie (Choo Choo) Justice, who became an All-America tailback in the single wing offense of Carl Snavely at North Carolina, was heavily recruited by Enright, who, along with former Gamecock star Lou Sossamon, had known Justice when he played for Bainbridge (Md.) Naval Base during the war.

Lawhorne: "Charlie came to Columbia in August (1946) and went out with Dumas Turner (assistant athletic director), a couple of others, and myself. When he left, he said, 'I'll see you.' I think he was to come back the following Tuesday and was gonna have his tonsils taken out. They even made reservations at the hospital here.

Ernie Lawhorne as a Gamecock in 1942.

We really thought he was going to enroll, but I understand that they picked him up and took him to Chapel Hill, and he stayed there."

But the loss of Justice to North Carolina didn't alter the close friendship between Enright and Snavely.

Lawhorne: "We used to scrimmage North Carolina before the season started. We'd go up there and spend about three days at Chapel Hill, or they'd come to Columbia. Snavely thought a lot of Enright's defensive mind, and Enright thought a lot of Snavely's offensive mind. (North Carolina used the single wing offense under Snavely.)

"We'd set-up our defenses prior to that, and the defense we planned to use for Clemson was tried—but we only tried it for six or eight plays and in certain situations. And nobody really would know we were changing. We'd practice it and film it, and that's really when we'd set our defense for Clemson.

"Coach Enright would think about that defense all through the season, and if there was anything he thought might change it—looking at films—he'd make that change then. Basically Coach Enright had Clemson in the back of his mind most of the time.

"We used to have closed practices for that game out at Capital City Park (baseball). He'd just throw it on our shoulders—didn't try to get us up too high—but the day of the game he had a way of keying you up and really make you get with it.

"One game (Clemson) we weren't playing too well in the first half, and he stuck his head in the dressing room door and said, 'Excuse me, I thought this was the Carolina dressing room, not the ladies' restroom.' Then he closed the door and left. We kept waiting for him to come back and make a big halftime talk, make changes, and so forth. But he didn't show up until about two minutes before we were to go back on the field. Several of the players had gotten up—like Bobby O'Harra—and ranted and raved. But all we did was go back out and play like we were supposed to have played in the first half.

"Enright was great at that type of thing. I guess he got a lot of that from Knute Rockne." (Enright played under Rockne at Notre Dame.)

Lawhorne's first post-college job was to help convert old Camp Croft, near Spartanburg, into a state park. However, about a year later he was offered the job as head football coach at Columbia high school, as veteran H.B. (Bee) Rhame was retiring from that position. Rhame had supervised Lawhorne in a practice-teaching situation at University high school, and he liked what he saw, and Ernie was his personal choice for his successor. Lawhorne's first season (1950) at Columbia was a successful 7-5, including an upset over Pinky Babb's Greenwood Emeralds at Greenwood in the opening game. It was unheard-of for Greenwood to lose at home, especially in the opening game.

Lawhorne: "After the season George Terlep left the University of South Carolina coaching staff to go to the Canadian League, and Enright called me and offered me a job as an assistant coach. In about three days I took the job without even asking the salary. It turned out to be four thousand dollars."

On the Carolina staff Lawhorne joined, among others, former teammate Earl Dunham, a halfback on the 1946 team. Dunham had the unique distinction of serving as captain of the football, basketball, and baseball teams during the same school year. Lawhorne had known Dunham as a high school teammate in Macon.

By that time Carolina had begun to suffer in comparison with arch rival Clemson, even though the Gamecocks had beaten the Tigers in 1946, 1947, and 1949 and tied them in 1950. Clemson had experienced unbeaten seasons in 1948 and 1950, plus winning the Gator Bowl over Missouri and Orange Bowl over Miami.

Lawhorne: "Clemson's success was hurting out recruiting, so that's one reason Enright placed so much emphasis on that game."

Lawhorne's first encounter with the Tigers as an assistant coach was successful, 20-0, as Carolina completely shut down Clemson's star tailback, Billy Hair, who had seen his predecessor, Bobby Gage, likewise frustrated against the Gamecocks. In that 1951 game freshman linebacker Leon Cunningham had a fine day, as did Harry Jabbusch, a senior.

Lawhorne: "The difference in the way Enright played linebackers against the single wing was that, unlike most teams that would have them in front of the blocking back, Enright had them a foot and a half behind the blocking back. Most people tried to knock down the blocking back and get the tailback, but Enright wanted to go in behind the blocker to get to him. We set our defense to turn everything in to the linebackers, so it wasn't unusual to see one of them make twenty-five tackles.

"I think Coach (Frank) Howard (Clemson) had a hard time seeing that. The tailback couldn't outrun our linebackers, because we had the angle. In fact, we used to give North Carolina (single wing offense) a fit when we scrimmaged them."

Lawhorne's nine-year coaching career, including five seasons as an assistant to Enright and five under Enright's successor, Warren Giese, was on the positive side. During that time the Gamecocks compiled three 7-3-0 seasons, two 6-4-0, two 5-5-0, a 5-4-0, and a 3-6-0, adding up to 51 victories against 37 defeats for a 58% batting average. Over that period the Gamecocks won five and lost four to Clemson, another yardstick of success for Carolina teams.

Lawhorne: They used to say that Enright would do three things. Beat somebody he wasn't supposed to. Lose to somebody he wasn't supposed to. And beat Clemson."

Several of the greatest victories in Carolina football history took place while Lawhorne was on the staff. Over Virginia in 1952, West Virginia in 1953, Army in 1954, Duke in 1956, Texas in 1957, Clemson in 1958, and Georgia in 1959.

Lawhorne remembers the 1953 team as one of the finest with which he was associated.

Lawhorne: "We had seniors in key positions, such as Johnny Gramling (quarterback), and Gene Wilson (halfback)."

Lawhorne reflected on an amusing incident that occurred during the final moments of the 20-14 victory at Morgantown, W. Va., over a West Virginia team that was unbeaten in eight games and eventually received an invitation to the Sugar Bowl. With the Gamecocks clinging to their six-point lead, and time running out, the Mountaineers were on the march around midfield.

This was the day before the large, lighted digital scoreboards, and the face of the game clock at one end of the stadium had disappeared in the late afternoon haze. Enright, pacing nervously on the sideline grabbed a young sophomore lineman by the arm and said, "Quick, son, run down and see what the time is." The obedient player vanished into the distance.

Momentarily he returned, dashed up to the Gamecock coach, who was awaiting the critical information. "Coach," the young man said, "it's quarter till four!"

Seconds later Enright's frustration was eased when end Clyde Bennett intercepted a Mountaineer pass to seal the victory.

Enright's final season, during which his health was failing, was a losing one, but it ended on the upbeat, when Carolina defeated Virginia in Charlottesville, Va.

Lawhorne tells of an incident that illustrates the feeling which coaches and officials alike had for Coach Enright: "We had a

The Lawhorne family in 1985. Seated, daughter Barbara Little, Lawhorne, wife Isabel, daughter Missy. Back row, son-in-law Bob Little, grandson Bob, and son Ernie.

twenty-one to fourteen lead and were attempting to run out the clock, and, of course, the quarterback called the plays back then. Mackie Prickett (qb) called a pass play to Buddy Frick (end), and the referee, who was retiring at the end of this game, called an official's time out, grabbed Mackie by the shoulder pads, and led him over to Enright. 'Somebody get this boy's pad straight,' he said in a loud voice. Then he whispered to Enright, 'Hey, Rex, did you know he called a pass!'

"All we had to do was fall down and run out the clock, which is what we did after that timeout."

The final four years of Lawhorne's coaching career were spent under Giese, who had been the top assistant to Jim Tatum, who was producing national championship contenders at Maryland.

Lawhorne: "Working for Enright was a lot different than working for Giese to me, simply because of my association with Enright as a player. Enright was very even keel—he was the same guy every day.

"Giese was a very excitable person, because he was a lot younger. I thought, as far as teaching the fundamentals of blocking and tackling, Warren Giese was the best I had ever seen. His downfall was that there was no gamble to him. You played it straight. Three yards and a cloud of dust.

"When we were behind there was no way to catch up. That was our problem. In our offense you could not afford to make a mistake. I remember against Wake Forest (43-20 loss in 1959) it would take us twelve plays to score, and it would take them three, throwing the ball.

"Warren believed that nothing good would come out of a forward pass. You either threw the ball wrong, the receiver would drop it, or the other team would intercept. As a result of not having anybody to throw the ball, we'd try to play pass defense, and there was nobody to practice against. We didn't know enough about the pass offense to play good pass defense.

"We had some good tough football teams. Giese had been under some fine coaches—like Tatum at Maryland—and was very astute in football. The players were sold on Giese and his system, and I thought we got a good, hundred per cent effort from them. I think we probably practiced and hit a little too much. Had some brutal drills we used during the season. We had great scrimmages on Tuesday, but we got a number of people hurt or in weakened condition. But Giese's record will speak for itself, although it wasn't an exciting offense.

"Giese's biggest problem was that he would isolate himself—didn't want to be close to anybody. I used to say he could get rid of a friend faster than anybody I knew.

"We never recruited first class quarterbacks. We just didn't go after them. We knew he would be very limited as to what he did. So, we didn't go after the Harvey White's (Clemson star), and so forth. It was real tough to get a topnotch quarterback to come in and run three yards and a cloud of dust.

"We had a great recruiting year the last year Coach Enright was here. Like King Dixon and Alex Hawkins."

One of the players Giese inherited from Enright was Sam DeLuca, a 230-pound tackle out of Brooklyn's Lafayette high school. DeLuca was named to the Associated Press third team All-America for 1956, received the trophy awarded to the best blocker in South Carolina colleges, played in the Senior Bowl, and later had a professional career with the San Diego Chargers and New York Jets. DeLuca had a short career as analyst for pro games televised by NBC.

Lawhorne: "Sam was getting to be just ordinary, so one day before practice Marvin Bass (line coach) said, 'I'm gonna make Sam DeLuca a football player today, or he's gonna be on the five o'clock train.'

"We had one-on-one drills, and Marvin got on Sam. Sam was crying, but I never saw a guy work as hard as he did. When it was over Marvin came over and put his arm around him. Sam was still crying, because Marvin had really worked him over. Marvin said, 'Sam, I just want you to know that you're a damn football player. You really don't know what you can do.' After that Sam got better and better."

DeLuca had been one of the better recruiting victories for the Enright staff, finally convincing Sam that he should enroll in Columbia, rather than Chapel Hill, N.C.

Lawhorne referred to the uphill battle Carolina faced in trying to recruit some of the more sought-after high school prospects: "Enright was trying to move Carolina up by playing a big-time schedule, but he was fighting a losing battle, because every time we put in five dollars, others were putting in twenty. It was hard to catch up. Our facilities didn't compare—part of the time we were eating at a boarding house, and we had no particular dormitory for the football players.

"We were sort of choosy in what we showed prospects. We only showed the best things we had. We tried to sell the rapport between the coaches and the players. These guys would fall in love with Enright. When he shook hands, you felt he meant what he was saying. He'd look you right in the eye. Wouldn't make any rash promises.

"Another thing, part of our visit with a prospect would be to President (Donald) Russell's office, and Mr. Russell would stop whatever he was doing and sit down and talk. It seemed like he always knew someone who was related to the young man. He was a great salesman for our program."

Thumb through a modern-day Carolina football brochure, and the only place you'll find Ernie Lawhorne's name is in the alphabetical list of football lettermen. No all-star teams, statistical records, year-by-year leader, or professional participation. But Lawhorne

represents one of the good things about Carolina football . . . someone who gained a lot from the program and later returned even
more to it.

You'll find a long list of friends and admirers from among the
people who played with him and for him, because of his willingness
to fit-in where he was needed and to lend a helping hand, on or off
the field, to those who reached out. His loyalty to Carolina hasn't
diminished since he left the coaching staff, and he has been one of
the founders and backbones of the USC Association of Lettermen.

The late Paul (Bear) Bryant, the Alabama coached considered
by many as his profession's all-time great, contributed his success
more to the over-achievements of players with average talent, than
to the performance of the super-stars. And, in that regard,
Lawhorne was a prototype of so many like him who helped to pass
the torch from one generation of Gamecocks to the next in the pursuit of excellence.

The Lawhorne years:

As a player
1943—Won 5, Lost 2
1946—Won 5, Lost 3
1947—Won 6, Lost 2, Tied 1

As an assistant coach
1951—Won 5, Lost 4
1952—Won 5, Lost 5
1953—Won 7, Lost 3
1954—Won 6, Lost 4
1955—Won 3, Lost 6
1956—Won 7, Lost 3
1957—Won 5, Lost 5
1958—Won 7, Lost 3
1959—Won 6, Lost 4

TOTALS—Won 67, Lost 44, Tied 1

1951-52-53

JOHNNY **gramling**

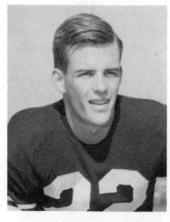

20

QUARTERBACK

A description of Johnny Gramling reads like the movie version of a star quarterback. However, Gramling seems to enjoy recalling the defensive aspects of his great senior year, which brought Carolina its first national ranking.

6 JOHNNY GRAMLING

When you go down the checklist of things that typify the traditional star quarterback of a major state university football team, Johnny Gramling emerges as normal as apple pie, hot dogs, and weekends at the beach. At the University of South Carolina he set passing records, made the all-conference team, was a class president, received the award as the school's outstanding senior, and married a beauty queen. Just like the movies.

The standard sequel to that would be a successful career in the National Football League, followed by a vocation, such as banking or other white-collar endeavor. He would reflect at times on his years of throwing a leather spheroid into the outstretched arms of dashing receivers.

This is where Johnny Gramling and orthodoxy come to a parting of the ways. Johnny passed up a draft by the Cleveland Browns of the NFL to play in the Canadian league, was conscripted from that to play armed services football, and eventually became a farmer. Plus, of all things, he likes to expound on his experiences with DEFENSIVE football!

Gramling came along the college route back in the early 50's, when two-platoon football was the order of the day, until, suddenly, when Johnny was a rising senior, NCAA rules were changed to limit substitutions. All at once, former offensive and defensive specialists found themselves facing two-way duty, and thirty-some-odd years later, Gramling was still talking about how he loved to play D.

Case at point: Even when reflecting on one of the Gamecocks' more impressive wins ever, a 20-14 upset of unbeaten West Virginia at Morgantown in 1953, he ignores his 40-yard touchdown pass to halfback Gene Wilson and two touchdowns that he scored on option plays.

His greatest thrill was, "I remember in that game I ran down a guy that had caught a ball for West Virginia and saved a touchdown." He also remembered a critical mistake in that game. "I don't know whose responsibility, but they threw a pass out in the flat—it wasn't my guy—but I saw the play coming, and I got out there, and that offensive end and I met at about midfield. I put my head down and made the mistake of going for his feet. He gave me a stiff-arm and went about fifty yards for a touchdown."

Harking back to the opening game of that year, Gramling said, "When we were seniors and had to play offense and defense, it was a lot to put-in right at the end of pre-season practice and get everybody ready. We played Duke in the first game, and, lo and behold, we were on defense, and I was a defensive back. We held Duke, and they had to punt. For some reason we hadn't practiced receiving punts, and I was the safety man. They punted the ball—it was a nice punt—and I caught it, and, just as I did, somebody just put my hat up in the skies. And Coach (Rex) Enright really got mad about that. He said, 'What are y'all doing letting the quarterback get back there to receive a punt?'"

The Gamecocks obviously learned instant defense well, as they held four of their opponents scoreless that season and gave up an average of only 9.7 points per game.

Gramling: "I love defense. When I was in high school I played defense all the time, and I liked it. I like to hit. We probably weren't as good offensively, but, then, the other guys had to do the same thing. If I'm a good offensive quarterback and a good defensive quarterback, and that other guy's gotta do the same thing—it works both ways.

"There was some substituting, but that West Virginia game is one game I know I played the whole game. You could substitute a punter, but the deal was, if you came out, you couldn't go back until the next quarter. We were happy with playing offense and defense. I know it was to my advantage, no question about it. When I played in the East-West (Shrine Game in San Francisco) I won the starting position out there, and I know the other guys were just as good as I was on offense. But I had 'em beat hands down on defense."

Before you get the impression that Gramling talks about defense in order to cover up inadequacies on offense, it should be pointed out that in this 1953 season under discussion, Gramling set new school records for pass completions (68) and passing yardage

(1,045). That boosted his career totals to 150 completions in 330 attempts for 2,007 yards and 18 touchdowns, also school records in those categories.

Among the pleasant memories held by Gramling, along with those magic moments playing defense, are participation in four straight victories over Clemson, if you include a 40-20 win by the 1950 freshman team. During Johnny's three varsity season the Tigers scored a total of one touchdown, and he had touchdown passes that provided victory margins in 1952 and 1953.

Adding insult to injury to the state's agricultural school, Gramling has stashed away his Carolina degree in Economics and become one of the state's outstanding farmers, or, if you prefer, agri-businessmen. Exhibit A is the Distinguished Service Award that he received in 1984 from the South Carolina Farm Bureau, based on contributions to the bureau and farming in general.

The land under cultivation by Gramling is part of an original settlement by Paul Gramling in 1735. "The records were destroyed in Orangeburg during the Civil War, but I imagine, at some point in time, that they owned twenty thousand acres of land," Gramling said.

The Gramling farm, some 3,000 acres in production, straddles Interstate 26 near Orangeburg, South Carolina, just 40-odd miles from Columbia. There he lives with his wife, the former Betty Lane Cherry, who was chosen "Miss USA" in 1956.

Gramling: "You read the papers enough. We're farming, and we're not making any money. We've just got a general farm, and we don't grow anything that makes money, like tobacco or peanuts. Cotton, corn, soybeans, cows, and hogs."

It was here that Johnny, an only child, used to spend hours throwing a baseball from an improvised mound at a strike zone painted on the door of the smokehouse. Other times he would hang a tire from a tree and practice throwing a football through it, as it swung back and forth.

Gramling: "I was a country boy and lived out where there weren't any paved roads back in those days. I went to a small country school, with two other people in my class; Four Holes School."

Obviously, there weren't enough boys around to constitute full teams in competitive sports, so Johnny went it alone for much of the time. However, there was precedent for sports in the Gramling family, as his father, "Jumbo" Gramling, is still considered one of the all-time greats at The Citadel, for whom he played tackle in the early twenties.

Johnny Gramling, farmer, in 1985.

Gramling: "I went to Orangeburg High School in the eighth grade, and a guy who ended up being my college roommate and was a good athlete himself—Warren Clarke—moved to Orangeburg. We got to be good friends, because we both liked to hunt and fish, and we also started playing sports together. He and I would practice throwing the ball back and forth. We went out for the high school team, and when we first started playing organized ball, he was a tackle, and I was a tackle. Then we went from tackle to both of us being quarterbacks. When we were sophomores we were both substitute quarterbacks, but when we were juniors he went to end.

"Cliff Morgan, now an automobile dealer in Orangeburg, was our coach, then Bill Clark came in when we were juniors, and we had eight-two and seven-three seasons.

"I didn't go to the Shrine Bowl, but Warren did. As for colleges, you got a lot of letters, and I visited Vanderbilt, Georgia Tech, Clemson, Furman, Georgia, and Carolina. I guess I went to Carolina because of a lot of local pressure and Mister Rut Osborne (Chairman of the Carolina Board of Trustees for a number of years), who was as influential as anyone. He said, 'You boys like to hunt, and if you'll take care of the birds, I'll give you the shells.' He was a devoted Carolina alumnus, and he really went after us.

"Then Coach Enright came down, and we just kinda fell in love with him. I used to go to Clemson to more games than Carolina, because I had an uncle who was a big Tiger fan.

"When I went up to Clemson to visit, you go out and run, and I think I was the slowest guy out there. Then you go in to see Coach (Frank) Howard. I walked in and Coach Howard was sitting there with a big pair of shears, cutting him off some tobacco to chew.

"He said, 'Gramling, I ain't gonna bull you now, and I ain't gonna bull you later; we want you to come up here.' And I told him, 'Coach, I'm too slow to play tailback, and I can't punt, and I'm not big enough to play anything else.' He said. 'Gramling, you could be a fullback.'

"At that particular time I think they were trying to keep some guys from going to the University, and they thought that I was going there. Carolina gave Warren and me scholarships, along with Clyde Bennett, who was from St. Matthews, and we had gotten to know pretty well. We hit it off, and Clyde and I decided we were going to school together. In fact, when we finished college, we both went to the same pro team.

"In nineteen fifty we had probably as much talent on that team as anybody, but we had four individuals that didn't stay at the University that went to other schools. Two of them ended-up being captains of major college football teams. Don Fritts went to Cincinnati, and he was a tremendous athlete—an end. He probably would have been a better end than Clyde Bennett. And we had another guy Dick Kolhagen, a tackle, who went back to Illinois, and he was a starter there. Dick called me just a couple of years ago when he was on his way to Florida.

"Oh that team were Bobby Drawdy (fullback), Gene Wilson (halfback), Jimmy Cox (halfback), Gene Kopec (tackle), Charlie Camp (tackle), George Martin (tackle) and some other good ones. The only team we played as freshmen that whipped us was Miami. I believe if we had played 'em here, in climate more normal, it might have been a different story."

As seniors, those freshmen were the backbone of one of the better teams at Carolina, gaining the school's first ranking in the wire service polls and registering a 7-3 record in 1953.

Gramling: "In retrospect, if there was one missing ingredient when I came along, it was that esprit de corps. I didn't realize how important it was until I played in the East-West game. Johnny Lattner (Notre Dame halfback), who won the Heisman Trophy that year, was a good athlete, and a nice guy too. But he wasn't any better than Gene Wilson. He was surrounded by a lot of talent. That year they had beaten Iowa by faking an injury and getting one more play in. The Iowa boys still wouldn't talk to them!

"I just think there was a missing ingredient when we came along, and I'm hoping that that's what Coach Morrison is getting here. That thing that you go out there, and you're gonna beat 'em all. I'm convinced that when I was a senior at the University, we could have beaten Duke and Maryland—and Maryland was national champion that year—if we thought we could have done it. It was just like Duke always came and beat you, so you went out there and didn't think you could beat them."

When Gramling was a sophomore he shared quarterback duties with Dick Balka, a junior, and Billy Stephens, a senior, both of whom met accidental deaths some years later.

Gramling: "I won the starting quarterback job, until we were playing George Washington, which upset us (20-14), and I fumbled the ball on about the two-yard line. I think Rex said, 'Enough of that,' and he started Balka in the final three games of that year.

"One thing, I would say, when we were sophomores and when Steve Wadiak was on the field, I can see right now that those opposing coaches would say, 'Let Bennett, Gramling, Wilson and all those sophomores do what the hell they want to do, just stop Wadiak.' You could get out there and just see how they would have things stacked in against where his strong points were.

"Steve was a hard individual to get to know. I don't think anybody up here really knew Steve that well. But, as far as I'm concerned, he was a hundred per cent. You put ten down, and you mark him ten on everything. He was a good person, a good athlete. Whether he was a good student or not, I didn't keep up with his grades that much. He never complained, and he was always there, if you wanted to give him the ball. He was a quiet guy, but he always did his part.

"Steve was a tough runner. I can remember throwing a couple of blocks, and you see him go for a touchdown, and think you contributed something to it. He was a good athlete; he wasn't tall, a stocky individual with very, very good balance and adequate speed. He didn't have the blazing speed, but if he ever got in front of you, I don't think you'd catch him. He had a lot of savvy it's just a shame

A collision with Clemson tacklers at the end of this run knocked Gramling unconscious in the first half of the 1952 Big Thursday game. However, Gramling's 22-yard touchdown pass to Gene Wilson earlier was enough to give the Gamecocks a 6-0 victory.

he didn't have an opportunity to play professional football. He's the kind of guy that would have stayed there a long time. And I don't mean this in any detrimental way at all to George Rogers, but George won't play professional football very long. Not like a Tony Dorsett, because George takes too many licks."

(Note: Steve Wadiak was killed in an automobile accident near Aiken, South Carolina in March, 1952, following his senior football season.)

Although the Carolina defense accounted for two of the touchdowns—a punt return by Stephens and an interception return by linebacker Harry Jabbusch—Gramling learned in the 1951 game that nothing can be finer than a win over Clemson (20-0).

Gramling: "I thought, if anybody had anybody's number, Coach Enright had Coach Howard's number. When it came to defensing the single wing, they just did an excellent job of scouting from a standpoint of what they (Clemson) did with personnel. They had a wingback one time that, I remember, we never covered the whole game. They could have thrown ten touchdown passes to him. Of course, I'm sure, after he caught one or two, we'd have covered him. But we never covered him. If he went downfield, we just let him go, because he couldn't catch the ball.

"I can remember Coach Enright telling Don Earley (tackle), 'Now, we're gonna put you here, and, if you don't make ninety per cent of the tackles that come your way, you aren't worth your salt. There's no way that guy can block you.'

"He knew Clemson's personnel, and he matched-up people, and we'd run a seven-one-two-one.

"We went into those games pretty doggone confident that we could beat'em. In nineteen fifty-two (Carolina 6, Clemson 0) they were still single wing—they went to the T the next year. We scored on them in the first quarter (22-yard Gramling-to-Wilson pass); and we were driving again; and I ran into somebody and got my head plastered. It was a fake pass and run.

"I don't know if he (Enright) called that play or not, but we practiced it the week before, because we thought it would work. I think Charlie Camp came back in the huddle and said, 'Run that fake pass to my side; I believe they're set up for it.' And, lo and behold, we did, and we got about fifteen yards on the play. And I got creamed trying to run over some guy—we didn't do then like they do now. (Drop to the ground or run out of bounds to avoid getting hit.)

"That's the only time I've been knocked unconscious, and I can truthfully say that I don't remember a thing. At the half I could barely read the scoreboard. In the second half I played some, but I wasn't really in it."

Actually, the intestinal fortitude shown by Gramling in putting his head down and challenging a linebacker didn't impress Enright, who was rather upset about losing his number one quarterback so early in the game. Still, Carolina, as most teams of that day, left most of the play-calling up to quarterbacks.

Gramling: "We'd get a play in from the bench maybe five times a game. If you had a time-out in a critical situation, you'd say, 'I'm thinking about this,' and he'd say. 'Why don't you think about this?'

"I think the way the game is now, the guy that's playing can't do as good a job of calling as someone else that can probably see what's going on a lot better than he can. I'm not saying that there's not times that the quarterback won't see something that the guy sitting in the press box won't see.

"However, I don't think play calling adversely affected the quarterback's performance. That's part of your responsibility of playing. You're not gonna win 'em all; if you did, you wouldn't be doing it. I just think it's part of the satisfaction of having done a good job.

"I would say that Bill Clark at Orangeburg had as good an offensive mind as any of the coaches I played under anywhere or was around. I think his basic philosophy, which I was indoctrinated with in high school, is something I still believe in. It gave me confidence in what I could do.

"One thing I didn't have enough confidence in—because I wasn't fast—was my running. If I had done it more, I would have been a whole lot better. I didn't have blazing speed, but I should have run the ball more on option plays. We had the split-T option. We started that when we came up here. They didn't have backs running it like they have now. They were mostly fake pass situations, where you fake a dive play and drop back to pass, rather than just a straight dropback. The philosophy then was, if you were gonna pass on anything but third down, use some type of running fake. If they knew you were going to pass, like it's third and long, then you'd just drop straight back. We also had a shift that ended up in the old Notre Dame Box. Same principal as the shotgun. I remember the Furman game my junior year, we threw four touchdown passes in the first half, and only one was on third down. It was, like, they knew we were gonna throw, but it was down the middle, wide open."

A passing attack is like the Tango—it takes two to do it, and Gramling was fortunate that his close friend, Clyde Bennett, was one of the finest receivers in Carolina history. Of the career school record of 150 pass completions set by Gramling, 64 were into the sure hands of Bennett. The St. Matthews native set Carolina records for most pass receptions in a season (34 in 1952), most yards on receptions (502 in 1952), most pass receptions for a career (64), most career yards on receptions (1,021), and most career touchdown receptions (10). This earned Bennett a first-team berth on the All-Atlantic coast conference teams chosen by Associated Press, United Press International, and the Southern Sports Writers Association. He was also named to the A.P. All-America third team.

Johnny Gramling (left) and teammate Charlie Camp during a pause in the action during the 1953 season.

Gramling was also chosen to the All-ACC team by A.P. and U.P.I. This was accomplished in a season when Bernie Faloney quarterbacked a Maryland team that finished Number One in the A.P. and U.P.I. polls.

Gramling: "It's hard to judge the speed of some receivers. I don't know what it is; just tough to throw to them. Bennett—I just knew where he was going to be. There's something about it that two people hit it off together, and they think alike. And, of course, he could catch the ball.

"The only one I ever saw him miss was when we were seniors up there at Wake Forest (19-13 upset loss on Thanksgiving Day at Charlotte). I hit him right in the stomach, and that kind of thing happens to everybody. I remember overthrowing 'em when they were wide open, too.

"How do I rate myself as a passer? I think I was somewhere in the top five in the nation, as far as completions went. The boy I played against in the East-West game, Bob Garrett at Stanford (fifth in the Heisman Trophy voting); I didn't think I was as good a passer as he was. He had a hell of an arm. That's one reason I didn't go to the Browns. I was a draft choice, but he was their bonus draft choice that year, like number one. And I was down the line. So, I said, 'There's no way I'm gonna beat out that guy.' As it was, he never played.

"I think my strength was that I had good projectory—a pass you could catch. I didn't try to knock your head off. The secret of getting the ball and completing it is, get it to a point, sometimes straight, sometimes looping it.

"Ball-handling? I had to do something right, because I couldn't run!"

Besides the upset victory over West Virginia's Sugar Bowl team, the 1953 season had several highs. The first victory over North Carolina (18-0) since 1944 in the first game ever televised from Carolina Stadium. A 14-7 win over Clemson on Big Thursday, a game that saw Gramling injured against the Tigers for the second time in three games with them. After throwing a 45-yard touchdown pass to give Carolina the lead, Gramling "pulled something in his leg" in a single-player accident, without even getting hit.

However, back-up quarterback Harold Lewis, who later became a Methodist minister, hit a wide-open end Joe Silas for a 21-yard TD in the third quarter to give the Gamecocks what proved to be their winning margin.

Johnny has only two regrets in reflecting on his senior season. One was the team's inadequate confidence and the other was a season-ending upset to Wake Forest that prohibited the Gamecocks from ending the season ranked high in the wire service polls. After beating West Virginia, they were rated No. 18, the school's first appearance ever in the polls, and they moved up to No. 15 the following week when they routed Wofford, 49-0.

Gramling: "Had we thought we could have beaten those teams (Duke and Maryland), we'd have gone down as one of the better teams in USC history.

"When we were freshmen we played Wake Forest's freshman team, and we administered to them the worst beating that I have ever participated in on a football team. We didn't throw a pass, but we beat 'em something like, thirty-four to seven. We never made a run that was over fifteen yards. We physically beat them to a pulp. It was one of the most gratifying games I ever played in. Those were the same guys that beat us when we were seniors.

"That boy, White (Wake Forest third-team quarterback who had a sensational game against Carolina) hadn't played much, but he was on that freshman team.

"Why did we lack confidence? There could be a whole lot of reasons. Once you do it, you know, we'd never beaten North Carolina or any of these teams; but once you do it . . . I think these football players around here now, Morrison's getting them to thinking they can beat anybody they want to beat.

"After you do it a couple of times, you believe it. What made Gene Wilson good was that he always hustled; he gave it a thousand per cent, if there is such a thing. Like when we were playing down at Miami as freshmen, when he said he was too tired to run the ball, you knew something was wrong."

One problem that Gramling didn't devote a lot of time to fretting over was short-yardage situations.

Gramling: "I had Frank Mincevich and Bob King at guards and Leon Cunningham at center, and we never worried about getting a yard with a quarterback sneak. In that Wake Forest game we ran the ball three straight times on their goal line right at their big tackle, Bob Bartholomew. Those were stupid calls on my part.

"Why in hell did I run over there, when I should have been running quarterback sneaks? Maybe it was because I didn't want to score myself. You know, everybody does it, then you get down to the one-yard line, and Gramling scores."

As for his coach, Enright, Gramling shared the opinion with others that his biggest failing was that his heart was too big.

Gramling: "Everybody loved him. I think he bent too much for us. If we looked like we were too tired, he didn't run us that extra lap that it would have taken to do the job.

"He'd make a speech like, if anybody does so and so, we're gonna kick you out of school. If it was a fourth stringer, that's okay, but if it was (Bill) Wohrman (fullback) or Mincevich, or somebody like that, he wouldn't do it.

"I don't think he was as much of a disciplinarian type guy, say, as Coach (Bobby) Dodd was at Tech. When he kicked Billy Teas (star back) off the ball club, Teas needed two more yards to set an all-time Tech rushing record. They were playing Duke, and he kicked him off the team; he never played again.

"Everybody respected the guy (Enright). He was just as fine a gentleman as I've ever been associated with. I think, if anything, he just didn't push us; he wouldn't make us sweat for his benefit, or our benefit, either. He could probably have pushed us and had a lot more wins. But he'd get out there and start feeling sorry for us."

The University was far more than just a place to play football, as far as Gramling was concerned. He was elected president of his sophomore class, was elected to Omicron Delta Kappa National Honorary Fraternity and Kappa Sigma Kappa Service Fraternity, and received the ultimate honor for a Carolina student in 1954—the Algernon Sydney Sullivan Award, which goes to the most outstanding graduating senior.

Another extra-curricular activity in which Gramling participated, the Air Force R.O.T.C., had an impact on his post-college life.

Gramling: "I was drafted by Cleveland in the twelfth round, and Clyde was a second-round choice of the New York Giants. I didn't even negotiate with Cleveland. Clyde and I decided we wanted to play together, so we went to Ottawa in the Canadian League.

"We only played there one year. We didn't know it at the time, but they were having 'drafts' in th service then. Any R.O.T.C. student that was an athlete, the Generals got together and called into the service. I lacked about three games of finishing the first season when they called me to active duty at Shaw Air Force Base (near Sumter, South Carolina). I went in on a Thursday and played a football game on Saturday. Jerry Barger, who played at Duke, was there also, and we shared quarterback duties."

Bennett made a career of the Air Force, completing enough years to qualify for full retirement.

Gramling: "I hadn't really committed myself to anything, but when I got out, I said, 'I'm an only child, and my parents are out there living alone. I'd be with them, for what it was worth, and make them happy for the rest of their lives. And I've enjoyed it. I considered farming, and I considered coaching. I could probably have come back to the University, maybe, as an assistant."

Between the various challenges that confront every American farmer, Gramling has been a close follower of Gamecock athletics through the years. And, as a major contributor to gaining the school its first national ranking, Johnny couldn't have been prouder of the high 1984 finish, if he had been playing on the team himself.

Gramling: "Could I play on Carolina's team now? If I were young, I'd sure be for giving it a try. I don't know if I could play under his (Morrison) system, but I could play somewhere. I don't

Gramling and family, left to right, Tracy, Lawrence, Johnny, Betty Lane (wife), Cherry, and John.

know if I'd be willing to pay the price; it's a physical fitness thing. We had only one or two guys who lifted weights when I was there— that was it.

"Oklahoma started it and was beating everybody, and people said, 'What's going on?' And they came to find out they were just stronger than everybody else. Now everybody does it. If you line-up across from a guy, and he's faster and stronger, he's gonna beat you. It's demanding, but it's rewarding (in terms of pro contracts).

"Clyde Bennett was offered twelve thousand dollars, a lot of money then, maybe. But not now.

"One of the main things for so long was that the organizational structure at the University wasn't like it should have been. I don't need to say anything else. Athletics in college is big business, and evidently they've got the right system now. Plus they've got the facilities, and they've got the money.

"Now, I'm a strong believer in trends, from a technical standpoint. People worry about Clemson, but Carolina's gonna be up there for a while. Clemson will come back, too, but I think Carolina will have the upper hand for three or four years."

On that happy prediction, Johnny Gramling turned his thoughts back to the farm and the approaching spring planting season. The Gramling's four children, two grown daughters and twin sons who are attending Lander College, are now out of the nest. So, Johnny and Betty Lane have it to themselves again, on a day-to-day basis.

Outwardly, Gramling doesn't show evidence of the intensity and pride that have been such important ingredients in the successes he has achieved during his fifty-plus years. And, to hear his talk, you'd think that the teams on which he played were underachievers made-up of unmotivated players.

However, 165-pound quarterbacks who try to run over man-eating linebackers; who love the hard contact of defensive football; who played "sixty-minute" games; who helped present an aging head coach his best-ever season; and whose record as a student matched his accomplishments as a player; are not exactly misguided or uninspired.

The University of South Carolina isn't overloaded with sports legends, and Gramling most assuredly doesn't try to make any claims at being one. Still, over three decades after he played with such distinction in jersey number "20," if a Gamecock quarterback, or any other position, is looking for an example of what a player should be or do; they could do a lot worse than the country boy with a radar arm, a coach's mind, and the heart of a lion—Johnny Gramling.

CHARTING JOHNNY GRAMLING
PASSING

YEAR	ATTEMPTS	COMPLETIONS	YARDS	TOUCHDOWNS
1951	52	21	253	1
1952	144*	61	709	9*
1953	133	68*	1,045*	8
TOTALS	330*	150*	2,007*	18*

*School records at that time.

Other school records: Single game:
Most yards passing—227 vs. Wake Forest, 1953
Most passes attempted—29 vs. Wake Forest, 1953
Most passes completed—15 vs. Wake Forest, 1953

KING **dixon**

20

HALFBACK

The Marine Corps motto, "Semper Fidelis," is a fitting summation of King Dixon, the football player, military officer, and citizen. He received his first military strategy lesson on the football field at West Point.

7

KING DIXON

i f King Dixon had been asked to list ten places he would like to be on this muggy day in 1967, chances are he wouldn't have included dangling on the end of a parachute behind enemy lines in the Da Nang province of South Viet Nam.

That's where he found himself, drifting slowly into the thick mahogany forest, where the unknown awaited. It could be anything from the serenity of a picturesque jungle setting, to an adult tiger in search of food. Or, perhaps, the Viet Cong, on a similar mission of intelligence gathering.

Dixon was there, rather than in a National Football League uniform in New York, or a business suit in South Carolina, because he possessed a sense of duty that came before personal desires and safety. It was that trait that had made him both one of the more outstanding football players in the history of the University of South Carolina and one of the finest student leaders ever to cross the Horseshoe.

In his even younger days King had made several choices that led him on a diametric course to that which brought him to the world's most controversial area. First, he thoughtfully made a decision to decline offers to attend the three service academies. Then, he signed a letter of intent to attend Duke University, with an ultimate goal of becoming a doctor. As a college student he moved in the direction of a career in politics, losing a race for the South Carolina House of Representatives by a scant margin. Even after entering the Marine Corps he pondered an offer to play in the NFL and end his Marine service at the minimum obligation.

Whenever Dixon approached crossroads, circumstances surreptitiously nudged him down the route that led to a military career. Therefore, it was with no second thoughts or misgivings that he descended into this potentially treacherous thicket 12,000 miles from his hometown of Laurens, South Carolina.

Dixon: "I've always felt very strongly about this country. I've always had a very strong patriotic feeling about it. I guess I inherited that from my dad, who was in the Navy, and I was an only child.

"Talk about a difference in individuals, when Coach (Warren) Giese came to Carolina, I remember one year we started going out to Fort Jackson to spend the night before home games. I was rooming with Alex Hawkins on the road, and we were staying in the B.O.Q. (Bachelor Officers Quarters). Alex couldn't sleep.

"He said, 'Do you realize that, if you were in the service, that you'd have to spend your life in a room like this?'

"It was a pretty nice room to me, but it seemed to bother Alex.

"I felt a very strong calling to defend my country, should I be called on to do so, when I took an oath to the President of the United States to defend this country and the Constitution. Again, I was a product of World War Two, and I had travelled a lot with my dad and learned with my mama how to endure the loneliness of the separation of a family. Consequently, when I joined the Marine Corps, I did go overseas on an unaccompanied tour for thirteen months.

"I came back, and when I got ready to go to Viet Nam, there was a war going on. An undeclared war. So, the time came for me to go to Viet Nam.

"Before that I was in jump school with the Army at Fort Benning; there were eight Marines in a class of about two hundred and fifty; you were one of the chosen ones. I received orders to 'pack your bags and go.' It was something I'd been training to do. I just wanted to make sure my family was taken care of and was all right.

"I went on to Viet Nam and was in a reconnaissance batalion for seven months and was commanding officer of a force reconnaissance company. While I was in that company I made one of the two combat jumps that were documented during that war in Viet Nam.

"A combat jump is nothing more than getting into an Army Caribou or helicopter and being able to jump into an area. It's like coaching—if you can land a helicopter, do you parachute into an area? It depends upon what your particular ideas and motives are. Do you walk in? Do you go in clandestine? Do you go by boat, up a river? Or, do you jump in?

"We were going in to maintain observation; we were an intelligence-gathering unit. We were to maintain observation over particular trails and networks leading in and out of the country, seeing how many things and what was coming in. This was around the Da Nang area, along the borders and back end, primarily in the northern part. We initially went into the Chu Lai area, right on the beach, but most of our work was done in the hills. Most of it was observation and calling in fire missions, when the situation warranted it. I enjoyed it.

"We parachuted into what was known as 'Happy Valley,' and the reason it was 'Happy Valley' is you were happy as hell to get out of it. When I was in there, so many people had been in there, that a lot of places in the hills were mined. You normally jumped out of helicopters to keep them from landing and setting-off mines."

When orders came, King Dixon responded in the true tradition of the Marine Corps, but it was a result of his loyalty and sense of duty, rather than because he had no personal thoughts about his country's involvement in Southeast Asia.

Dixon: "After I got back and saw what really took place, I regret that a lot of people lost their lives over something we very possibly should not have been in. I don't see how you can go into combat and not fight to win.

"Now, in retrospect, I don't read too much about it, because it would probably make me mad, and you never really know the truth. In the years of maturing in my life, I have begun to question a few things now more than I would have at that time.

"I picked up my bag and went, and I was happy to serve."

Just the act of serving in Viet Nam doesn't necessarily make Dixon another Nathan Hale, but his mental attitude and conscientious approach in facing this national dilemma provides insight as to why he has excelled in all of his endeavors.

At Carolina he was a key player on teams that compiled 7-3, 5-5, and 7-3 records, and in his senior season, 1958, the Gamecocks ranked 15th in the final Associated Press poll, the first such ranking in the history of the school; in fact, the only one until 1984. He also ran the dashes for the track team.

As a student he was elected to Phi Beta Kappa national scholastic fraternity, was president of Omicron Delta Kappa national service fraternity and Kappa Sigma Kappa local service fraternity, held several class offices, and received the Algernon Sydney Sullivan Award as the University's most outstanding graduating senior in 1959. You couldn't get any argument that he was the model athlete, student, and person.

As of 1985, he had not been elected to the University's Athletic Hall of Fame, although he had been so honored by the State of South Carolina's honor "hall." The Marine Corps honored him with the Bronze Star Medal, Navy Commendation, and the Vietnamese Cross of Gallantry.

From a football standpoint, Dixon stands with his backfield mate, Alex Hawkins, as one of the finest all-purpose backs ever to wear a Gamecock jersey. Statistically, he led the team in rushing in 1956; in kickoff returns in all three of his varsity seasons; in punt returns in 1956; and interceptions in 1957.

Until 1984 he shared the school record for the longest kickoff return, a 98-yarder on the opening kickoff for a touchdown against the University of Texas at Austin. That record was not without its price!

Dixon: "When they sing, 'The Eyes of Texas Are Upon You,' it really puts chills up your back. At that time Walt Fondren was their quarterback and was allegedly the richest quarterback in the country, because of his family.

"I happened to have a little flu and didn't know about it; I didn't know if I was going to play in that game. We received the opening kickoff, and I remember cutting about the forty-yard line, and The Hawk just wiping out their safety, who was Walt Fondren.

"I cut back of him to score, a ninety-eight-yard kickoff return, and when I planted my foot and cut back . . . we had new uniforms, white with elastic trousers. It was right there that I realized my stomach had problems—and I changed the color of my trousers when I cut back! It was most embarrassing.

"We ran off the field, and everybody was patting me on the back, and I asked the coach, 'Can I put on a cape?'

"He said, 'Why?'

"I said, 'I got some problems. I went to the bathroom in my britches!'

"I had to run all the way around the stadium, go back under, and change.'

"That got us off to a good start, but Texas came back and scored twenty points. As I remember, it (newspaper write-up) said, 'When The Hawk got mad, Texas got sad.'

"I remember The Hawk playing some tremendous ball games, and in the last two or three minutes of this ball game, Hawk did some beautiful running. A large part of that (comeback to win, 27-20) was Alex.

King Dixon (20) eludes a Wake Forest tackler, as running mates Alex Hawkins (41) and John Saunders (33) provide blocking.

"Later on, when I came back to play in the North-South game, Darrell Royal (Texas head coach in 1957) was head coach of the South team. I played for him, which is a lasting relationship with Coach Royal."

Dixon's relationship with and attitude toward his college coach, Warren Giese, were in sharp contrast with his running mate, Alex Hawkins. Again, his sense of duty and loyalty overshadowed personal considerations, and he has nothing but positive things to say about his dealings with Giese. In fact Dixon's youngest son, Lee, a freshman at Carolina, also serves as a page for Giese, who was elected to the South Carolina State Senate in 1984.

Dixon: "In my opinion, Coach Giese put football into perspective. When I say into perspective, in my opinion there possibly was, in years gone by, some divisiveness, because of what someone may be receiving and someone not receiving—through the alumni. I have suspicions of that. When everybody is treated fair and equal, it sets the course. And when someone says, 'You're expected to be a student, and you need to pass your courses . . .'

"I have several friends today that said two things: One, is they want to give Coach Giese credit for them graduating from college. Two, if it had not been for the academic standards of the Atlantic Coast Conference, they would not be where they are today—being a successful businessman. Had they not had that burning desire to play football and become a student of the game under Warren Giese, they may not have been the success they are today.

"So, in my opinion, Coach Giese brought in a tighter organization. He put football in perspective, and he taught people to deal with pride, and to get along with one another, and treat them as equal. He brought a different caliber of intellect to the game of football. He was a real student of the game, in my opinion.

"Now, having said that, I'm sure there'll be a lot of folks who'll disagree with the type of football that he brought in. That's a matter of, if somebody says today, I'll pay twelve or fourteen dollars to go see a football game, regardless of the type of football they're playing, if I'm close to that school. But I won't pay twelve or fourteen dollars to go see someone take an exam in the classroom.

"There was some exciting football under his regime. It could have been more exciting—I don't know. I don't know if we would have done better, or done worse.

"I very definitely think recruiting was a problem. Number one, I left—I left—I went into the Marine Corps and had my hands full at Quantico and in the Far East. So, I became removed from the situation at Carolina. But I would suspect two things: One, to have the seven-three, five-five, and seven-three, and then the six-four and the three-six, you start on a losing trend.

"As I recall, there was a great deal of discontent over Coach Giese's relations with the press—that might be an understatement. When you start getting negative publicity—let's compare it to what happened in nineteen eighty-four. When you're winning big; and you have the exciting things going for you; and you're getting everything positive in the press; people want to come. Kids today want to be a part of a winner. They know if you play for a losing ball club, it's not going to help you get in the pros.

"It's been my experience over life, now, that, if you become a negative target, the target has to be removed, before your program will prosper."

Dixon obviously didn't need any outside motivation for being a student, as well as an athlete. Along with maintaining a B-plus scholastic average, serving as vice-president of his freshman, sophomore, and junior classes; playing football, running track, serving as president of two honor fraternities; and being an active member of a social fraternity (Kappa Alpha); Dixon served as a page in the state legislature for three years; and was enrolled in the Marine Platoon Leaders Class.

As if that were not enough activity, Dixon was a candidate for the South Carolina House of Representatives, where his father had served, during this senior year. In a field of eight candidates, he finished fourth, missing being one of the three elected by only 83 votes.

The girl Dixon would later marry and his high school sweetheart, Augusta Mason, was also a student at Carolina and was initiated into Phi Beta Kappa along with Dixon.

Had Dixon not been an eye witness to surgery at Duke Hospital in Durham, North Carolina, during his senior year in high school, Carolina would have been deprived of an outstanding student, exceptional athlete, and one of its more loyal alumni. He was a heavily recruited halfback when he was playing under Jack Adams, and later Jerry Boland, at Laurens High School. And, as the script would have it, he played in the Shrine Bowl game at Charlotte and was named the game's most outstanding player.

Dixon: "During that period I had one of the most difficult times of my life, trying to decide what I was going to do with my life, and where I was going to school. I always put a lot of stock in my dad, and he said, 'Go where you want to.'

"It was the first year of the Air Force Academy, and I had an opportunity to go to all three academies. I decided at the time not to. Kinda ironic—didn't go to any of the academies and ended up spending twenty-two years in the Marine Corps!

"I did have an opportunity to go to several schools. My dad was very much interested in Georgia, because his friend Wally Butts coached at Georgia. I had an opportunity to go to Duke, with which I signed at first. Ace Parker (assistant coach) and Bill Murray (head coach) were good friends of my dad.

"I signed a letter of intent, but I accepted a scholastic scholarship. I had good grades at that time and thought I wanted to be a doctor. After I signed, once I got there (Duke), I visited the hospital and medical school and actually saw an amputation. I decided that wasn't for me. I knew right then I didn't like the sight of blood, as I saw it there in that amputation.

"About that time my father was elected to the South Carolina House (in 1954). I had already been very highly recruited down at Carolina, particularly by Earl Dunham and Ernie Lawhorne, and they seemed to me lifelong friends. I got to know Coach Enright and decided I really wanted to stay in the state.

"The attitude and type of example that was set down at Carolina—the way the coaches handled themselves, particularly Coach Enright, Dunham, Lawhorne, Weems Baskin, and Hank Bartos. So, I had to go to see Bill Murray and tell him I wanted to come to Carolina.

"The fact that Carl Brazell and Mike Caskey (like Dixon, small running backs) were doing real well influenced me. I looked at Georgia Tech very carefully, too. Bobby Dodd was there, and they had a winning tradition. It was awfully appealing, if you wanted to be an engineer.

"I was more interested in political science, so I opted to come to Carolina.

"Coach Frank Howard (Clemson) and my dad were best of friends—chewing tobacco, fishing, and hunting friends. I never will forget—we were the Laurens High Tigers, and when I got ready to sign, I told them I was going to sign by a certain date. I got a telegram from Frank Howard saying, 'You've been an outstanding Tiger for the last four years. Don't *fowl* it up today.'

"I had to appear before conference commissioner (James) Weaver and give sworn testimony as to why I changed. The complaint didn't come from Clemson; it came out of North Carolina, and it didn't come from Duke.

"Then I played in the South Carolina All-Star game (Columbia in August). We played in this humidity, and I wondered if I had made the right decision!

"Our freshman team (1955) was supposed to be the best quality team in the school's history, and we couldn't wait until we joined the varsity. The hardest game I experienced at Carolina was when we scrimmaged the varsity, after our freshman schedule was over. They took it out on us (for losing season). We were the highly-touted freshman team that got all the good ink and publicity. They really socked it to us—they were tough. If they had played every ball game like they played the freshmen, they would have been tough.

"I came to Carolina for the reasons I mentioned. Again, I

believed in Coach Enright as a coach and as a person, who to me was one of the finest gentlemen I've ever met. Donald Russell (USC President) also did a super job in talking to athletes and making them feel at home.

"At the time when Coach Enright retired, it really put a lot of questions in some of our minds, but we had gotten used to Carolina.

"The biggest change I think it made when Giese came—he was the youngest head coach in the country (age 32)—the biggest impact it made on me was when he called us all in individually and asked us why we came to Carolina. What other remuneration, what

This is the attire worn by Gamecock footballers, as they arrived at the Miami, Florida, airport in 1956. Left to right, King Dixon, Alex Hawkins, coach Warren Giese, Julius Derrick, and Heyward King.

other inducement were we promised, other than a straight Atlantic Coast Conference scholarship—books, tuition, fifteen dollars a month spending money?

"I told him exactly what I had been promised, and nothing else. I had heard that some other players, who weren't as fortunate as I was, had some family problems, or didn't really have an extra shirt, very possibly had been promised something by—I'm sure it was alumni. I never questioned the coaches' integrity."

The 1955 Carolina freshman team brought together two halfbacks that formed an exceptional combination, offensively and defensively. Years later Gamecock supporters referred to the "Dixon and Hawkins teams." Both Hawkins and Giese became the subjects of many conversations, both for their football and their personalities.

Dixon: "After playing with Hawkins my freshman year, I knew that Alex was one of the finest athletes and toughest I'd ever seen in my life. He told coach Giese, if he couldn't get what he'd been promised, he'd have to look elsewhere to go to school. I don't know how he and Coach Giese worked that out.

"I think we were all blessed that Alex stayed at Carolina. Certainly, Coach Giese was a real student of the game; to me a real student of psychology. But I don't think he'd ever had a test case like Alex Hawkins. And Alex proved to be one of the things that really challenged Giese.

"How he was able to handle our particular group under the circumstances and get the results he did was a real tribute to him. A lot of folks say they had some hang-ups in Coach Giese's offense. I didn't—I'm a winner. I was one—as long as we could get on that field and win consistently—as we did our sophomore year, when we were seven and three—and here's a group that was a large percentage of sophomores—the caliber was there.

"It was a matter of providing the leadership and the direction, with the ability that you had there. But to be able to turn a season around—and you can call it 'three yards and a cloud of dust.' I enjoyed playing whatever way it took to win. I had a lot of confidence in that coaching staff. I wasn't blessed with a lot of other things we OUGHT TO DO. I more or less did what the coaches wanted to do.

"Alex Hawkins is the toughest, most hard-nosed, hardheadedest football player, pound for pound, I've ever seen. In 1958 we were elected tri-captains, and coach Giese called Alex, Dwight

(Keith), and me in. We were expected to workout at the Y.M.C.A. so many days a week to get ready for spring practice. If you missed three workouts, they took your fifteen-dollar laundry check. He called Alex in and said, 'Look, you've missed three now; we don't mean to hold up your check. But you're the one setting the example for the young players. If you don't come up there, they won't come, and it's not creating the situation we'd like to have.'

"Alex said, 'Coach, I don't have the money I need to sustain me through school. That was taken away from me two years ago. I'll be ready in spring practice. I don't need all these workouts. I'll be ready. I'm out there selling ads—I'll probably get more of a workout running here and there selling ads for the bowling program than I would be up there. I can still beat anybody here in handball, anyway.'

"'No, Alex, you don't understand; you need to be there.'

"'Coach, I don't need to be there, and, if you don't like what I'm doing, I resign—if it's my example you're looking at.'

"So, Alex got up and walked out of the office. Coach Giese said, 'That's strange; that's most unusual.'

"How do you wrestle with something like that?"

Following an excellent sophomore season, in which the Game-cocks finished 7-3-0 and defeated Duke for the first time since 1931, Dixon entered a junior year that was shortened by a leg injury.

Dixon: "After coming off the season we had in fifty-six, you'd expect great things, and we did. We did have some key injuries that year, and that was probably the difference in our season. But, you know, we scored more points (202) than any team in the history of Carolina at that time.

"Against Duke in the first game, it was the largest crowd to witness a game in the two Carolinas. There were forty-four thousand at the Duke ball game; this means a lot to me, now, when I go down to Carolina and see the seventy-two thousand people. We had more at the Duke game than we had out at Texas—the stadium would only hold forty thousand when we played them that year.

"On the Tuesday before Big Thursday we were concluding our last practice, and Bobby Bunch (quarterback) and I collided on pass defense. Bobby's knee pad got me up under my right thigh pad, and I broke a blood vessel in my leg, and was put in the infirmary. Bobby hurt his knee pretty bad, too, and both of us were pretty much out. It wasn't some kind of ploy, like we were faking it.

"I was in the infirmary for two days with ice packs and something to take the swelling out of my leg. The swelling did leave my thigh and went down to my knee, and they worked it out of my knee, down toward the calf. By game time I could run about three-quarter speed, and they had made a special type of steel thigh pad that was heavy.

"I was standing around kinda feeling sorry for myself—when game day comes, you want to play. Coach Giese looked over there right before kickoff—we received—and said, 'Can you run?'

"I said, 'I can run, coach.'

"He said, 'Get in there.'"

With half the backfield much below par, Carolina's offense lacked scoring punch, and the Gamecocks were shutout by the Clemson Tigers, 13-0. Holders of a 3-2 record at that point, the Gamecocks won only two of their final five games to finish at 5-5-0 for the year. Of course, the win over a Texas team that ended its season with a Sugar Bowl bid was a highlight and one of the great victories in Carolina football history. Dixon had other recollections of that year.

Dixon: "We had several revolutions. One was watching closed circuit TV on the sidelines, which was something in itself. It's difficult to put it into perspective—how can you be on the sidelines and not be wanting to watch the game? You do have a better angle, but how do you tie that in with the scouts in the box? For a coach to be able to manage that on the sideline was rather unusual. It was something we hadn't seen before, and I don't know how well it worked. We were infrequently called to look at it.

"I got hurt in the North Carolina game right before halftime. Caught a punt and extended my leg, and a guy tackled me—good tackle—but I wound up with severely strained ligaments. My leg was in a cast for the next two weeks. (Missed Carolina's final three games.)

"I wasn't dressed out for the N.C. State game, and State was the only undefeated team in the A.C.C. (won the conference championship and finished with an overall 7-1-2 record). We had so many injuries going into the ball game, they should have beaten us handily. However, Alex Hawkins played one of the finest games I ever recall seeing someone play. The team played 'way above its head.

"Once again it was one of those games, 'when The Hawk got mad, other people got sad.' There was a penalty on the last play of

King Dixon was in good company when he received the Washington Touchdown Club award as America's most outstanding service player in 1959. Left to right, Billy Cannon of Louisiana State; Roger Davis of Syracuse; Ben Martin, head coach of Virginia; Joe Bellino of the Naval Academy; and Dixon.

the game. They had driven to our thirty-five yard line, and pandemonium broke out when the clock ran out. And I learned what it means 'it ain't over till it's over. They called pass interference on Tommy Addison. That was it. Dick Christy kicked the only field goal he ever tried in college (35 yards to give State a 29-26 win).

Dixon's knee responded to four weeks in a cast and therapy that had him ready, not only for spring football drills, but to run the sprints on the track team.

Dixon: "Ironically, that spring I had my best time in the hundred. In our first meet I ran against Dave Sime (Olympic sprinter from Duke), and I was timed at nine-six. Sime ran a nine-three. I could see headlines about forty or fifty yards out; I was ahead of Sime. Then he passed me, and I felt like I had a piano on my back!"

The Gamecocks opened the 1958 season with an 8-0 victory over Duke, prior to travelling to West Point, N.Y., to play an Army team that was to be the final one coached by Earl Blaik, and one of his finest. The Cadets surprised everyone by bringing a new wrinkle to college football, lining-up one end (Bill Carpenter) wide, while the rest of the team huddled. It was immediately tabbed "the Lonesome End."

Dixon: "In retrospect, when I think about the Army game, I appreciate that I see where Earl Blaik is coming out now saying he had to do something special for that game, because he had a lot of respect for Hawkins and Dixon at Carolina. So, he put in something special, so they wouldn't be embarrassed. I show those clippings to the boys, but I don't tell 'em the score (45-8)!

"I learned what the element of surprise meant, and what it meant to be inflexible, prior to going into the Marine Corps. One of the principles of war is the element of surprise. I think that when we went up to play Army in nineteen fifty-eight, we were as well prepared, physically, mentally, in every way, that you could possibly be to go up there and play. We had one of the best workouts at Bear Mountain that we've ever had. I remember our kick-off kicker was kicking the ball through the uprights in practice. We had more spirit, and we had scouted (Pete) Dawkins (Heisman Trophy winner in 1958), (Bob) Anderson (halfback), and Carpenter. I wouldn't remember Carpenter, had it not been for the next day.

"Alex, Dwight, and I knew we were in trouble when we went out there for the coin toss. Pete Dawkins was as tall as Dwight (6-4) and bigger than Alex and me combined. When they came out with the end never coming to the huddle; and their philosophy was to run a play every fifteen or twenty seconds; the Lonesome End just provided some distraction; because you never knew what he was gonna do.

"The Lonesome End would never have bothered us that much, except that we didn't know what to do. Everything we did was a zone type defense—no man-to-man coverage. On the snap of the ball, you took two steps back, and you reacted from your keys. When they came out there running the plays as fast as they did, it didn't take long for us to realize that we were in deep trouble, psychologically.

"Then, when we started adjusting which took us quite a while, they'd run a little shovel pass right up the middle. At halftime I remember Coach Giese saying, 'Gang, we've been together three years now. Go out there and hang tough, and I'll guarantee you, before the third quarter is over, we'll have this diagnosed and be able to adjust to it.'

"That was one of the few times I really didn't look forward to the second half!

"Finally, The Hawk says, 'To heck with it; wherever he goes, I go, and you take the second man out of the backfield.' Which made a lot of sense to me. I think we started doing better on defense.

"But, again, it was the thought of our inability to adjust, because we were so set in our ways. We didn't expect the element of surprise, and, of course, when you play Army, that's a military tactic, to be able to do that.

"Every time they scored, the sound of that gun and the smell of gun powder . . . after that game I was a seasoned veteran and ready to go into the Marine Corps!"

After the Army game, Carolina defeated Georgia, Clemson, Furman, Virginia, North Carolina State, and Wake Forest, while losing only to North Carolina and Maryland. This gave the Gamecocks a final record of 7-3-0 and a ranking of 15th in the Associated Press poll. During his three varsity years the Gamecocks were 19-11-0 for a 63.3 winning percentage, leaving Dixon with many fond memories of his football days at the school.

Dixon: "When I think about our senior year—we were second in the A.C.C. and fifteen in the nation. Jack Scarbath came to join the staff. I think coach Giese realized that we needed to open up a little bit more. (Scarbath was an All-America quarterback at Maryland.)

"I got to thinking over the years how very important your quarterbacks are. That's an understatement. Think about our last year; go back and think about the quarterbacks—what all they bring to the game—their ability to handle situations on the field, and their ability to communicate with the coaches. I'm seeing a different breed of quarterbacks now than when we played.

"When I was coming along the quarterbacks were schooled on how to call plays on the field—to go through certain motions. The quarterback is supposed to execute exactly what the coach wants on the field.

"I think Mackie Prickett was different from any quarterback I played with in college. Mackie had come up under a different set. He was a gifted quarterback, and, as far as anyone having to adjust, Mackie had the biggest adjustment to make, of the guys we played with. As you recall, following Johnny Gramling and a real passing attack, Mackie Prickett all of a sudden becomes three yards and a cloud of dust.

Laurens banker King Dixon and family in 1985. Standing behind King and his wife, Augusta, are sons King III, Gus, and Lee.

"I think, with his personality and leadership, he was able to adjust. And for him to come from a three-six to a seven-three is quite a tribute to Mackie, to be the leader out there on the field that he was.

"All the quarterbacks following that—Sammy Vickers—double dislocations in his shoulders, and knee problems. Bobby Bunch had several physical problems. Jack Hall had several problems along that line. Stan Spears came along and had some problems, physically. We never had real athletic ability, compared with what you see in quarterbacks out there today. We had the minimum requirements to get the job done. And in those days it was hand the ball to the halfbacks, or to be able to call the plays, based on the coach's philosophy. I don't think we were blessed with the best talent, but the guys we had did a great job with what they had.

"When you're out there on the field, playing that much of the time (offense and defense). How much it takes out of you, playing both ways. It comes back as a tribute to the type of athlete that was recruited here.

"The greatest thrill to me is to be able to line up and to be able to block for somebody. And I say that, because you've gotta do everything that's called upon you. Or, be able to be given that football, and everytime you've got it, with the hopes that you're gonna score. I had it, anytime I got the football.

"You don't block any different for a long touchdown or short touchdown. It's what you do when you get that football. Of course, the defense always has one more man on the field that the offense— they've got eleven, you've got ten. And you're carrying the ball. If they can handle ten, you oughta be able to handle one!"

Dixon's football career didn't end with his final collegiate game, as, upon graduation, he was commissioned a second lieutenant and sent to basic school at Quantico, Virginia. Football was in high gear in the armed forces at that time, with most major bases producing teams.

In 1959 the Quantico team won all of its ten regular-season games, then defeated McClellan Air Force Base by the unbelievable score of 90-0 to win the All-Service championship. For his role in that accomplishment, Dixon was voted the outstanding service athlete for the year, receiving an award from the Washington Touchdown Club. Other honorees at the awards dinner were Louisiana State's Billy Cannon, national back-of-the year; Syracuse's Roger Davis, national lineman-of-the-year; Virginia's Ben Martin, Washington area coach-of-the-year; and Navy's Joe Bellino, 1960 Heisman Trophy winner, Washington area player-of-the-year. Good company to be in!

Later he played for the Marine team in the Far East, was player-coach of the San Diego Marines in 1962 and 1963, and head coach at San Diego in 1964, posting a 10-1 record. In 1968 he coached the Quantico team, which played an all-college schedule, except for Pensacola Navy, which was quarterbacked by Roger Staubach, Heisman Trophy winner at Navy in 1963 and later all-pro for the Dallas Cowboys.

Dixon: "When I got ready to graduate from Carolina, I was five-eight, a hundred and sixty-four, and had a significant knee injury. When the pro draft came about, I didn't expect to be drafted at that size. I had talked with Peahead Walker at Montreal. He liked little guys.

"At Quantico I went up to a hundred eighty-five and was on an undefeated team. I packed some weight and was able to maintain my speed.

"Interestingly enough, the time frame we're looking at is nineteen fifty-nine, and the immortals, like Alex Webster, were retiring from the New York Giants. The Giant organization was scouting all the services then, and I had a very fine opportunity to go with the Giants. I received a very nice contract offer to go with them in nineteen sixty-one, but I still had another year remaining on my service obligation. I thought heavily about that. Tommy McDonald (Philadelphia) was about my size, and he was out there catching passes.

"I decided I was able to play in the service and coach in the service, and I had a pretty good salary. I decided that I just didn't want to live that type of life. I was more of a family man. That meant more to me than football.

"The point is, if I'd gone to the Giants I'd have gone there about the time of Joe Morrison."

Dixon does have one connection with a member of Morrison's staff at Carolina, as tight end coach Tom Kurucz played for Dixon at Quantico in 1968.

Dixon retired from the Marine Corps as a Lieutenant Colonel in 1981. Returning to Laurens, he is now vice president and city executive for Palmetto Bank, a financial institution with over $100 million in assets and nine offices. His oldest son, King, followed in his footsteps and is a second lieutenant in the Marines, following graduation from the University of Virginia. A "middle" son is a senior at Virginia and heading for Carolina Law School, while the youngest, Lee, is a freshman and Carolina Scholar at the University in Columbia.

Although the Marine Corps adopted its motto, "Semper Fidelis" (Always Faithful) in 1868, it seems that the people who selected it must have had King Dixon in mind. There is no greater exemplification of that characteristic.

To God, Country, family, friends, and school, there are no two better words to describe what makes him something special—almost unique—among University of South Carolina athletes and alumni.

King Dixon—"Semper Fidelis."

Charting King Dixon

YEAR	RUSHING			PASSING			RECEIVING		KO RETURNS			PUNT RETURNS	
	NO.	YDS.	AVE.	NO.	COMP.	YDS.	NO.	YDS.	NO.	YDS.	AVE.	NO.	AVE.
1956-	136	655	4.8	11	6	61	7	126	7	199	28.4	5	13.4
1957-	73	272	3.7	9	3	20	3	53	7	293	41.9	2	12.0
1958-	79	323	4.1	14	6	65	10	189	11	263	23.9	11	8.1
	288	1250	4.3	34	15	146	20	368	25	755	30.2	18	10.0

YEAR	SCORING			INTERCEPTIONS		PUNTING	
	TD	EP	PTS.	NO.	YDS.	NO.	AVE.*
1956-	4	0	24	2	6	15	32.5
1957-	5	0	30	NOT AVAILABLE		14	32.7
1958-	5	2	32	5	51	29	32.3
	14	2	86	7	57	58	32.5

*Under NCAA statistical rules in effect during Dixon's career, if a punt went into the end zone, the punter was given credit for the distance to the 20-yard line only. In other words, if he punted, with the ball at midfield, and it went into the end zone, the punter received credit for a 30-yard punt.

ALEX **hawkins**

From Monday through Friday Alex Hawkins was a coach's nightmare. On Saturday he was a coach's dream and what many consider to be the finest all-around football player to represent the University of South Carolina.

41

HALFBACK

8

ALEX HAWKINS

i f Alex Hawkins had lived in 18th century America, he would have been host at the Boston Tea Party. As an ancient Greek, he would have remained with Leonidas at Thermopylae. In the War for Texas Independence, he would have volunteered for Alamo duty.

His motivation wouldn't necessarily be patriotism; it's just that Alex Hawkins loves a confrontation about as much as Dale Carnegie liked making friends.

To say that Hawkins is an individualist would be monumental understatement. He no doubt considers Robin Hood a rigid conformist; Howard Cosell, too timid; and Mohammed Ali, lacking in confidence.

Yet, a strong case could be made for calling him the finest all-around football player ever to wear a University of South Carolina football uniform. Statistics never tell a complete story, and often, none at all. But they do help make a point about Hawkins. During his varsity career, 1956 through 1958, for at least one season, he led the Gamecocks in rushing, passing, receiving, scoring, punt returns, and interceptions. Had they counted tackles in those days, he might have led there, too. If DEFIANCE had been a measurable category, Hawkins would have led the NCAA. The world should have known what was coming when Alex made moves out of high school that were in direct contrast to what was expected.

Most colleges were interested in him as a basketball player when he was at South Charleston, West Virginia, High School. So he chose football. It was considered heresy for a West Virginia star to consider any school other than the state university at Morgantown. So, Alex bolted to South Carolina.

Hawkins: "I was a better basketball player than football player. I didn't make all-state in football; might have made second team. I had twenty-three basketball scholarship offers, and I was heavily recruited to go to several schools, but I only had three football scholarships. Fact is, Clemson offered me a basketball scholarship and didn't offer me a football scholarship.

"I felt at the time that I was a ball handler more than a shooter, and you could see the larger people were starting to come in. I felt like my future was better in football, even though I had made the all-state teams in basketball and baseball.

"I knew I wanted to get out of West Virginia. I just wanted to try some place else, but I wasn't sure where I was going. At that time you just didn't get out of West Virginia. Bobby Barrett (enrolled at Carolina in 1954) was about the only boy who left the state. Pappy (Art) Lewis was coach up there (WVU), and he put so much heat that most coaches wouldn't even recruit up there. They had to register under false names and all that.

"We had the West Virginia all-star game in July, and I hadn't made up my mind at that time; I didn't want to commit. I was chosen the most valuable player in the game, and right after the game Ernie Lawhorne, who had been watching the practices, enrolled downstairs under an alias. Pappy Lewis was that physical and intimidating, and all that. He sneaked up the back stairs, and talked to me, and arranged for me to visit Carolina. I came down and went out to Arcadia with Lem Harper and a few others, and I went water skiing. That was the first time I had seen clean water ever in my life. They had a real attractive girl who was a helluva water skiier, and that afternoon sealed the whole thing, as far as I was concerned. Clean air, clean water, and pretty girls—they had none of the three in West Virginia. I made up my mind right there.

"When I signed the letter of intent I went straight to Charleston (W. Va.), and people would, honestly, throw things at me. They'd boo me when they'd see me on the street, because it had been announced in the paper. I couldn't get out of there quick enough. I reported early, as a matter of fact, just to get out of West Virginia."

All of the recruiting noise around Columbia concerned the signing of King Dixon, the all-everything back from Laurens, and few Carolina followers had heard of Hawkins. It wouldn't take this maverick long to get their attention.

Carolina's 1955 freshman team, the final one recruited by Rex Enright, who would retire from coaching following that season, was one of the school's better ones. A number of future varsity stars came from this squad, forming the nucleus of teams that would record 19 victories against 11 defeats in the three years to come.

They also developed a winning attitude that Hawkins projected, and he found it puzzling that everyone didn't have that fierce desire.

Hawkins: "I dated a girl who was a beauty queen up at Duke, and I visited her up there. They were wealthier people going to Duke, and all that. I kinda felt inferior, because Duke does have a wonderful campus.

"I remember when we were going to play Duke (1955 varsity), and we had such a losing attitude—the varsity did. When it came time to play them, a group of seniors in the dormitory were laughing about how bad Duke was gonna beat 'em. (Duke won the game, 41-7).

"That was the team I wanted to beat, so when my sophomore year came I was pointing to Duke. Having not grown up in South Carolina, the Clemson game really didn't mean that much to me. I just couldn't understand the intense rivalry. So, looking back on that first year, the Duke game, when we beat them seven to nothing, as far as I was concerned, that set the stage for our whole year. We went ahead and lost to Clemson, after dominating them throughout the game. But it wasn't a particularly bitter loss for me, like it was for Nelson Weston, Mackie Prickett, and Buddy Frick, because they were from South Carolina. They just couldn't get over my reluctance to accept that Duke would be a bigger loss than the Clemson game."

While the 1955 freshman team was winning all but one of its games, the varsity suffered through a 3-6 season, during which it became apparent that Enright's health was declining. He died less than five years later.

Did the coaching situation, the losing season, and negative attitude on the part of some of the players trigger second thoughts about his decision to attend South Carolina?

Hawkins: "No, because we had such an outstanding freshman team. I think we lost to Clemson (actually tied), even as freshmen, but we had the talent. I think off that freshman team there were five boys that played professional football. (They were tackles Tommy Addison, Sam DeLuca, and John Kompara, guard Don Rogers, and Hawkins.) I had never played on a losing team, so I still couldn't imagine someone sitting there laughing before a game about how bad they were gonna get beat. The attitude was such that they more or less expected it."

Immediately after the season Enright announced his retirement and introduced Warren Giese, former assistant to Jim Tatum at Maryland, as the new head coach.

Hawkins' reaction to this: "I liked Rex Enright as a person so much. I thought he was just a great man and everything. So, I just took that with a grain of salt, 'We're gonna have a new head coach in here, and I didn't think much of it. I wasn't particularly impressed with Warren Giese at all. Of course, back then a number of players were getting some 'extras'.

"The first thing Warren Giese did when he came in was to have a meeting, and he said, 'Payday's over; nobody's getting paid. If you don't like it, name three schools you'd like to go to, and I'll recommend you.'

"So, naturally, I did. I said, 'Kentucky has offered me a farm.' I'll go to Kentucky or Texas, and I don't remember what the other school was. I didn't hear from the other schools, and he didn't contact any of the schools and tell 'em I was lookin' to transfer, or anything.

"During the summer months I was working in West Virginia; construction work, breaking rock and all that, and I was in good shape and looking forward. I had already fallen in love with the University and the state of South Carolina, so I just let it die at that and went back to school. We never had any more words about the financing."

"Giese and I never really did get along the entire year. But, I'll tell you what he did do. I remember what a difference he made with a particular athlete, Julius Derrick (end who played for Epworth Children's home in Columbia). Derrick had kinda the losing attitude that exemplified Carolina football. He was one of those players laughing about how bad they were gonna get beat; that sorta slanted my values on him. But Warren Giese had such a positive effect on him. I don't know what he did special to Julius, but he became one of the most tenacious competitors we had on the ball club. That's a good thing he did for him.

"I didn't know enough about football to be able to judge Giese as a coach or strategist, but when you didn't throw a forward pass, and other teams threw it against us—I felt like that was operating at a disadvantage. When you only had one defense, and other teams had several defenses, I suspicioned that that was a little bit too elementary there.

"He never let it interfere with our relationship at all. He did call King Dixon and Dwight Keith in my senior year and told 'em that he was seriously concerned about one of the tri-captains. So, since I wasn't there, I figured it was me. He said I'd either end up as a millionaire or in a straight jacket, and neither one has taken place so far.

"We had some run-ins. We only had one check-off system, and that was to change the same play to the other side of the line. Bobby Bunch was the quarterback at that time, and it was generally conceded by most people that Sammy Vickers was a better leader and quarterback than Bunch. I said, 'Either put me on the second team with Vickers or move Bunch to the second team.'

"He said, 'I'm not going to do either.'

"At that time they were playing two-platoon, anyhow, and it didn't make any difference, because I was on both platoons. He'd only put ten men in the game. I think I averaged fifty-six minutes my senior year. It was a ten-man two-platoon thing.

"Ernie (Lawhorne) recruited me, and we were great friends the whole time. You know, you worked with the offensive backfield coach, and Giese sorta stayed removed from the scene, anyway. Ernie and I got along beautifully, so Giese came to him my senior year and said, 'Ernie I want you to find out why Hawkins is not talking to me.' I had just quit talking to him altogether after his refusing to move Bunch and Vickers around. So, we didn't talk my whole senior year. He called Ernie in and said, 'Hawkins won't talk to me, and I want you to find out why.'

"So, Ernie came out on the field and said, 'What's wrong with you and Warren?'

"I said, 'Nothing.'

"He said, 'Why won't you talk to him?'

"And I said, 'Because I don't like him.'

"He said, 'What else?'

"I said, 'That's it. I don't talk to him, because I don't like him.'

"He goes back in after practice, and Giese said, 'Did you find out what it was?'

"He said, 'Yes.'

"'What was it?'

"'He said he doesn't like you, so he won't talk to you.'

"Warren said, 'Okay.' And that was it. We didn't have any run-ins, because we didn't talk."

Carolina's 1958 team would be rated one of the finest in the school's history, winning seven of ten games and finishing the season ranked 15th in the Associated Press poll. It was the first Gamecock team to be ranked in the final poll, and, as of 1984, was still the only Carolina team, other than the '84 squad, to hold a final ranking.

After an opening 8-0 win over Duke they lost to an Army team that introduced the famous "Lonesome End (Bill Carpenter) and featured Heisman Trophy winner Pete Dawkins, a halfback. The Cadets were unbeaten that year, tied by Pittsburgh, and ranked sixth nationally.

The Gamecocks held key wins over Georgia at Athens, Clemson, and North Carolina State.

Hawkins was named to the Paul Williamson All-America team, third team All-America by Associated Press, and the Atlantic Coast Conference Sports Writers Association selected him as the league's Player-of-the-Year.

Hawkins: "I had a good season, there's no question about it. Even in games we lost, I played well offensively and defensively. I was real proud of getting as much as I did out of my ability, speed, size, and what have you."

The Georgia game, won 24-14, by the Gamecocks was an excellent example of the respect commanded from opposing coaches by Hawkins and his natural talent. Alex put the Gamecocks ahead in the first quarter by intercepting a pass by Bulldog quarterback Charlie Britt and returning it 45 yards for a touchdown.

Hawkins: "Wally Butts (Georgia coach) had told 'em not to throw to my side of the field; I was the defensive left linebacker. Well, when the wide side of the field was to the right, for that particular game, they moved me to the right side. When I intercepted the pass, they figured they were throwing to the other side of the field, but I was on the right side for that situation. It was about the only defensive adjustment we ever made.

"We had a big fight after the game. They had a boy named Dave Lloyd, who was crazy; he was the center for them. He reached out to Lawton Rogers (Carolina center) after the game, like he was gonna shake hands, and Lawton had his helmet off, and shook hands. Lloyd took his helmet and hit him and broke his nose, and the fight started.

"I didn't like the odds—it was about fifty thousand to two hundred at the time. So, I took my wife, who was a cheerleader at the time, and I ran to the open end of the stadium. I took care of the cheerleaders!"

The win over Georgia had followed the opening frustration against Army's Lonesome End, which Hawkins recalled with clarity.

Hawkins: "At that time we only had one defense—it was a five-four. So, technically, I was a linebacker, and we never made an adjustment the entire year.

"We opened the season at West Point (actually, it was the second game), and they had the Lonesome End (lined-up on the wide side of the field, without going to the huddle). so, we made-up a defense.

"If that damn King Dixon hadn't been so regimented when we went up to West Point, we'd have come out a little better. I saw the Lonesome End out there by himself, and we didn't know what to adjust. We had never seen it before, so, here we are in a five-four defense—in tight. And here's a guy out there by himself. I knew how disciplined King was, and I said, 'Get out there!'

"He said, 'No. You turn the play in, and I'll make the tackle.'

"And I said, 'There ain't gonna be no runnin' plays, until we get into some other formation.'

"And this went on till they scored, and we never made it. So, finally I said, 'This is ridiculous.' I went to one of the coaches and said, 'You've got to get another defense. This defense will not contain them, and I don't know one. But you're the coach, make-up one.'

"He said, 'This is the only one we've got. Warren won't change it.'

"So, we would take turns, after they'd scored two or three touchdowns, doing this: Dixon would go out one time, and I'd go out the next. And we really didn't get settled for the entire year, for the Lonesome End.

"Later, against Virginia, here I am trying to cover Sonny Randle (wide receiver with blazing speed, who was one of the nation's best with 47 catches in 1958, and later starred in the NFL). I had no experience with that at all, and that wasn't pleasant. All I did was line-up about ten yards off of him and hoped to wear him out when he caught it underneath me on the short ones.

"We were told in the scouting report that he didn't like getting hit. I hit him frequently—forearms and things of that nature—strictly legal—whenever I'd get a good shot! I think he caught about six passes, but he didn't get the long one. If he did, he didn't get it off me. I knew what speed he had, so I lined up 'way off him. I was the deepest linebacker what ever played! He was the hardest one to cover I played against in college.

"We didn't have receivers spread out like that until our senior year and the Army game. That Carpenter; I didn't even know what kind of potential he had, but he was a helluva receiver. We were so unprepared for that game, we had no chance at all."

Another low point in the 1958 campaign was a 6-0 loss to North Carolina at Chapel Hill in what was the most lackluster performance of the year by the Carolina team.

Hawkins: "That North Carolina game—I was in the hospital all week with laryngitis, flu, and I don't know what all I did have. Friday, they came and got me out of the bed, put me on a plane, and I still couldn't breathe or anything. I didn't start the game, but I played pretty much the whole game.

"I was as weak as I could possibly be. I don't remember much about it; I was exhausted just from the trip up there. It was a hot day, too, and I made a long run pretty early in the game, and, for all practical purposes, I was pretty well spent.

"We did have a little five milligram pill that we used to take— sneak and take. It was the psychology of the whole thing. You wouldn't even let the guy in the locker beside you know you were taking one. They just appeared. As a matter of fact, we'd find them on the top of our little locker; no one ever knew who put 'em there. We'd sneak and take 'em. They never did you any good. It made you think you had something, because of the mystery of finding an illegal substance in your locker. A five milligram thing? Little ol' housewives take fifteen milligrams. The only person I ever saw it affect was John Dorsett. He was allergic to them. He fell down the stairs; he just acted hysterically.

"It was the psychology of the thing. I never have known them to help anybody; give them any energy or anything."

In spite of Carolina's very successful teams during his sophomore and senior seasons, Hawkins talked as if it was in spite of the system, rather than because of it.

Hawkins: "We had no offense, to speak of, except you beat the guy—you obliterate the person—you're playing against. We'd laugh at the meetings, because all the blocking was simply, here, here, here, and here. There were no cross-blocks, traps, or anything like that. It was just as fundamental and basic as you could get an offense.

"It was the same one that Jim Tatum's was. You have people that are better than the people they're playing against. You knock 'em back four yards, and the back will get two on his own. So it would be second and four. And that's honestly what he operated under.

"Did it work? Obviously, it did. Until recently he (Giese) had as good a record as any coach in the history of Carolina. What we did is—we had tremendous talent—John Kompara, Don Rogers, both played pro football. We just had a helluva lot of talent—Corky Gaines, Jake Bodkin, Sam DeLuca. We had some tremendous players at that time."

Alex did consider the system a problem for recruiting, particularly in attracting capable quarterbacks.

Hawkins: "I think the system was the problem more than anything. It was so fundamental. I don't know of any high school coach who was more fundamental than he was, as far as his imagination, blocking techniques, and overall thinking.

"Whoever invented the forward pass—when you have that at your disposal and don't use it, with the quarterback draw—it makes you wonder. Really and truly, a quarterback dropping back and throwing a pass, my senior year, we finally used it against Clemson. Buddy Mayfield was something like thirty yards behind the defense, because we didn't have one. (Carolina's first touchdown in a 26-6 win was set-up by a 26-yard pass from Bunch to Mayfield to the Clemson 12-yard line.) I talk and laugh about it with Frank Howard to this day.

"He said, 'Y'all were simple; you couldn't score, because we knew you weren't gonna pass the ball. So, all you gotta do is put eleven men on the front.' And, really and truly, you could. But we succeeded, so that doesn't say very much for the opposing coaches, does it?

"Frank (Howard) and I were always good friends. I still kid him about not recruiting me; Clemson offered me a basketball scholarship, but never offered me a football scholarship.

"I said, 'Why was that, Frank?'

"He said, 'Because you weren't any damn good!'"

Although the 1957 season was a disappointing five wins and five losses, it provided one of the most satisfying victories for Hawkins. The Gamecocks scored 20 points in the fourth quarter to beat Texas, 27-21, at Austin. In the rally Hawkins threw a 36-yard touchdown pass to Dixon and scored on runs of one and 18 yards. He also kicked the three conversions.

Alex Hawkins in his 1958 Gamecock jersey.

Hawkins: "It was Darrell Royal's first game as coach, and we didn't know anything about Darrell Royal; nobody did. It was his first game, but it was the only time we'd played that far away from home. It was exciting for us; I don't think any of us had ever been to Texas. You had heard about how rabid the Texas football fans were, and how big football was in Texas. We played a night game down there, and it was our second game of the year (actually, the third). Dixon ran the opening kickoff back for a touchdown (school record 98 yards), and they came back. We scored with about three minutes to go to win the game.

"And those Texas fans ended up cheering for us. When we were coming off the field, they were applauding just good football; that's how much they liked it. I knew then I was gonna like the Texas people."

Hawkins and Dixon are recognized as one of the better backfield combinations in Carolina history, along with such duos as Steve Wadiak and Bishop Strickland; Al Grygo and Stan Stasica; George Rogers and Johnny Wright; Kevin Long and Clarence Williams; Thomas Dendy and Kent Hagood; etc. Which leads up to Hawkins' association with his teammates.

Hawkins: "How did we get along? I don't know; I didn't pay much attention to them. Jake Bodkin was always a real good friend; we played high school ball together. Heyward King and I always got along very, very well. John Dorsett, John Saunders. King (Dixon) and I got along wonderfully. We didn't have much in common. Off the football field, we were almost never together, because his way of living was quite different from mine.

"But Sam Vickers and Nelson Weston were good friends. I got along with about everybody. Bobby Bunch and I were not as close as we might have been, and I wasn't as close to Lawton Rogers as I might have been.

"Dixon and I were a good combination, but it could have been moreso, had we utilized King a little better to his ability. The agreement was, when it came to spring drills (1956)—I was playing behind Carroll McClain, who had an outstanding junior year—he (Giese) said, 'I'm gonna keep 'em together. Either both will start, or neither.'

"So, Dixon was beating Frank Destino out for the job, and I was playing behind McClain. I wasn't beating him out, and that's the way it was through early-season practice. They were keeping us on the second team, but Carroll, unfortunately, had an injury. He ran the right side, and Dixon and I tackled him; and he missed the rest of the year; and we became starters. We didn't try to do anything, but the two of us were on the tackle, and he hurt his knee.

"That welded us together, and we became inseparable when we got our shoulder pads on. Off the field, it wouldn't have worked."

A self-analysis by Hawkins comes off rather objective:

"I was probably a better overall defensive player, and I was better against the run than I was against the pass. I was a linebacker, but I didn't have the great speed to be a threat in the open field, as far as an offensive back goes. They didn't time us in the forty; the only thing I know is everybody I ran against beat me at it.

"I had my own strength program during the summer—breaking rock in West Virginia. I did lift some light weights, but I didn't tell anybody, because they didn't want you to. At that time lifting weights was considered a bad thing; made you tight, slowed you down, and what have you.

"I think the overall best game I played was against North Carolina State my junior year. We lost the game 29-26, but I think I totalled more yards than Dick Christy (State All American who scored all of his team's points). I outrushed him, but he ended-up winning the game after it was over. (Hawkins intercepted a State pass on the final play, but it was nullified by a penalty against the Gamecocks, giving the Wolfpack one more play from the Gamecock 25-yard line. Christy responded with a game-winning field goal.)

"That's when I should have scored, but I had played so much of the game. I ran almost seventy yards with the ball and was run down from behind by the entire North Carolina State team at the twelve yard line. Not one person—every one of them! That's as good a ball game as you'll ever see.

"Incidentally, I have a record that nobody knows about. One year I led the team in receiving and passing in the same season. That will never be broken."

The record is that Hawkins led the Gamecocks in receiving with ten catches for 91 yards in 1956, then was the team's top passer in 1957, completing nine of 12 attempts for 153 yards. Still, statistical records don't reveal any Carolina player who has led the team in both passing and receiving even in separate seasons.

Hawkins: "When the second platoon would come in, I'd stay on the field. We didn't have but a halfback option pass, to the right and to the left. So, I was catching it from Dixon, Heyward King, and Destino, and I was throwing to them."

Before reflecting on his professional career, Hawkins couldn't resist one more backward glance at his college days and coach. His remarks might well be prefaced with the fact that University of Maryland teams under Jim Tatum as head coach and Warren Giese as assistant were ranked in the nation's top ten four times during their last four years at that school. Both departed, Tatum, to North Carolina, and Giese, to South Carolina, after the 1955 season.

The Terps were ranked third in 1951; first in 1953; eighth in 1954; and third in 1955.

Hawkins: "Warren's a fine man; he's better off in the business he's in now than he was in coaching, that's all. (Giese was elected to the South Carolina State Senate in 1984.)

"He was an English major, and he wrote Jim Tatum's book. Jim Tatum didn't know a helluva lot of football, either. That's how he (Giese) got the job."

Hawkins had plaudits for two of the backs who teamed with him and Dixon in 1956 and 1958.

Hawkins: "I think Mackie Prickett could have been really out-standing. He was a good athlete; had a great head; and he was a good leader; well respected. John Saunders was a fine football player; damn good competitor; good defensive player; good offensive player; excellent blocker; a pleasure to play with."

Just as Hawkins entered the University in less-than-quiet circumstances, it was appropriate that his exit was similarly unorthodox.

Hawkins: "The last game I played in was Wake Forest in Charlotte (Thanksgiving Day, 1958). I threw three touchdown passes in that game, and I hardly remembered it at all. (The passes were for 12, 45, and 8 yards, all going to Dixon.)

"What I remember was that, after the game, Sam Vickers, King Dixon, Nelson Weston and I went to the beach and celebrated our college career together. I came back on Monday, and whoever was in charge of housing had packed my bags from the fraternity house, and had 'em out there, and I got my walking papers that day. I was thrown off the campus, out of school, the whole deal. Why? For very deserving reasons. I had broken every rule that I had already bent. And they had put up with me just as long as they were going to. I richly deserved everything that they did. No question about that."

This led to Hawkins entry into the professional ranks, which technically began with his participation in the Senior Bowl at Mobile, Alabama.

Hawkins: "I was the thirteenth player picked in the draft; the first man in the second round (by Green Bay). We (Don Shula, Hawkins' coach at Baltimore) laughed about that. Shula, was scouting for the Detroit Lions, and he labeled me 'can't miss, offensively or defensively.'

"After he was with the Colts, years later he was trying to justify keeping me on the squad, because I could play six positions. He told me about that and said, 'That goes to show you how wrong a man can be!'

"At Green Bay I ran into Vince Lombardi. I was trying to live my life like I always had, and Lombardi didn't see it quite that way. He didn't put up with my B.S. or lack of discipline whatsoever. He put me on a plane and sent me to Baltimore—a nothing for nothing trade is what I think it was. I think they (Baltimore) had to give them the five hundred dollars they had given me for signing.

"I was used on special teams, until they had an injury to a halfback. At that time, sometimes, you didn't have a replacement at all. L.G. DuPree got hurt, and I started one game, against the Packers, and hurt my knee, and was out for the next couple of weeks. They activated a boy off the cab squad, and I played on a limited basis the rest of the year."

During Hawkins' career with the Colts he received quite a bit of national publicity for a nickname he received—"Captain Who?"

Hawkins: "I had gone to Shula his first year (Weeb Eubanks was the Baltimore coach when Hawkins joined the team). He and I got along very well, immediately. He was a similar type athlete that I was—competitor and wanted to play, but didn't have a lot of talent. He was cornerback for the Colts till he was traded to the Redskins, and Ray Berry caught nine passes on him; then he was released and started his coaching career. We had a meeting.

"He said, 'Do the best you can. You've got limited ability, but I'm gonna be fair about it. If you're doing better than whoever it is, you're gonna make the ball club.'

"I wasn't doing much. I was playing back-up everything— tight end, fullback, wide receiver, and a little bit of cornerback, too. About the fifth or sixth game a boy named Wendell Harris (Louisiana State) and I volunteered to be on the 'suicide squad'.

"Shula said, 'You'd get killed; those people are too big.'

"I reasoned that, in the open field, because we were faster and more mobile than the linemen, 'don't worry about us gettin' hurt.' It worked out beautifully; we dominated special teams from that moment on.

"The next year we were playing our first pre-season game in Hershey, Pennsylvania, and right before the game Shula says, 'For the coin toss I'm gonna start something new this year. I'm going to have a captain of the special teams.'

"And I said, 'I'm not going out there; it's embarrassing.'

"He said, 'You're going to do it.'

"I said, 'I'm not going out there; nobody knows who I am; and I'm going out there with Gino Marchetti and Johnny Unitas?'

"He said, 'You're going to do it, or you aren't going to be on the ball club.'

"And I said, 'You've convinced me!'

"Sure enough it became a laughing thing. At that time no pro team had more than two captains; some only had one. I went out, and the referee comes over and says, 'Captain Unitas, how are you? Captain Marchetti.'

"And I give him my name, Alex Hawkins, and he said, 'Who?' Johnny and Gino laughed, and we went to the middle of the field. The same thing happened with the captain of the Eagles—'Johnny,

"Captain Who" of the Baltimore Colts.

Gino, Who?' It just kinda caught on. Captain Who?

"Shula just turned those teams over to me, and I'd grade film on Monday. I had complete control over them—who I wanted on the team; how I wanted it done. He just eliminated that from what he had to do.

"To make this thing fun and get a little esprit de corps, I offered a hundred dollars for whoever graded out highest—out of my own pocket. Of course, I did the grading, and, unfortunately, nobody ever won it but me. But we had a lot of close seconds!"

Eight of Hawkins' nine years in the NFL were spent with the Baltimore Colts, but he went south to help the Atlanta Falcons through their inaugural year in the league.

Hawkins: "I saw a lot of receivers playing first string that I didn't think were as good as I was, but I was playing behind Raymond Berry, and there's nobody better. I knew I never would be a starter for them.

"I had an agreement with Shula, if they ever had a team in the South—an expansion team—that he'd put me on the list to be traded. So, the Falcons came up, and I liked the idea of living in Atlanta, someplace in the South, and they picked me up.

"That experience was horrible, but I did find out that I'd rather be a second team receiver on a good team than a first stringer on a bad team. I did lead the Falcons in receiving.

"Norb Hecker and I . . . . there seems to be a pattern forming here, doesn't it? Didn't get along with Paul Brown (coach in the Senior Bowl); didn't get along with Vince Lombardi; didn't get along with Warren Giese; did get along with Shula; got along fair with Ewbanks; and I got along with Ernie Lawhorne. So, I'm three for six!

"Norb Hecker and I just didn't see things eye to eye, either; not at all. It was a miserable existence for both of us. We mutually agreed that we weren't happy, so he worked out a deal and sent me back to Baltimore.

"I started till the last game of the season and had my best season ever. After the Jets beat us (1969 Super Bowl), I held my own press conference in Baltimore at Unitas' restaurant, in the back room.

"That was a beauty. I made Shula come back from vacation. I got hold of him and said, 'I'm here to announce that I'm quitting. I'm not retiring; my career hasn't been that good to justify retiring. So, I'm having a quitting party.'

"He came on up for it. During the course of the evening I made everybody get up—I guess there were about twenty-five people there—sports writers, friends, and a few players. I said, 'I've been catching all this flack for years; now everybody's gotta stand up and say one nice thing about me, since I'm paying for it.'

So, everybody takes turns getting up, saying this, that, and the other. After about the sixth person did, I got up and acted like I was touched.

"I said, 'After all this, I didn't realize I was that good, so I'm not gonna quit!'

"Shula threw down his napkin and left! But, really, that was it; you don't quit but once."

After leaving the Colts, Hawkins made his home in Atlanta, involving himself in a number of endeavors, including the commercial trash collection business; writing a sports column; television work, local and network; and recent exploration into imported products.

Hawkins: "I got along with corporate heads of networks about like I got along with Vince Lombardi. I was a little ahead of my time; I was doing a Don Meredith thing before Don Meredith was popular. I worked for CBS for six years (on pro football telecasts), with Lindsay Nelson, Don Criddy, Jack Buck, Vince Sculley, Pat Summerall, Frank Gifford, and Al Michaels, at one time or another.

"The first time I was fired, I was doing a game in Dallas, Texas; the Pro Bowl, and nobody especially wanted to play in the Pro Bowl by then. Back when I was playing, everybody would kill to play in the Pro Bowl, but salaries soared, and it didn't mean that much any more.

"Jake Scott (former Georgia star) was an old school player, and he reported with both hands in a cast. They said, 'You can't play in the game.'

"Jake said, 'I just played in the Super Bowl with both hands in a cast. The only time it bothers me is when I go to the bathroom. That's when I know who my real friends are.'

"And I related that story and was fired before we got off the air."

"A couple years later I was hired back and was doing one of the playoff games. I just saw a picture on the monitor of Roger Staubach; it was one of those things that just comes up; and he was kinda joggin' off the field. He has an unusual gait and I made the comment to Vince Sculley, 'You know, Roger kinda runs like a sissy.'

"They interpreted that as gay. That was when there were three gay quarterbacks in the league; but I didn't mean anything by that at all. It was interpreted that way, and they got something like five thousand phone calls to CBS, and I was dismissed again.

"You've heard Meredith and them say a helluva lot worse things than that, but, at that time, you treated it like it was a cathedral sport. You just didn't say certain things.

"I was hired back again, and they offered me half a season; instead of sixteen games, eight games. So, I retired."

Although he works hard at his image of the maverick, non-conformist, rebel, or what have you, Hawkins still maintains a strong loyalty to the school at which he made a name for himself. He took special pride in recruiting a high school quarterback from Atlanta for Carolina in 1979.

Hawkins: "Gordon Beckham was probably the best high school quarterback I've ever seen. I just happened to go to one of his games on a Friday night, and he reminded me of Bob Griese (Miami Dolphins). I got to going to his games and helped recruit him for Carolina. He was a straight A student. He never played one game for South Carolina as well as he did in high school, unless it was the North Carolina game. (Beckham was named national back-of-the-week for his role in a 31-13 victory over the third-ranked Tar Heels at Chapel Hill.) It just didn't come together for him.

"He loves it over here (Columbia), and he's going to be a credit to the University. He's doing post-graduate work in Europe right now."

Statistically, Beckham finished his career as seventh in pass completions and eighth in passing yardage in all-time Carolina records.

Of the present Carolina coach, Joe Morrison, Hawkins says, "I don't know Joe that well, but I played against him for ten years. I had a great deal of respect for him. Getting Joe down here is the best thing that's ever happened to the football program."

His marriage 26 years ago to that cheerleader—Libby Bagnal of Manning—has produced a son (graduating from Carolina in 1985) and a daughter (working for a brokerage firm in Atlanta).

When discussing himself, Alex Hawkins becomes his worst critic. As an example he comments, "I gave up golf; I don't have enough character to play. I never could beat myself."

Even when pointing out that he was a very high draft choice in the NFL, you get the idea that he is hinting at some hidden meaning in that he was Number 13. He was also the 13th person chosen for the Carolina Athletic Hall of Fame, but that also means one of the earliest to gain such an honor.

At Carolina, it was said about him, that he never had a good practice, but never had a bad game.

One teammate recalled that during a practice session one afternoon, a sudden lightning storm sent players and coaches dashing for the cover of the Roundhouse. Hawkins was said to have walked slowly in the middle of the stampede, saying wryly, "I don't know why everybody's in such a hurry. They oughta know that, if lightning is going to strike anybody, it's gonna be me!"

Whatever you say about Alex Hawkins, it couldn't be that he's dull, non-committal, or afraid to face-up to a situation. Nor could it be that he wasn't a helluva football player who put all of his ability on the line every time he suited-out in No. 41.

Now that his accomplishments are fading in the memory of fans, amid the advent of new stars wearing Garnet and Black jerseys, this might be a fitting epitath to Hawkins' football career:

Alex Hawkins

1956-1958

A coach's nightmare during the week.

A coach's dream on Saturday.

Charting Alex Hawkins

YEAR	RUSHING NO.	YDS.	AVE.	PASSING NO.	COMP.	YDS.	RECEIVING NO.	YDS.	SCORING TDs	EPs	PUNT RET. NO.YD.AVE.	INTERCEP. NO.	YDS.
1956-	130	566	4.4	16	8	140	*10	91	5	11	3-51-17.0	*2	14
1957-	109	*450	4.1	*12	9	153	4	37	4	11	5-43-8.6	N/A	
1958-	100	474	4.7	13	8	120	*10	141	5	12	11-*133-12.1	3	107
TOTAL	339	1490	4.4	41	25	413	24	269	14	34	19-227-11.9		

*Led the team.

Hawkins also returned 11 kickoffs for 239 yards, an average of 21.7.
Hawkins led the team in scoring with 41 points in 1956; 35 in 1957; and 42 in 1958.

1962·63·64

DAN **reeves**

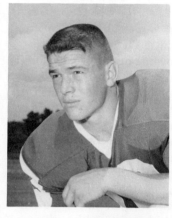

12

QUARTERBACK

He never experienced a winning season at Carolina, but Dan Reeves valued the solid football foundation he received from his coach, Marvin Bass. Three decades later they were together again, as Reeves became NFL coach-of-the-year with the Denver Broncos.

9

DAN REEVES

rom all outward indications Dan Reeves could have well been a bank president on this 12th day of February in 1985. It was a busy day at the office, and he excused himself for a moment.

"It's my boss calling," he said, "so I'd better take it."

Waiting in the wings were several others, ready for a meeting to discuss personnel and other matters.

Those who would guess that the schedule of a head coach in the National Football League is somewhat relaxed a month after the Super Bowl has been played and months before rookie camp begins, couldn't be more wrong. The Denver Broncos front office was a bee hive of activity, and Reeves was the main bee.

Dan Reeves—engulfed in a profession that he abandoned and wanted no part of when he was still young enough to consider other options. Just 12 years before he had walked away from pro football with the feeling that there had to be a better way to make a living, and, if so, he was going to find out, first hand. He needed to re-introduce himself to his wife and children, put behind him frustrations that he had encountered as a player-coach for the Dallas Cowboys in 1972, and reinstate weekends as a retreat, rather than a crisis.

By 1971 Reeves had worked his way from the University of South Carolina, where he experienced a fine career as quarterback, through a free agent entry into the Dallas organization, for which he performed with distinction at, of all places, running back, to player-coach status.

Reeves: "I was going to strictly be a coach in seventy-two. Then during pre-season that year Roger Staubach (who had won the Heisman Trophy at Navy in 1963), our quarterback, dislocated his shoulder, and Coach (Tom) Landry had me come back as a player-coach, and as a back-up quarterback.

"It was not a good experience. I really had some misgivings about being a coach. I had to work with Duane Thomas (running back who had great talent and greater personal problems) for a couple of years, and that was not a good experience for me, because of the problems we had with him. I was really second guessing myself, as to whether coaching was what I wanted to do."

Compounding Reeves' situation was the hiring of Sid Gillman by Dallas to coach the backs, as Reeves concentrated on quarterbacks. It was no secret that Reeves and Gillman didn't hit it off well.

Reeves: "I had my children at an age when I felt I needed to spend more time with them. And coaching was a profession that we spent six weeks every year in Thousand Oaks, California, away from your family. You were travelling a lot, you worked late hours. I really thought about going into private business—which I did in nineteen seventy-three.

"The year that I was out of coaching, I was in the real estate development business. During that time I really missed the game of football, so I was very fortunate to get back into it in 1974 as a special teams coach for the Cowboys.

"The year that I was out was valuable to me, because I think a lot of times there are guys who coach that maybe think they could be happier doing something else. There's no question in my mind now that I'm doing what I want to do. I enjoy the teaching aspect of it. I enjoy being around the young players, and I think it's a tremendous opportunity to really help young men mold and develop themselves for life after football. I enjoy the tremendous competition that you have week in and week out. It has great highs in it that I don't think any other business can offer to you. But it also has tremendous lows.

"It's an exciting business to be in. I feel like it's a business I'm knowledgeable about and feel comfortable that my knowledge of the game is as good as anybody's. You know, the key thing is getting people to play hard and making sure that you prepare them each week. I enjoy what I'm doing. I'm very fortunate to become a head coach at an early age (he was the youngest head coach in the NFL when he went to Denver in 1981), and I think I was able to do that because I was a player-coach, you know, at a young age.

"I've been around some of the best coaches, I think, throughout my career. In high school with Jimmy Hightower. In college with Marvin Bass. And pro football with Tom Landry. These three men helped develop my coaching philosophy and my life."

The individual speaking in such confident terms was the same Dan Reeves in whom only Carolina showed an interest when he was a senior quarterback at Americus (Georgia) High School in 1960.

The same Dan Reeves who was shunned by every National Football League team in the 1961 player draft. The same Dan Reeves who never gave a passing thought to being a coach until Dallas added that to his playing duties in 1970. The same Dan Reeves who said, "There's got to be a better way to make a living," in 1972.

And this is the same Dan Reeves whom the *Denver Post* gave the honor of holding "No.1" on its list of "10 WORST JOBS" in the Denver area, ranking ahead of the guy who cleans the restrooms at City Park and the woman who handles complaints from airline passengers. The newspaper explains, "Imagine having more than 70,000 people looking over your shoulder when you do your job; everyone of them second-guessing every mistake you make. And there is only one measure of job performance—win, or else."

Reeves added some credence to the selection with, "There are twenty-eight teams and head coaches (in the NFL), and only one of them will end the season feeling good about what they've done."

Although Reeves was not the ONE he described as feeling good about themselves, the fact that he was chosen the NFL Coach of the Year by five organizations couldn't help but ease the pain of "not feeling good." The Broncos record of 13 wins against only three losses and the AFC Western Division title in 1984 earned the coaching award from *Sports Illustrated, Pro Football Weekly, Football News, College and Pro Football Newsweekly*, and the Kansas City 101 Club.

If Reeves ever had any further thoughts about breaking the coaching habit—or addiction—the 1984 season was no way to go about it. The 13-3 of that year followed a 9-7 in 1983, 2-7 during the abbreviated 1982 campaign, and 10-6 for his first year as a head coach in 1981. Like a smoker or alcoholic, Reeves really can't put his finger on the moment when he became incurably hooked. Perhaps it had been in his blood forever, without his knowing it. Or, more likely, it is a communicable disease that he contracted gradually form the likes of Hightower, Bass, and Landry.

In 1960, when Dan was stretched out in the operating room of the county hospital, as surgeons prepared to insert an eight-inch steel pin to help mend a broken collarbone, his best bet for participating in sports beyond the high school level was small college basketball.

Reeves: "I wasn't a highly recruited player out of high school. My senior year I broke my collarbone and missed four games. I came back and played in the last three, and we ended the season

Reeves keeps for some tough yardage. (Photo courtesy of The State, Columbia)

eight and two. We beat the eventual state champion, but we lost a game while I was out that cost us the sub-region championship.

"We went on my senior year to win the state championship in basketball and baseball. I had some offers from small colleges for a basketball scholarship. But coach Weems Baskin came down during basketball season and asked me if I had any interest in going to the University of South Carolina on a football scholarship."

Baskin, who had been an assistant football coach at Georgia before joining Rex Enright's staff at Carolina, had been recruiting football players in the Peach State for many years. He could drive the roads of South Georgia blindfolded. Someone told him that there was a quarterback over at Americus that he should check into.

One thing that impressed Baskin was Dan's response to the question of how many passes he had completed before he hurt his shoulder. He replied, "I don't remember how many completions, but I do remember five interceptions."

That told Baskin that he was more interested in correcting his mistakes than thinking about his accomplishments.

Reeves: "My dad and I drove up to Columbia and visited. John Caskey, who was captain of the team my sophomore year, lived in Columbia, and he took me out and showed me the campus. I was really impressed with the school. At that time Coach Bass was not in town, and Jack Scarbath (All-America quarterback at Maryland in 1952), who coached quarterbacks, asked me if I'd like to go to South Carolina, and I told him I would. He said, 'All you've got to do is sign here—this scholarship.' And I couldn't sign it fast enough. That was the only school that had offered me a football scholarship.

"So, I signed with South Carolina and played in the all-star game in Georgia that summer. I got the MVP (most valuable player) award, and after that I had a lot of schools to offer me scholarships. I just felt like South Carolina had taken a chance on me, really, when nobody else did. I kind of felt an obligation, and I was impressed with Coach Bass, whom I met after that all-star game. He came down and talked to me and met with my dad and me.

"Then, after the all-star game, other colleges contacted me— Georgia Tech, Alabama, Florida, Georgia, F.S.U. (Florida State). The one I considered more seriously was Florida, because several of my friends were going there. When coach Bass came down to visit I had just gotten back from visiting at Gainesville with Coach Ray Graves. Of course, Coach Graves was at Georgia Tech (assistant) when my older brother was manager of the football team there, and I knew him and was a little bit interested in that. But when I met coach Bass, there was no question where I wanted to go.

"At that point I didn't really have an idea what I wanted to do with my life. I just felt like this was an opportunity. I enjoyed football more than basketball or baseball. When I went to South Carolina I never anticipated or thought about pro football. That just seemed to happen also. I was one of those guys who was just fortunate to get the opportunity, you know, to go to college.

"I probably would have gone to college, because I had some basketball offers, somewhere on scholarship. You know, I would have had a tough time to have gone, had I not gotten a scholarship. But I would have done it, I'm sure, because my mom and dad worked real hard on a farm, and my daddy was starting a construction company at that time. But I would had to have worked and gone to school."

The Reeves farm was actually at Andersonville, close to Americus, and only 15 miles from Plains, where another famous Georgia family lived.

Reeves: "Yes, we knew the Carter family. Everybody knew everybody in Americus and Plains. There was nobody that you didn't know. We used to play Plains in basketball and baseball, but they weren't big enough to have a football team. There were four or five families in Plains—the Shorts, the Jennings, the Carters, and the Chappells.

"When I was playing with the Cowboys, when he (Jimmy Carter) was Governor of Georgia, I went over and hunted quail on his farm and visited with him a little while. He was a real nice guy. You know, being President of the United States is sort of like coaching. You get second-guessed from everywhere. But the guy who has the tough job is the guy who's in the arena—coaching. In a small scale it's the same as the President's (job)—very small scale."

Reeves was on the first freshman squad recruited by Bass and his staff, as Bass succeeded Warren Giese as head football coach.

Reeves: "We had a pretty good freshman team. Won four and lost one, and beat Clemson. That was coach Bass' first recruiting year. and we had some great players that came in. Marty Rosen, Larry Gill, and Pete DiVenere were the backs, and we eventually ended up being the backfield at Carolina when we were seniors. They were also, except for myself, the second team backs my sophomore year.

"We had J.R. Wilburn, a great receiver from Virginia. Steve Cox, a big tackle from Easley. Len Sears, another big guy. Doug Senter was tight end. We had some real good football players who came in that particular year. We thought there was a foundation there for a good team coming up."

As Dan and his freshman colleagues labored under Bill England, the Carolina varsity registered a 4-6 record for Bass in his initial season. However, it was a respectable showing, considering a one-point loss to Duke, a three-pointer to Georgia, and a 21-14 victory over Clemson, which had beaten Giese's teams four times in five years. That team had a senior quarterback, Jim Costen, leaving that position "wide open" for Reeves' first varsity competition.

Tommy Pilcher, a senior, had some experience at quarterback, but the other candidates were the same ones who were on the 1961 freshman team.

Reeves: "I had a good freshman season, and I felt like I was getting better as a quarterback, and we all felt like we were going to be better. And we felt like the freshmen coming up would give us some depth. We really did have a good team (1962). We were four,

Dan Reeves was America's youngest starting college quarterback in 1962.

five, and one that year, but we lost some close games. I won the starting quarterback position in spring practice. I had a good spring, although I injured my knee, and I felt like that, if I came back in condition and had no problem with my knee, there was a good chance that I could start as a sophomore."

Prior to the start of the season a sports writer interviewing members of the Carolina squad expressed doubt that a boy as young as Reeves (his 18th birthday was in January of that year) could command the respect from his teammates necessary to be an effective quarterback and team leader. One of the players up from the freshman team with Reeves quickly spoke up, "We'd walk on water, if Dan told us to!"

The wise men of college football rule-making had created substitution rules that bordered on making it necessary for officials to carry computers. Suffice it to say that it drove college coaches to employ three units, instead of two, therefore accomplishing just the reverse of what the rules were *supposed* to do.

It must not have made much of an impression on Reeves, because he didn't recall it in 1985, but Carolina came up with names for its three units to correspond with breeds of Gamecocks. The number one, or two-way unit was named "Warhorse," the team of offensive specialists, "Bushwhacker," and the team of defensive specialists, "Stonewall." That made Dan a "Warhorse," whether he knew it or not, with a side order of "Bushwhacker," because he also quarterbacked that unit.

Carolina's opening opponent of 1962 was Northwestern, which was in one of its better eras of football under Ara Parseghian, who did such a fine job with the Wildcats that Notre Dame hired him.

Reeves: "A guy named Tommy Myers was quarterback at Northwestern. In fact, I was just a few days younger than Myers was, and that made me the youngest starting quarterback in the nation. Well, he broke Otto Graham's (Nothwestern, 1953 and later a star for the Cleveland Browns) record; I remember that. They were not supposed to be a passing team, but I think he completed, like, twenty-one out of twenty-five passes that day (actually 20 of 24), and they beat us pretty good (37-20). They ended up eight and one and the only game they lost was to Ohio State.

"I do remember the thing that stuck out in my mind is the first play of my college career we scored a touchdown on an end sweep by Sammy Anderson. We recovered a fumble down around the twenty, and on the first play I went into the game, ran a sweep with Sammy, and we ended up scoring.

"The quarterbacks were still calling the plays then, but I had always called the plays. We were sort of an inside-outside belly team, as they called it then, with a pro set of the I and the pro formation. And we rolled out quite a bit to throw the football."

Two games later, following a loss to Duke, Reeves faced his home state University in his first game in Carolina stadium. The result was a 7-7 deadlock with the Bulldogs.

Reeves: "Actually, Georgia tied us. We had a seven-nothing lead with about a minute to go in the game, and I was playing safety. Larry Rakestraw threw a pass to a big tight end (Mickey Babb), and I missed the tackle. The guy went about eighty yards (actually 68) and tied us right at the end of the game. I don't remember how we scored—seems like you always remember the bad things. I remember going up to make the play on the ball, the guy catching it, and missing the tackle; and the guy being gone."

Better memories were in store the following week against Wake Forest, bringing Reeves his first taste of varsity victory and producing his first touchdown pass. That was the first of four victories during a 4-5-1 season, others coming over Virginia, North Carolina State, and Detroit.

Reeves: "That was the best season I had there. I think the biggest problem we had is we didn't have a lot of depth. Our first team every year I was there could play with anybody. But our back-ups were not as strong, where we could count on somebody coming in. That was always our problem at Carolina.

"The North Carolina game, which we lost nineteen-fourteen, I threw a pass to Sammy Anderson, and he stumbled and fell right at the goal line and had yellow chalk all over his jersey. But they spotted the ball at the one-yard line, and we didn't have time to get off another play. That's another game we could have won.

"We lost a game to Maryland (13-11). They beat us with a field goal right at the end of the game (50 seconds remaining), after they called pass interference on what I thought—and still think—was a bad call.

"In the Clemson game (20-17 loss) we were in position to kick a field goal and tie it at the end of the game, but we decided to go for the win, which I still think was right. But, in that ball game, we were ahead, seventeen-ten, at halftime, I believe. But I threw a touchdown pass to Sammy, and they called it back, saying we had an ineligible receiver downfield. The film showed that our center, Rich Lomas, was not downfield. That touchdown was called back, and we ended up getting beat by three.

Carolina had threatened at the end, when star halfback Billy Grambrell returned a kickoff to the Tiger 49, following the go ahead field goal. Then Gambrell took a short pass from Reeves to the Tiger 20, where four pass plays failed.

"We had an excellent team that year and could very easily have been seven and three. It was a season that could have been much better. We lacked a little bit of depth there that could have made us an excellent football team. I had a good season, for a sophomore, because I was surrounded by a good team. That was the best team I was on while I was there."

In measurable categories Reeves was impressive, completing 66 of 131 passes for 930 yards and rushing for an additional 471, giving him a school-record 1,401 yards of total offense for the season. His eight touchdowns surpassed by one the 1954 total by Mackie Prickett, Carolina's scoringest T-formation quarterback.

Bass, observed that Reeves often violated some basics by carrying the ball on his "inside" arm and throwing off the wrong foot, but added that he wasn't about to change him. This was the formative year for a Bass-Reeves mutual admiration society that was still meeting regularly in 1985.

Of Bass, Reeves said: "He was a father figure, as far as I was concerned. It was like having a dad away from home, I thought he was a good coach. Looking back on it now, I think he was a guy who was extremely easy to play for. And maybe our players took advantage of it, and we didn't play as hard for him as we should have. He was not a hard-nosed type of guy that made you do things. He was the kind of guy that tried to get you to play at your best, but left a lot of it to be self motivated, and some of our players weren't self motivated.

"He was a great guy to play for. I couldn't have played for, not only a finer person, but a finer coach, and I learned a great deal about football from him. He was an extremely intelligent coach. I think he had a great grasp for the game. You know, he was basically the reason I went there, and had he not come down and visited me after those other schools wanted me, I would definitely have gone somewhere else."

The subject of considerable turnover in the coaching staff during Bass' tenure came up, but Reeves didn't attach a great deal of significance to it.

Reeves: "I know I had some good coaches. Jack Scarbath, our quarterback coach, his wife's dad gave him an opportunity to go into private business. I don't think it was because he was unhappy with coaching. So, we lost Jack. Then Ken Shipp came in, and he moved on also. I had a different coach every year I was there." (Don Watson was offensive coordinator in 1964.)

There's one word to describe Dan's junior season—OUCH!

Reeves: "That was an injury plagued season. I had to practice with both my knees taped up the majority of the season. I ended up missing the Georgia game with a ruptured blood vessel in my eye that I hurt against Maryland (a 21-13 Carolina victory). That was the only game I missed while I was at Carolina."

Bass still retained vivid memories of Reeves' eye injury, even after becoming a member of the Denver staff, and he told this story to *Rocky Mountain News* writer Dave Krieger to illustrate Dan's determination:

"He was in total darkness for three days. He had his eyes covered with some medical patches or something. I think on a Thursday they took the patches off his eyes in the infirmary. We were playing Georgia that Saturday. We left on a Friday. Of course, we took him on the trip, and he wanted to play. The doctor told me that he shouldn't play.

"So when we got to Athens, Georgia, on that Friday night, he came to me just before dinnertime and said, 'Coach, I'd like to play tomorrow.' And I says, 'Well, Dan, I don't think you can play, but I'll go and check with our doctor and see what he says.'

"And I went to the doctor, and he says, 'Marvin, I don't think he should play, because if he gets a jolt or something, he might cause some internal bleeding in his eye. If a guy gets in a tussle, these things might flare-up on him.' So, I went back and told Dan.

"Well, he went to his room and started a tussle. It was just a friendly tussle, with his roommate. And he came back to me about twenty-five minutes later and said, 'Coach, I can see fine. I just went back to my room and had a little tussle with my roommate, and it hasn't bothered me a bit'."

Bass didn't allow Reeves to play, but it underscored what he had already known about his intestinal fortitude and determination.

Twenty-two years later Bass was looking at his former protege from a completely different vantage point, as an assistant to Reeves, and he is still impressed.

Bass: "His knowledge of football—the technical aspect of the game—is superior to any coach I've ever coached for. I don't think I've seen anybody put a game plan together any better than what Dan does. I think he studies football all the time. Even as a college player, even as a high school player, I'll bet you he studied the game."

A study of the 1963 season isn't something that Reeves particularly relishes.

Reeves: "I was hurt the entire season. Not that that was the reason we were one-eight-one, but that's the main thing I remember about it. We were a young football team; had lost a lot of seniors from the team the year before, and we just didn't play well.

"Morale? One of the most difficult things in sports is to bounce back after being on a losing team. To gain the confidence that you need, and certainly, after that year, our confidence was really hurt.

"It was a case of not having a good recruiting year the year before (1960). We didn't have many seniors (10 listed on the pre-season roster). We were juniors that year, and there weren't many seniors who were starters (three). You know, it was basically a sophomore and junior team that year. I think the lack of success went back to a poor recruiting year the year before I came there."

Carolina had the dubious distinction of ending the nation's longest major college losing streaks twice within the season, dropping a 20-7 decision to Tulane on November 2, and falling to Wake Forest, 20-19, two weeks later.

Reeves drives for good yardage in leading Dallas to a 56-7 win over Philadelphia in 1966.

Reeves: "We had Wake Forest nineteen to nothing at the half, and they beat us twenty to nineteen on a Brian Picolo extra point. You try to forget those bad experiences, so I don't recall a lot about that season."

A national tragedy that was a reminder that winning or losing in football pales in importance to life's more meaningful areas also marred the 1963 season. The assasination of President John F. Kennedy took place on Friday, November 22, thereby dictating postponement of the Carolina-Clemson game from the 23rd to the 28th, which was Thanksgiving Day. Reeves passed for two touchdowns and compiled 116 yards in offense, but the Gamecocks lost again, 24-20, in a close but uninspiring game under the mood existing in America at that time.

Dan's senior year was an improvement, but still not the success that he would have preferred. Yet it had its highs and ended on the upbeat.

Reeves: "We felt like we had a good ball club, and we were looking forward to our senior year. We had another good freshman team coming up as sophomores that we thought would really help us to become better.

"We tied with Duke (9-9), but there were a couple of controversial calls in that ball game, which we could very easily have won. That's when they scored, kicked off to us, and we returned the ball out to about the forty yard line. And they gave the ball to Duke. Said we were called for holding while the ball was in the air, which is the only time that has ever been called in college football. That would have been a great start for us, had we won that ball game.

"In a seven-seven tie with Georgia we missed a field goal at the end of that game that was shorter than an extra point. They ended-up going to the Sun Bowl. (Vince Dooley's first year as head coach.) That was a good day for me (passed for Carolina's touchdown). We did a good job of moving the ball, and J.R. Wilburn caught a bunch of passes.

"Nebraska (at Lincoln) had us about twenty-one to nothing with seven minutes gone in the first quarter, and our game plan was out the window. I remember drawing up plays in the huddle—routes for the receivers. I think I broke the school record that day for passes completed (18 for 240 yards, both school records), and we ended up getting beat, twenty-eight to six. On the last play of the first half, we had a halfback (Jule Smith) to catch a long pass and got caught from behind and knocked out on their one-yard line.

"They ended up going to the Cotton Bowl that year. They were better than anybody we played while I was in college. Memphis State (9-0 winner over SC in 1963)—they were a heck of a football team. They were like eighth or ninth in the country. Florida (37-0 loss in 1964) was a good team. Steve Spurrier (1966 Heisman Trophy winner) was at quarterback then. He impressed me, and they had a great running back, Larry Smith."

When the Gamecocks met The Citadel in Columbia on November 7 they were possessors of the nation's longest winless streak of 15, dating back to the second game of 1963. Carolina broke the fast with a 17-14 victory, but Reeves said, "It really wasn't anything I had anything to do with."

What Reeves really had "to do with" was scoring Carolina's winning touchdown against the Bulldogs in the third quarter on a three-yard run, after setting it up with a 39-yard effort.

A mild streak was in progress when Carolina defeated Wake Forest, 23-13, the following week, Reeves passing for 72 of the yards in an 80-yard touchdown drive and hitting Bobby Bryant on a 69-yard pass play for the go-ahead touchdown with 34 seconds left in the first half.

The star performer for Wake Forest in the 1964 game and in the previous year was Brian Picolo, whose career with the Chicago Bears and friendship with Gayle Sayres was dramatized in the movie, "Brian's Song." Picolo was a victim of cancer.

Reeves: "Brian and I played against each other every year. I knew him when he was at Wake Forest—went up there to play baseball my junior year, and he was on the team there. A guy who was on the team with him at Wake Forest was from Americus, and he and I were real good friends. So, I got to know Brian when we were freshmen. In nineteen sixty-three he rushed the ball that day thirty-something times for a bunch of yardage and ended up kicking the extra point that won the game, because their kicker had gotten hurt."

The victory over Wake in '64 had a painful ending for Reeves, who recalled, "Toward the end of the game I ran a quarterback sneak on the five-yard line, and a guy tackled me. And when he did, he tore my ankle up. I didn't practice all week, and I went up to Clemson (final game of the season), and my ankle was still bothering me. They gave me some shots to numb my foot, and I played.

"Late in the third quarter I got hit, and I could feel it; and I figured, if I could feel it with all that novacaine they'd put in my foot, that something was wrong. So Jim Rogers came in and took us down on a drive and ended-up winning that game (7-3)."

In spite of playing for a team that won only eight games against 18 losses and four ties, Reeves had an outstanding career as a quarterback, statistically and otherwise. He established these records for the University:

SINGLE GAME
Most yards passing—240 vs. Nebraska
Most passes completed—18 vs. Nebraska

SEASON
Most touchdowns scored—8 (tied with four others)—1962
Most total offense—1,401 yards—1962
Most passes attempted—164—1964
Most passes completed—83—1964

CAREER
Most yards passing—2,561
Most total offense—3,376
Most touchdown responsibility (pass & run)—28 (16 pass,
    12 run)
Most passes attempted—441
Most passes completed—211

This obviously didn't impress scouts for National Football League teams.

Reeves: "I thought I might get a chance to play, but not as a quarterback. I thought I might be able to play as a defensive back, but I never thought about being a running back.

"I was a quarterback because I could do both (run & pass). I wasn't a great passer, and most pro teams were looking for guys that really threw the ball a lot, and there were a lot of them that year. The (Joe) Namaths, the (Craig) Mortons, the (Jerry) Rhomes— all those great quarterbacks were coming out that particular year.

"I was more of a scrambler. I never had time to sit back in the pocket. We never had good enough protection. I was always scramblin' for my life, throwin' the ball on the run. I felt like I was a better runner than I was a passer.

"I got banged up. I knew pro football wouldn't be any tougher, because nobody was gonna take the beating that I had taken in college. I took a beating in every game.

Coach Dan Reeves of Denver.

"I think one of the toughest things—this is looking back on it—that made it tough to win at South Carolina is the majority of players were going to be recruited out of the state of South Carolina. Those guys in high school did not have spring practice. I think, being from Georgia, that's where I learned football. That's where the basic fundamentals were taught, because you had twenty days that you could hit and not worry about getting hurt. In South Carolina those guys didn't work on fundamentals, because they had to get ready to open the season. And nobody wanted to hit and block and tackle a great deal, because you didn't want to get somebody hurt right before the season started.

"So, I don't think the caliber of high school football was where it should have been. Clemson, at that time, was out-recruiting Carolina in the state, and they were getting some top players from throughout the South. Frank Howard had built a good foundation, and they were getting good athletes.

"I just felt like it was tough to win there, looking back on it, when you were competing with the Alabamas, Tennessees, and all the great teams that were recruiting where they had spring practice."

While the Mortons, the Namaths, and the Rhomes were awaiting the pro draft with great anticipation, Reeves was wondering if anybody out there was really interested, although he did hear from a few.

Reeves: "Not anything but the normal thing that everybody got. The Cowboys came down and gave us some tests, about six or eight of us. There'd be some scouts around every now and then, but nothing like it is today, when there's so much of that going on. That was not a big thing then, but that was during the war between the N.F.L. and A.F.L., and I felt like I'd get a chance. I felt like I might be drafted, but I wasn't. I was just fortunate to sign with the Cowboys as a free agent.

"When the season was over I was contacted by the Cowboys and the San Diego Chargers. A guy named Harry Robinson came down to represent the Cowboys, and Bud Asher came down for the San Diego Chargers. The money was the same, but, really and truly, I signed with the Cowboys, because I figured, if I didn't make it in th N.F.L., I still would get a chance at the A.F.L. And really, Robinson was just a nice man that I felt very comfortable with. And Dallas said they'd give me a chance at every position. San Diego said, basically, my only chance was at defensive back.

"I had a long stride, and I was faster than most people thought I was. That was not something we ever timed at Carolina. But there were very few people on our team faster. J.R. Wilburn, Sonny Dickinson, and a few of them.

"I didn't make it as a defensive back, and they switched me to running back for a while. I got a chance to play running back, because some guys got hurt, and I was able to play well enough for them to keep me on the football team. My second year I was able to start as a running back. I was just in the right place at the right time.

"I played about half the time as a rookie; alternated with a guy named Perry Lee Dunn; and then Dunn was picked-up in the expansion draft the next year by the Atlanta Falcons. My second year they moved Mel Renfro from defense to running back, and set their offense around him, because he had led the league in punt returns a couple of years. So, they changed the offense to fit his abilities, and he got hurt. I ended up having some success while he was out, and they moved him back to defense. I was the starter for the rest of the year. We won the Eastern Division championship, and I led the league in scoring. We got beat in the championship game by Green Bay, thirty-four to twenty-seven."

Although Reeves had no inkling that his career was moving into the direction of coaching in the National Football League, he couldn't have been serving an apprenticeship under a better teacher than Dallas head coach Tom Landry.

Reeves: "He's just a solid person that has great coaching ability. Extremely knowledgeable about both offense and defense, and very thorough. We were always prepared. Nobody ever beat us because we weren't prepared to play them. He's a guy who's a stickler for details, and he wanted you not to beat yourself. Make the opponent beat you. And we were always in great condition.

"Landry had tremendous vision to see where a player was going to be two or three years down the road.

"I never thought about coaching until I got my knee torn up in sixty-eight. I came back in sixty-nine, having been the starter those years, and I got beaten out by Calvin Hill. He was rookie-of-the-year, and for the first time in my life I sat on the bench. After that season was over, Landry asked me about being a player-coach, and that was the first time I ever really considered or even thought about coaching.

"I always felt like that, because of my background as a quarterback, that I knew what everybody was supposed to do, not just what my assignment was. Therefore, I had a pretty good idea what we were trying to do. I had called plays all my life. I always had to look at it from a strategy standpoint. So, I probably had more knowledge than, say, the average guy that played running back. Strictly because of the way I had approached the game from the time I was in high school.

"My first year as player-coach was seventy, and we went to the Super Bowl, and we got beat by Baltimore. My second year we went to the Super Bowl and beat Miami. So, I thought I was the greatest coach alive! I WAS JUST JOKING! I coached running backs and had responsibility of getting those guys ready, and I was still playing myself a pretty good bit. I had ideas and thoughts in putting the game plan together, but my main responsibility was strictly to prepare the running backs and get them ready, so that they knew what and why and when they were supposed to do things."

Then came the turbulent year of 1972, during which Reeves re-evaluated his life's direction, questioned whether coaching was what he wanted to do, and came up with the temporary answer that it was not. After he re-joined the Cowboys in 1974 Reeves earned a growing reputation, moving up to offensive coordinator for his final three years with the Cowboys. Dan was the subject of rumors on several occasions when coaching vacancies occurred in the NFL, and many speculated that he would be Landry's successor when he decided to retire from active coaching.

Reeves: "That was always a rumor. It was never something that was ever mentioned to me. First of all, I don't think anybody knows when Coach Landry is going to retire. I think this business is such—as I mentioned before—it gives you an opportunity for such tremendous highs and tremendous lows—it's an extremely tough business. I think as long as Coach Landry has good health, I think he's gonna coach. I think he'll be coaching for a number of years. So, that was something that I felt like, I needed to move on.

"I felt like I was prepared and ready to be a head coach, if the right opportunity came along; then certainly I was gonna move on. Denver turned out to be an excellent opportunity for me. I had a chance to have a control over my destiny. A lot of times I had been interviewed for jobs during those years, but I never had an opportunity where I had control over the football part of it. I think that's important for a coach—that, if you're making a decision, and, for some reason you don't succeed, it's not one of those deals where you wanta look around and blame it on somebody else. If I don't succeed here at Denver, I don't have to look any farther than myself to find where the fault was. So, I've got a great opportunity here, and it was a good opportunity at the time; and four years later I think it's a GREAT opportunity."

Although Reeves is totally involved in the Denver program, having been made a vice president of the organization in February 1985, giving him further input in personnel matters, he still stays in touch with the University that gave him his start. He knows Joe Morrison, played against him in the pros, and agrees with many that he is an excellent coach. He had called a few high school prospects for the Gamecock coach, and agreed to help Morrison with a clinic for high school coaches in March.

Still very much the family man, Reeves and his wife, formerly Pam White, whom Dan dated all through high school and married prior to his senior year at Carolina, have two daughters, ages 14 and 19, and a son who plays football at Cherry Creek High School.

"He's smarter than I was," Reeves smiled. "He's a linebacker. He likes to hit, instead of getting hit!"

Search through a modern-day Carolina football brochure, and, under "School Records," you won't find the name of Dan Reeves listed anymore. Tommy Suggs and Jeff Grantz saw to that.

In the "Athletic Hall of Fame" listing, Dan's career at Carolina is summarized simply, "Lettered in 1962, '63 and '64."

The statisticians may have forgotten Dan Reeves, but those who watched him perform in garnet jersey No. 12 still remember the effort he exerted and his quest for excellence in three trying years for the Gamecock football program. He remembers them as good years, not for percentage of wins, but for the foundation he received for a productive career in an exciting field. The friendships he made and continues to maintain. And for the coach who made coming to Carolina an easy decision. The coach who is still there when Dan needs him . . . . right down the hall.

BOBBY **bryant**

Bobby Bryant set the standard for defensive backs at Carolina. Then he became one of the mainstays of the Minnesota Vikings, as they became regular participants in the Super Bowl.

20

DEFENSIVE BACK

10 BOBBY BRYANT

for football purists the 1966 University of South Carolina highlights film might have been edited down to one play. The main character of this footage was Bobby Lee Bryant, a senior whose talents and contributions to the Gamecock athletic program deserved much better than the 1-9-1 season that ended his college career.

You'd have to thumb your way through the Carolina records book all the way to 1897, when the school lost its only three games, one to Clemson and two to the Charleston YMCA, to find a worse season, mathematically. And it could have been worse had not Bryant made one of the most spectacular plays in Gemecock football history.

It came during the introductory season of Paul Dietzel as head coach and could have well been responsible for avoiding a winless season. The scenario was the fourth game of the season, and Carolina was helping North Carolina State to dedicate brand new Carter Stadium. The score was tied at seven-all when State's Jim Donnan projected a punt that ultimately travelled 60 yards and sailed over the head of Bryant, the safetyman.

Bryant: "I don't have any trouble remembering that one. It went over my head and kept bouncing toward the goal, then it took a couple of good bounces that made it easy to field. I never thought about letting it go—didn't know how close I was to the goal. My thought was just to get some of the yardage back."

Bobby got a lot of it back, 98 yards to be exact, and a touchdown that shot South Carolina into the lead and provided the momentum for an ultimate 31-21 victory. Enroute he received key blocks from Bill Dickens, Toy McCord, Wally Orrel, and Bob Cole.

Bryant: "The good thing about a punt like that is that you get a lot of those big guys spread out, and I was faster than they were. So, I got a couple of good blocks and was able to make a couple of moves; and then it was a foot race to the end zone."

Bobby, who could have run on the track team at Carolina, had he not been playing baseball, didn't lose many foot races to other football players.

Bryant: "It was sort of funny. Coach Dietzel told me later that when he saw the ball going inside the ten-yard line he said, 'Oh no, Bobby, what are you doing?' Then he saw me break through a couple of holes and get into the clear, and he said, 'Oh, I see what you're doing!'"

During his three varsity football years at Carolina Bryant did many other good things, always striving to meet his own standards of excellence, regardless of how the game or season was going. The fact that he came off a big loser in football and pitched for a so-so baseball team, but was still chosen for the Anthony J. McKevlin award, given annually to the best athlete in the Atlantic Coast Conference, was a sports miracle. Yet, an even greater tribute than if he had performed for big winners, as is usually the case with the recipient of such awards.

If Bobby had stuck by a decision he made as a junior in Willingham High School at Macon, Georgia, the trophy would be now displayed in someone else's den. Bryant was a starting halfback (both ways) during the first two games of 1961, but he never finished the season.

Bryant: "Actually, I was a little burned out on sports, because I was playing everything. You know, basketball, baseball, running track, and playing football, too. One day we were just doing a lot of extra running, and I was really tired for some reason—I was in a bad mood, or whatever.

"Coach (Billy Henderson, former assistant under Warren Giese at Carolina) was making us run for something I didn't think was reasonable, and so I just stopped running. He said, 'If you don't want to run, go on and turn in your equipment.' So I did.

"So I played in just a couple of games my junior year in high school, and then my senior year I decided to come back out. And coach invited me back out, so I did play my senior year. But the fourth game of the season I broke my wrist, so I played in the first four games and finally came back and played in the last game. So that made only five games my senior year in high school.

"I was recruited by Weems Baskin, who was the track coach at Carolina (also assistant football coach). Weems really wanted me to run track, but when I got up to Carolina I wanted to play baseball, and he certainly understood that.

"Track scholarships were limited, so he (Baskin) was always on the lookout for people who could do both. He said he had come to watch Willingham play . . . Weems was a diplomat also . . . he told me that he had come to scout a couple of other players—a wide receiver and quarterback—but he went back and told the people at South Carolina that he liked me better than the others. The fact that I did run track certainly didn't hurt me at all.

"I had a couple of offers to go to some smaller schools, like Georgia Southern and University of Tennessee at Martinsville. But I didn't have any other offers to a major college. South Carolina was the only one. I didn't know anybody at South Carolina. I did know that Dan Reeves from Americus (about 65 miles south of Macon) was playing there."

When Bryant enrolled at Carolina Marvin Bass was in his third year (1963) as head coach, having experienced two straight losing seasons—4-6-0 in 1961 and 4-5-1 in 1962. One factor that prevented alumni and trustees from becoming uncontrollably upset was that Clemson was also struggling, losing to Carolina in Bass' first season and winning a narrow 20-17 decision at Clemson in '62.

Freshmen were ineligible for varsity play under rules of this era, so Bryant began his college career with 43 other recruits under Ed Pitts, former All-ACC tackle at Carolina.

Bryant: "One of the players on our freshman team was Mike Johnson, the big center from Church Hill, Tennessee, who died of cancer our sophomore year."

Johnson, a 6-3, 220 pounder, was considered one of the prize catches for the Gamecocks, and the 1964 football brochure described him as "a star of the future." In the same publication Bryant was described as, "Slim, rawboned, quick type . . . impressed with frosh and considered a varsity comer . . . pitched for freshman baseball team and displayed blazing fastball . . . lefthander."

Bryant: "We had a good freshman team. I don't know how tough a schedule we played, but we won four and tied one (Clemson). As it turned out we had 50 or so (actually 44) freshmen, and by the time I was a senior we only had four or five guys still left from that team who were playing much. A lot of guys went by the wayside." (The 1966 Carolina roster lists 17 of the players who were named on the 1963 freshman list.)

Meanwhile, the 1963 varsity was experiencing a season that would make the previous two years spectacular successes by com-

Bryant jumps in front of New York Jets receiver to claim an interception for the Minnesota Vikings.

parison. Carolina defeated only Maryland and tied Virginia in a ten-game schedule that featured losses to Tulane and Wake Forest when each was possessor of the nation's longest major college winless streak at the time. The Gamecocks, thus, inherited that distinction.

Of the varsity frustration, Bryant observed: "It made me think that it wouldn't be as hard to make the team the next year. Back then we didn't have a lot of affinity for the varsity, because we hardly ever practiced together. Pretty much like we were a separate team, which we were. So, we never even had a chance to know the varsity players until we were sophomores. We realized they (the varsity) were having a bad year, but we were undefeated, so we felt pretty good.

Bryant: "My sophomore year I didn't start—I played a back-up position. Our starting halfbacks were Larry Gill and Marty Rosen (both seniors), and Phil Branson (junior) was the fullback. The first game I ever got into, except for special teams, was when we played Georgia (third game of the season). The first time I got into the ball game was to return a punt, and I think I returned it about fifty yards (actually 42). So, I had a pretty good game returning punts— also a couple of others about twenty or thirty yards."

Bryant's recollections were basically accurate, except for the order of events. The Gamecocks tied with Vince Dooley's first Georgia team, 7-7, on a touchdown that was set-up by Bryant's 24-yard punt return to the Georgia 38. Late in the game Bryant turned-in his 42-yard runback to the Bulldog 23, and the Gamecocks moved to the four-yard line with a chance to win the game. However, time ran out, as Reeves was thrown for a loss on fourth down. There was no field goal attempt, although kicker Jack McCathern made three of seven attempts during the season, including a game-winner against The Citadel.

Georgia went on to a great season and defeated Texas Tech, 7-0, in the Sun Bowl.

Although Carolina tied with Duke, 9-9, in the season's opener, the winless streak reached nine, and a loss to Maryland made it ten. Following Georgia was Big Eight power Nebraska at Lincoln.

Bryant: "Nebraska just outplayed and outclassed us (28-6). About the only thing I recall about it was that Dan (Reeves) had a good game, running the ball. He didn't do much passing, but he really impressed me with his gutsy play—getting beat-up like he did.

"Nebraska had a great defensive back named Kent McCloughan, who later became one of the outstanding backs with the Oakland Raiders. I guess he was the one who invented the "bump-and-run." The first one to use that technique for playing defensive halfback."

Losses to Florida and North Carolina maintained the Gamecocks' winless ways, and a 72-yard run by North Carolina State's quarterback late in the game deprived Carolina of its first victory in a 17-14 decision. The fast was broken on November 7, when Carolina edged The Citadel, 17-14.

The following week Wake Forest, featuring national scoring champion Brian Picolo, came to Columbia, and the Gamecocks established a winning streak by prevailing, 23-13, over the Deacons. The play that placed Carolina in the lead, 14-13, occurred with only 34 seconds remaining in the half and Carolina in possession on their 31-yard line. Bryant scored on a spectacular 69-yard pass play from Reeves.

Bryant: "That was a fortunate play for us. I remember running the pattern the play before that, and Dan had tried to throw it somewhere else, and I was wide open. So, I went back to the huddle and said, 'Dan, I was wide open,' so he called the same play again and just threw it up there and got the ball to me. Two defenders got there just as I caught the ball. They hit me and just fell off, and the impact from both sides held me up. The ball was down on my side between my arm and my body—enough for me to hold onto it. And I was all by myself. It was my first college touchdown, as a matter of fact."

The Carolina streak reached three in a 7-3 win at Clemson, and Bryant's major contribution was recovering a fumble with 3:19 left in the game, halting a potential game-winning drive by the Tigers. The late-season victories gave Carolina a record of 3-5-2 and kept hopes alive that Bass could create the consistent winner that Carolina supporters had sought for decades.

Bryant: "Marvin Bass was one of the finest persons I've ever had a chance to play for. I had a great deal of respect for him and really liked him. A super, really good person; and that was a consensus of the squad.

"I think people took advantage of him sometimes, because he was as good a man as he was. He let players get away with things he shouldn't have, and I don't know what the problem with assistant coaches was, but we had a lot that came and went."

Bobby Bryant, the Gamecocks' All-America defensive back and punt return ace, set an Atlantic Coast Conference record as well as turning in the longest punt return of the year nationally when he ran Jim Donnan's 60-yard punt back 98 yards in the Gamecocks' 31-21 victory. **1** *Bryant fields the punt over his shoulder on the first bounce at his two-yard line;* **2** *heads upfield as two members of the Wolfpack close in at the eight;* **3** *eludes them and two others*

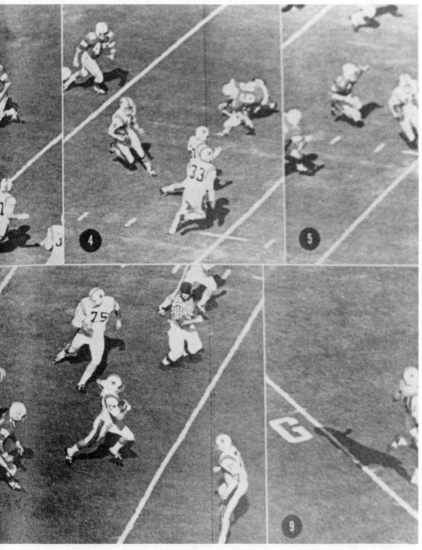

at the 13 after a good block by Bill Dickens (60); **4** *Toy McCord blocks #68 as Bryant cuts behind Wally Orrel (27) and Bob Cole (33);* **5** *is pursued by two defenders at the 20, but* **6** *outspeeds them as Stan Juk (16) arrives to throw block;* **7** *bursts past #14 into the clear;* **8** *and heads for the goal line 75 yards away;* **9** *Bobby scores with no one else in sight.*

There were five assistant coaches on the Carolina staff in 1965 that weren't around the previous year, as Bass sought the combination that would produce a winner.

Bryant: "Our record shows that we didn't have a whole lot of success under coach Bass, but his main strength was his ability to empathize with the players. Sometimes that was a disadvantage. They knew how vulnerable he was and took advantage. It really didn't help the discipline on our team. We didn't have a very well disciplined team."

Another young man that made an impression on Bryant was Reeves, who was a senior during 1964: "Dan was a great leader. I didn't know him real well personally, but he had a lot of ability—was smart and tough. I was very impressed with him. He was a good, strong running back, but I never had the idea that he would be an outstanding running back in the pros. But he fit right into the Dallas system, because of his ability to throw the halfback pass. But he was always a smart player and knew the offense down in Dallas very well. That helped him get into coaching."

Finally, in 1965, Bryant was able to enjoy at least a taste of honey. The Gamecocks shared the ACC championship with Duke, both having won four and lost two within the league. Carolina's overall 5-5-0 mark wasn't anything to brag about, but it was progress, and, without a doubt, another victory over Clemson abated speculation about coaching changes, although the shuffle of assistants would continue.

Bryant had launched the Gamecocks toward an opening win over The Citadel at Charleston with a 43-yard punt return to the Bulldog 16, leading to Ted Wingard's quarterback sneak for a touchdown. This team was aided by new blood from a good 1964 recruiting year, including quarterback Mike Fair, halfbacks Benny Galloway and Ben Garnto, center Jimmy Gobble, middle guard Don Somma, and Jimmy Poole, who would become the first in a long line of outstanding placekickers at Carolina.

The Gamecocks opened their ACC schedule with a narrow 20-15 loss to Duke, a game in which Fair led a second half comeback and established himself as Carolina's quarterback for the next three years. Victories over N.C. State, Wake Forest, and Virginia, and a second conference lost to Maryland, led to a confrontation with Clemson that would determine the league championship. The Tigers had a 4-2 mark entering the season-ending battle in Columbia, with Duke also figuring in the title picture.

Carolina won the game when linebacker Bob Gunnels deflected a pass in the end zone on a two-point conversion attempt after Clemson had scored with 40 seconds remaining. Bryant had contributed to the 17-16 win with an interception at the Carolina 12 to avert an earlier Tiger scoring threat. The victory, along with Duke's win over North Carolina, deadlocked the Gamecocks and Blue Devils for the conference championship.

This, perhaps, assured Bass of another year as head coach, although the Board of Trustees declined to give him a multi-year contract. Although Bass' team lost five games, three were to Alabama, which won the national championship by downing Nebraska in the Orange Bowl; Tennessee, a top ten team and Bluebonnet Bowl winner over Tulsa; and L.S.U., which won the Cotton Bowl game over Arkansas.

Bass was still attempting to fine-tune his staff, as 1966 spring practices approached. He added Lou Holtz from the Connecticut staff, and Pride Ratterree from The Citadel, but the two were present for only ten practice sessions under Bass, who suddenly announced his resignation to accept the job as head coach of Montreal in the Continental Professional League.

Ten days later Paul Dietzel had accepted the job and made plans to complete the spring sessions.

Bryant: "When we heard that Dietzel was coming down from Army we were pretty excited, because he had success at L.S.U. I was playing baseball, but I did take part in some of the drills. But I was pretty much excused.

"He (Dietzel) had a squad meeting and talked about what we had to do. He was an organized person—sort of like Bud Grant (Minnesota Vikings)—but he was a good motivator, too. Tried to make you believe you could win and would win. He had a style about him, very polished and very smooth. Talked about how we would be a better team than we had been. As it turned out, we didn't have a whole lot of success his first year.

"We had a lot of seniors, and I'm sure it hurt a lot trying to learn a new system. Anytime you change systems right before a season, you really don't know what you're doing."

Carolina fans were hyped-up, as this was the first time the school had hired a head football coach with bonafide credentials from another major school. The confidence that Dietzel would deliver permeated the Carolina community, even when his first year—1966—carried the school to new gridiron depths. Ironically,

Salesman Bobby Bryant of Prior Lake, Minnesota, in 1984.

Dietzel's first opponent was L.S.U., where he had won the national championship in 1958.

Bryant: "Coach Dietzel was certainly excited about going back down there. He told us stories about how they'd be poking that Tiger with a stick, trying to make him growl. And they'd have him out there by the dressing room door where we had to go out, tryin' to get you nervous and scared. But it was fun; we weren't scared.

"They just had a better program (LSU won, 28-12) than we did at that time."

One of the Gamecocks' touchdowns came on a 77-yard punt return by Bryant, a young man who seemed to fit-it, regardless of the system.

A devastating schedule didn't make it any easier for Dietzel to establish his system. It included Georgia, which ultimately finished 10-1-0 and downed SMU in the Cotton Bowl; another great Tennessee team; and Bear Bryant's Alabama squad that was undefeated in 11 games and posted another Orange Bowl win over the Cornhuskers.

The aforementioned game with North Carolina State was the lone ray of sunshine in a season of dark clouds, but Bryant's final game for Carolina was a two-way disappointment. First, the Gamecocks lost by a 35-10 score at Clemson, and, second, Bryant suffered a broken wrist.

Bryant: "That was one of the few injuries I had in college—a couple of sprained ankles. However, I was still able to play in the East-West Shrine Game in San Francisco and the Hula Bowl in Honolulu."

For his play, even with a one-win team, Bryant was impressive enough to be named to the All-Atlantic Coast team as a defensive back and to two All-America teams—The New York Daily News and the Detroit Sports Extra. In the spring he would receive the highest award presented by the ACC, the selection as the league's most outstanding athlete.

Bryant: "I was certainly surprised, because there were some outstanding athletes in the conference, such as Ken Willard (North Carolina back who later played with the San Francisco Forty-Niners), who also played baseball, and Jeff Mullins (All-America basketball star for Duke.) A lot of the guys just played one sport, so anybody who played two certainly had an advantage."

Bryant was an outstanding pitcher for the baseball team, posting a three-season mark of 18 wins against 6 defeats and was the first Carolina pitcher to strikeout over 100 batters in a season. Consequently, he was drafted by the Boston Red Sox in 1967 and by the New York Yankees in 1966.

Bryant: "The Yankees didn't offer much of a contract, and I wanted to finish college and get my degree. Their offer wasn't enough to make me want to quit school.

"During the 1966 season I got letters from a lot of NFL teams, but I had no idea I'd be drafted by the Vikings, because they were one of the few teams I didn't hear from. I was also drafted by Boston Red Sox in baseball, so I did have a chance at baseball. They didn't offer me a lot, and I knew that, if I went to the NFL, I'd either make it or not make it. I'd be with a major league team—not sent to the minors. So I decided my odds were better at Minnesota, and I could find out right away, if I could play."

Thus, Bryant, a seventh-round choice by the Vikings, joined the other rookies reporting to camp and began his efforts toward making it in the National Football League.

Bryant: "The first week in training camp I tore cartilage in my knee. It was really an injury I received during my senior year at Carolina. I just never did have it checked thoroughly and taken care of, so I thought it was okay. I did play a little bit in exhibition games but ended-up on the injured reserve the whole season (1967). They had a need for defensive backs, so that really helped me.

"The next season I made the regular roster but didn't start, although I played in several games. The first game I played in was against the Saints in New Orleans—I intercepted two passes and ran one back for a touchdown. So that made an impression on Bud Grant. I played on special teams, too, but never started. We made the playoffs that year.

"Then in 1969 I was a starter the whole season until I was injured in the ninth game. We were playing the Pittsburgh Steelers on a frozen field. J.R. Wilburn (played with Bryant on the 1964 and 1965 USC teams) was playing tight end for them. On a particular pass pattern I hurt my knee again—tore cartilage—and had to have another operation. So, I missed the playoffs and the Super Bowl (vs. Kansas City).

"Beginning in 1970 I was a starter again until 1980. During my career with the Vikings we played in four Super Bowls. I was also injured late in the season the year we played Pittsburgh (1975), but I played in the Super Bowl against Miami (1974) in Houston and Oakland (1977) in Pasadena.

"During training camp of 1981, I was 37 years old and playing cornerback. They put in a new defense—we were running up, playing bump and run on wide receivers—and we had a couple of young corners who were doing really well. It was obvious that I wasn't going to be starting at corner, and they didn't see fit to use me at safety, where I might have been able to play some. But I just wasn't physically able to handle the type of defense the Vikings were trying to institute, so that's when I decided to retire. Before the 1981 season started."

Bryant's observations of Bud Grant were typical of those who have had close association with the highly successful Minnesota

Bobby Bryant in 1965 Carolina jersey.

coach, who returned to the team for the 1985 season, after having retired from the job several years earlier.

Bryant: "Bud's a great organizer. He doesn't get into coaching that much. He's just a great organizer and leaves coaching up to his assistants. He demands discipline. If a player isn't (disciplined), he won't be on Bud's team very long. Bud always placed a lot of value in a player being experienced. Felt like a player who had been in a situation before would probably react the right way, more than a guy who had never been in that situation. That's why Bud never played rookies a whole lot. There were a few exceptions, like Allen Page."

Bryant can look back on a successful NFL career, spiced with memories of covering receivers such as Armad Rashad at St. Louis, Carroll Dale of Green Bay, and Oakland's Cliff Branch. And the challenge of making open-field tackles against the likes of O.J. Simpson, Earl Campbell, and Walter Payton, not to mention Larry Brown and Larry Czonka.

Bryant: "Larry Czonka was just a big load. He couldn't run around you or put a move on you, but he didn't have to. He'd just put his shoulder down and carry you for five or ten more yards!"

In his latter years as a Viking, Bobby purchased a company that scheduled the Minnesota Vikings basketball team, composed of players who stayed in the area during the off-season. The team made spending money by playing 50 to 75 games for fund-raising groups, meeting all-star teams throughout the upper Midwest. Bryant was one of the players, as well as manager and booking agent for the group.

Following retirement from football Bryant also went into the light construction business, later giving-up both of his interests to join the Norex Company. Owned by a friend and neighbor, this company assists other corporations in buying and selling computer equipment, an activity that Bobby conducts in Southern California. This requires several days a month "on the road" around Los Angeles and San Diego.

The rest of the time Bryant can be found at Prior Lake, Minnesota, about 25 miles south of Minneapolis/St. Paul. His marriage in 1975 to Stephanie Bakos of Milwaukee, has been blessed with two sons, as of 1985—Blaze, age 5, and Brady, age 3.

Does that mean more Gamecock football players on the way? Not necessarily.

Bryant: "I don't know. It (football) seems so dangerous, once you're not doing it. It's crazy to have young kids banging into each other; they seem so young and frail. However, if my boys want to play—and they're already talking that way—I'll support 'em and encourage them to do their best."

Bryant has been able to follow the Gamecocks only through the Sunday sports pages since his departure from the University, but he was able to see three games during the "magic" 1984 season.

Bryant: "I watched the Florida State and Notre Dame games on television, and I was down for the Georgia game; and I really enjoyed that one. While I was down I went out to the stadium and did meet Joe Morrison just briefly before practice."

Bobby, like other Carolina supporters, appears to guess that Morrison, whose 14-year career with the New York Giants barely overlapped Bryant's entry into the league, has Carolina on the road to winning consistently.

Fourteen years in the NFL has qualified Bryant for a good pension, which he may begin receiving at the age of 45, if he chooses. Meanwhile, the lure of the Sunbelt continues to beckon to this Georgia boy who has two retirements from football in his background. Once as a high school junior in Macon, and again as a veteran of the world's most glamorous professional sports league.

The University of South Carolina's Athletic Hall of Fame included 17 football players, as of 1985, and only one of those was chosen because of excellence as a defensive back. Although he happened along in a period in which the Gamecocks were struggling amidst a game of musical chairs among their coaching personnel, Bobby Bryant established a standard to which all Carolina defensive backs through the years could aspire, and with which any claims of greatness must be inevitably compared.

CHARTING BOBBY BRYANT

| YEAR | PUNT RETURNS | | | INTERCEPTIONS | | KICKOFF RETURNS | | |
	NO.	YDS.	AVE.	NO.	YDS.	NO.	YDS.	AVE.
1964	10	128	12.8	2	23	9	181	12.8
1965	11	161	14.6	3	43	3	63	21.6
1966	11	242	*22.0	1	32	16	334	20.9
CAREER	32	531	*16.6	6	98	28	578	20.6

*School record

(Also holds school record for longest punt return, 98 yards vs. North Carolina State, 1966)

1966—All-Atlantic Coast Conference team; New York Daily News All-America; Detroit Sports Extra All-America; Captain of the Carolina team.

1967—Anthony J. McKevlin Award as Outstanding Athlete in the Atlantic Coast Conference.

1979—Inducted into the University of South Carolina Athletic Hall of Fame.

1967-68-69

FRED **zeigler**

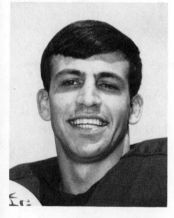

No college coach was willing to risk a football scholarship on Fred Zeigler. That was before he re-wrote the pass receiver's recordbook at Carolina.

WIDE RECEIVER

11

FRED ZEIGLER

f you attempted to select a former record-setting pass receiver who is now an Associate Judge from a lineup of ten people, Fred Zeigler would be your tenth choice. In his college days you would have guessed that he played tuba in the band. In 1985 you would have positioned him as proprietor of the general store at Reevesville, South Carolina.

Zeigler's down-home surface conceals the drive and intensity that turned him into one of the University of South Carolina's most accomplished athletes and, later, a successful attorney and Associate Judge for the South Carolina Industrial Commission. Zeigler appeared on the Gamecock scene during years in which Paul Dietzel mesmerized Carolina fans into illusions of grandeur by dangling before them a 1958 National Championship team he had coached at Louisiana State University. Fifteen years after he played his final game for Carolina the records section of the school's football brochure still carried the following listings:

Most receptions
Game: 12, Fred Zeigler vs. Virginia (1968)
Season: 59, Fred Zeigler (1969)
Career: 146, Fred Zeigler (1967-69)
Most yards gained (receptions)
Game: 199, Fred Zeigler vs Virginia (1968)
Season: 848, Fred Zeigler (1968)

He also shared the mark for most touchdowns in a game (three vs. Virginia in 1968) with two others.

Quite an accomplishment for a young man who had actively sought a football scholarship at The Citadel, Furman, Presbyterian, and Wofford, with the common response of "don't call us, we'll call you." Which they didn't.

Zeigler's hometown, Reevesville, a farming community about 70 miles southeast of Columbia, wasn't large enough for a high school, so Fred played at nearby St. George and later at Carlisle

Military Academy at Bamberg. Carlisle was unbeaten Zeigler's senior year, but the opposition was out of the mainstream of South Carolina high school athletics, and, thus no college scout wasted time on such insignificant confrontations.

Young Zeigler had never become caught-up with college football, but he aspired to a higher education, so he enrolled at Carolina mainly because his Reevesville neighbor and former high school teamate, Donnie Myers, was there and on the football squad. Myers persuaded Zeigler to try out for the team, which he did, and a week later he was a fulltime student, nursing a broken arm, acquired while he was on the team running Citadel plays in preparation for the 1965 season opener at Charleston. Zeigler credits his break to a pile-up under Steve Cox, a bulky lineman nicknamed "Lil' Abner," for physical reasons.

After five months of healing, Zeigler was ready to give it another try in spring practice, which was interrupted in midstream by the resignation of head coach Marvin Bass to head-up the Montreal staff in the Continental League. New hope was injected into the Carolina camp with the hiring of Dietzel, whose success at Army had not matched that at LSU, but he still possessed the image of a big winner, and the Gamecocks were ready to make it big with the man with the Pepsodent smile.

Zeigler: "I don't remember Coach Bass very well, because I was out only a short time while he was here. Coach Dietzel's coming had everyone buzzin', because he had a national name. I remember Coach Dietzel's first practice. There was a thunderstorm, and a big bolt of lightning came right over the Roundhouse (USC athletic office building). It was kinda ominous."

One move that Bass had made before his decision to leave Carolina was to hire 29-year-old Lou Holtz, a Kent State graduate who had served the past two seasons as an assistant coach at Connecticut. Holtz, as even the most casual football fan knows, made a name for himself later as head coach at North Carolina State, Arkansas, and Minnesota, with a one-year stop-off to coach the New York Jets in the NFL. Although his primary duty at Carolina was to coach defensive backs, Holtz made a major contribution to the offense by recognizing the potential in young Zeigler, who was a member of the redshirt or scout team headed-up by Holtz during the 1966 season.

Zeigler: "We were called 'Holtz' horses'. John Marcotsis was the quarterback, and Warren Muir, who had transferred from Army, was our fullback. I didn't do much during spring practice, but they told me, if I made the squad, they'd give me meals.

"Coach Holtz was sort of my promoter—thought that I had potential—and he was the one that talked 'em into giving me a shot at playing the next year. Also Bobby Bryant had gotten to be a friend of mine, because he was Donnie Myers' roommate, and in scrimmages he let me catch a pass or two—made me look better. (Bryant was an All-Atlantic Coast defensive back who played for the Minnesota Vikings from 1968 to 1981.) Bobby would let me make a cut on him and wouldn't play me so hard every now and then.

"Coach Holtz was a real fireball. He liked for folks to be rah-rah and real energetic. I remember he'd go (Zeigler clapped his hands three times) when he called everybody together. And we had to (three claps), too. He really caught your eye."

That isn't the only thing Zeigler caught, and when the 1967 season arrived Zeigler was listed as the back-up receiver behind Roy Don Reeves, brother of Dan Reeves.

Zeigler: "Reeves hurt his knee, Benny Galloway had a bad injury, and we had to do some shuffling around. As a result, I got to start.

"I remember the first game of the 1967 season. We played Iowa State, and that's when people really began to support Carolina and fill-up the stadium. We had close to a full stadium, and I hadn't played a real football game in three years—since I was a senior in high school.

"Mike Fair was the quarterback, and the first pass he threw to me—I just went a little buttonhook about two yards—and I caught the ball and didn't move. I just stood there. And the guy (defensive back) was way off of me. I had plenty of cushion, but I just stood there until he tackled me. I was awed by just being out there!"

Dietzel's 1-9 record during his first season had failed to dim the enthusiasm of Gamecock supporters, who had visions of great recruiting and big wins, as the Dietzel program matured. An opening 34-3 rout of Iowa State, followed by a 16-10 victory over North Carolina, and 21-7 over Duke had the faithful thinking that when Dietzel stated that he was not a miracle worker, he was just being modest.

Zeigler: "That (the Duke game) was the stadium dedication for Wallace Wade Stadium. You know, back then we got all the stadium dedications and homecoming games, which, at least, gave us plenty of time to rest at halftime. The only game we won in 1966—N.C. State—was the dedication for their stadium."

The wheels didn't exactly come off after the three opening victories, but there were some flat tires along the way, and the result was a 5-5 record.

Zeigler: "It was just an average year, but we felt that we were making progress, and we had some pretty good freshmen (ineligible for the varsity in 1967), such as Tommy Suggs (quarterback). We played a respectable game against Alabama (0-17). I believe Ken Stabler was their quarterback then."

One of the disappointments of the season was a 23-12 loss to Clemson, which was more than a loss to an arch-rival, as it cost Carolina a three-way tie for the ACC championship with Clemson and N.C. State, gave the Tigers the title outright, and deprived Carolina of its first winning season since 1959. One of Carolina's touchdowns, both of which came in the fourth quarter, was set-up by a Fair-to-Zeigler 33-yard pass completion to the Clemson three.

Fred would have swapped a win in that game for the fact that he lead the ACC in pass receptions with 35, good for 370 yards. So, this sophomore walk-on had made it big, giving Dietzel and Game-cock followers a lot to talk about during the off season, as they anticipated even bigger things in 1968.

Judged by points scored (214), the season was a success, as the Gamecocks ran-up the second highest total in the school's history. Based on wins and losses (4-6), it was a disappointment, although several of the losses were by razor-thin margins. Duke, 7-14; Georgia, 20-21; Maryland, 19-21; and Florida State, 28-35.

Zeigler points to two games that helped take some of the sting out of being an overall loser.

Zeigler: "Against North Carolina at Chapel Hill we were behind, 27-3, near the end of the third quarter, as I recall, and there were two things I remember about that game. One was that Don Bailey had the longest non-scoring kickoff return in ACC history, and we failed to score. It was like 90 yards, and he got tackled on the six. We had practiced using me as a holder for field goals, because I was a lousy blocker, and you could only substitute two people at that time. So, on fourth down we tried a field goal, and, dadgum it, if I didn't fumble the snap. Butch Grenoble was kicking, but I went ahead and admitted that it was my fault.

"Although we were 'way behind, Johnny Gregory, who was co-captain, and never lost his enthusiasm, was real excited. Well, I

Zeigler teamed with quarterback Tommy Suggs (above) to form the most productive passer-receiver combination in Carolina history.

scored on the first play of the fourth quarter on a pass (from Tommy Suggs), and we got on a roll."

Carolina won the game 32-27, for Dietzel's second straight win over North Carolina, as he moved toward an ultimate 5-0 advantage against the Tar Heels during his tenure at USC.

Although he set a school record of 12 receptions for 199 yards and three touchdowns against Virginia (49-28), Zeigler only recalls from that game two long touchdown pass plays from Suggs to Benny Galloway, who drifted out to the right and took short tosses before making great runs. He also remembered Frank Quayle, outstanding Virginia back who had asthma.

Zeigler: "It was a hot day, and I can remember him on a run close to our bench, and when he was tackled he was just suckin' for air."

Despite the record, both Zeigler and Suggs had sensational statistics. Zeigler set school records of 59 catches and 848 yards, while Suggs had school records for most pass completions (110), most passing yardage (1,544), most touchdown passes (13), and most total offense yards (1,658). In addition defensive back Pat Watson established a new school mark for interceptions (7).

One of Zeigler's regrets was that Galloway was handicapped by so many injuries during his three varsity seasons.

Zeigler: "He could have been a great one. You know, he ended up playing defensive back one season and made all-conference. He had everything—he was a perfect athlete, except he had bird legs, and had all that knee surgery. He would have been, in my mind, just a great back, but his knees failed him."

Zeigler's 1968 statistics were accomplished in only nine games, as he suffered a broken collarbone in a 17-6 loss to Virginia Tech on a rainy night in Columbia and had to sit-out the finale against Clemson at Clemson. Zeigler pointed out rather sadly that he never had the chance to play in Clemson's "Death Valley."

However, he was on the sidelines and had an excellent view of Tyler Hellam's 75-yard punt return that gave Carolina a 7-3 victory. Zeigler had a recollection of another Hellams capability—acting.

Zeigler: "We always got a kick out of Coach Dietzel having written the words to the Carolina Fight Song (USC obtained rights to the Broadway show tune, "Step to the Rear"). At the beginning of each year the squad had a variety show, and each class would put on a skit. One of the skits was Coach and Mrs. Dietzel sleeping, and Tyler Hellams played Coach Dietzel. And he got up in the middle of the night and said, 'I can't sleep. I think I'll go down and write a fight song.' We never had a variety show after that—there were two or three other things that were responsible for that, too.

"He (Dietzel) made everybody know the fight song and the alma mater, and we had to practice. When I was a redshirt, Dave Berry (tackle) was the chorus leader. It was a pretty foul sound! Coach Dietzel was big on things like that. But he was a tremendous promoter and marketer. No question about that."

With what has proven to be easily the most impressive passing-receiving combination in Gamecock history (through 1984) returning for the 1969 season, there was again reason for optimism. Suggs, the thrower, and Zeigler, the catcher, also had impressive running backs to keep opposing defenses honest. Rudy Holloman had led the team in rushing in 1968 with 530 yards, while Warren Muir, injured for part of '68, had an impressive 805 yards in '67.

Zeigler: (Commenting on the question of what made the Suggs-to Zeigler combination so effective): "We just had one pass play. It was called a tailback pass—a play action pass. A fake to

Muir off tackle, and Suggs would roll out. I had the option of taking an out, if they gave it to me—I always ran the out pass. That's why I caught a lot of passes around 12 yards. If it wasn't there, I ran the curl. If the curl wasn't there, I went up. We had that one pass that we used to me, when I was the primary receiver, and we had three options off that.

"Suggs could read the defense the same time I did, so he knew where I was going. And he could whip it when I made my break. Tommy had a strong arm and real football savvy. He knew the game real well, and, of course he was real short (5 ft. 9 in.), but Doug Flutie (1984 Heisman Trophy winner at Boston College) was short, too. I don't know why some pro team didn't give him a shot. He could run the ball well. I remember he made a long touchdown run against Duke in nineteen sixty-nine, and I threw a block for him. I hope he remembers that, because I didn't throw many!"

That run was a 48-yarder by Suggs in the opening game and launched a season to which Gamecock fans had looked forward since the Atlantic Coast Conference was formed in 1953. The 27-20 win over the Blue Devils featured 113 yards rushing by Holloman, including a 60-yard scoring run, and was the first of six ACC wins against no defeats, for Carolina's first outright conference football championship. It was also the first of five sellout crowds of 42,000-plus in Carolina Stadium, and this stimulated talk of stadium expansions in the future.

The highlight of a 14-6 win over North Carolina in the second game was a sensational touchdown pass reception by Zeigler, who deflected the ball away from a defender and made a lunging catch in the end zone.

A 41-16 road loss to Georgia was soon forgotten in the satisfaction of a third straight conference win, 21-16, over North Carolina State, in which sophomore Jim Mitchell had a 72-yard punt return for a TD. Then, although it wasn't a league game, came the most exciting finish of the year, a 17-16 win over Virginia Tech at Blacksburg on Billy DuPre's school record 48-yard field goal with only nine seconds left on the clock.

Zeigler: "We thought Coach (Scooter) Purvis was having a heart attack when we kicked the field goal, but it turned out that he just hyper-ventilated. Doug Hamrick made a super catch that put us within field goal range. (The Gamecocks drove from the SC 11 to the VPI 40 in 49 seconds.) Earlier I had to stay in the game on an extra point, and they had a tackle that was tough as nails. He

Fred Zeigler shows record-setting form for the Gamecocks.

hit me and I just went past where the kicker and holder were, like I was shot out of a cannon. We lined-up for that field goal, and I turned to him and said, 'Man, don't hit me again.' He said, 'Are you really gonna kick it,' and I told him, 'I swear to God we're gonna kick it. Just don't hit me again!' And he didn't, so we just walked off the field together."

Suggs passed for 190 yards in a 17-0 win over Maryland to give Carolina a 4-0 ACC mark, but a trip to Florida State was a 34-9 disaster. The Gamecocks turned in an outstanding performance against nationally-ranked Tennessee at Knoxville but succumbed to two fourth-quarter touchdowns, 29-14.

Zeigler: "In that game I made up a play in the huddle. I saw that I could pick the linebacker, so we worked it out in the huddle; that's the only time we ever did anything like that. But we did, and Holloman had about a 30-yard scoring pass from Suggs, and nobody touched him.

The temperature was 33 degrees at Winston-Salem, N.C., when Carolina met Wake Forest in a game that resulted in a 24-6 win and clinched the ACC championship for the Gamecocks. Suggs had three TD passes in a fairly relaxed win.

Zeigler: "We were really excited about winning the ACC, but about all I remember about the Wake Forest game is that my mother was standing outside the locker room when I walked out."

A season-ending 27-13 win over Clemson was anti-climactic, but it was a great day for Zeigler, who caught nine passes to run his ACC career record total to 146. Another reward for the Gamecocks was an invitation to play West Virginia, headed by future USC coach Jim Carlen, in Atlanta's Peach Bowl.

A crowd of about 54,000 turned out on a terribly rainy night, but Zeigler might as well have stayed home, failing to catch a pass. Even so, the Gamecocks were trailing only 7-3 midway through the fourth quarter and had a first down at the Mountaineer seven. However, a 15-yard holding penalty stalled the drive, and West Virginia scored with 23 seconds left in the game to widen the final margin.

Zeigler: "It was the most horrible weather. I had mud in my ear lobes, eyes, everywhere. West Virginia had a strong running game and a great running back (Jim Braxton, a future NFL star). The weather really hurt us, because we had a wide-open game, and they didn't."

Thus Zeigler ended his playing career with every Carolina and ACC passing record worth mentioning in his possession, and

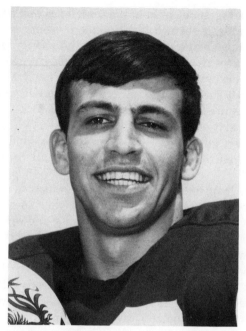

Fred Zeigler — the ultimate "walk-on."

Suggs also had enough school passing records to warm his memories for many years to come. Muir's 969 yards rushing was just short of Steve Wadiak's 998 season's record, and it placed Muir second on the all-time career list with 2,234 yards.

As it turned out this was the last season for South Carolina in the ACC, as the school's trustees voted to withdraw and become an independent.

Zeigler: "Everybody felt like the North Carolina schools ran the ACC. Coach Dietzel's thinking was that football in the ACC was below other conferences and national independent teams. He felt like, if he went out of the conference, he'd have an easier time recruiting, and he might could make us more prominent by opening up and playing other schools.

"Right after South Carolina got out they lowered requirements in the ACC. But I still don't think the ACC is a real factor in football. Obviously, we suffered in basketball, but I don't think we have in football. Most people thought it was the thing to do at the time. Of course, later everything changed.

"After being undefeated in the conference and pretty good out-side in sixty-nine it seemed like nineteen-seventy was going to be the year we turned the corner. I think the changing mood of the times was a factor in 1970. There was a whole change from conserv-atism into liberalism in the late sixties and early seventies, and I think the times sort of moved away from him (Dietzel) a little bit. He was more suited to the conservative, hard rock times of the fif-ties and early sixties. He was regimented—always had time slots at practice—fifteen minutes for this—ten for that—and was always a real planner, real scheduler. Down to the details and that type of thing.

"He was involved in practice about as much as any head coach would be, although you were really under your specialty coach. Of course, I was a graduate assistant in seventy and seventy-one help-ing with the freshmen, so I still had contact with the team. The hippy thing was underway, and people with long hair. Coach Dietzel liked short hair.

"I tried to grow sideburns one time. We were getting ready for an away game, and Roy Don Reeves and I decided we were gonna grow sideburns. He (Dietzel) saw us at breakfast, and we were gonna leave at mid-morning, and we had to go shave-off what little we had grown.

"He was a stickler for appearance—everybody wore travel dress, which I thought was ugly. Double-breasted garnet coats, black pants, and white turtleneck shirts. That was one year—I had never worn a double-breasted coat in my life. Now, I think every-body wears what they want to wear, but we were like a herd of cattle.

"Coach Dietzel did realize that Clemson was the big game, however, and he put a lot into beating Clemson. Special plays, and that type of thing."

Dietzel's record against the Tigers in his nine seasons at Caro-lina was four victories against five defeats, and his final game as USC coach was a 39-21 loss at Clemson in 1974.

Zeigler felt that the Gamecocks were blessed with good leader-ship from within during his three varsity years. Mike Fair in 1967, Johnny Gregory in 1968, and Tommy Suggs in 1969 and 1970, to name a few.

Zeigler: "Mike (Fair) is now in the House of Representatives from Greenville County—but he's in the wrong party (Republican), as far as I'm concerned!"

In 1985 Zeigler was an Associate Judge for the South Carolina Industrial Commission.

After undergraduate school at Carolina Zeigler finished the USC law school and was admitted to the bar, practicing in St. George, S.C., near his hometown, for three years. He returned to Columbia and spent a year-and-a-half in the Attorney General's office, before entering into private practice again in the state capital. In 1981 he was appointed to the South Carolina Industrial Commission as an Administrative Law Judge by Gov. Richard Riley, a position he still held in 1985.

In 1982 he was married to Jane Boatwright of Ridge Springs, and his mother died during the same year.

Zeigler: "Mother was born and died in the same house in Reevesville.

Zeigler has known the Carolina coaches who have succeeded Dietzel, including Jim Carlen, Richard Bell, and Joe Morrison. He pays Morrison the supreme compliment.

Zeigler: "I really like him. He's so down to earth and easy going—almost like he's from Reevesville. Like a good, solid country fellow; I know he's not from the country, but there's no pretense about him."

How would he fit into Morrison's veer offense?

Zeigler: "I ran short routes. They seem to run all deep—30 yards or nothing. And they use more receivers. I used to play the whole game."

Ziegler (center) posed with friends at the 1982 Belmont Stakes.

There wasn't a more excited Gamecock fan than Fred Zeigler when the 1984 Carolina team compiled a 10-2 record, was ranked as high as No. 2 nationally during the season, and received a bid to the Gator Bowl. This, he agreed with so many, was the beginning of the era for which so many had waited so long, but he still has pride in some of the milestones of the past.

Zeigler: "Lots of folks look down on Coach Dietzel's era, but we played pretty well with the teams like North Carolina, Clemson, and so forth, back then. Later those teams left us—got better than us. We got a reputation—I think falsely—for firing coaches. If anything they've stayed too long. Coach Dietzel stayed too long, but he was good about it. He resigned and left with time on his contract. It would have saved us a lot of heartache, if he had left earlier and stayed as athletic director.

"But things got so bad, and he announced his retirement after the Duke game (second game of 1974 in Columbia), and the horns were blowing, and the people were real happy—but I wasn't. I wish he had quit coaching earlier and taken over as athletic director. He was a better A.D. than coach.

"Coach Carlen came in, and he had some winning seasons, but Clemson just seemed to take off and leave us. The thing that bites on everybody is that we haven't had success in relation to the input . . . at least until 1984."

Despite his record-breaking success as a Gamecock receiver, Fred Zeigler never got carried away with himself, preferring to laugh about his failures, rather than try to glory in his accomplishments. Now in the growing years of a successful legal career, he's still "Reevesville" through and through.

And he's one of the reasons that when an awkward-looking country boy with no visible athletic assets walks onto the practice field and wants to tryout for the team, coaches still pay attention.

Who knows, it just might be another Fred Zeigler!

Charting Fred Zeigler

YEAR	RECEPTIONS	YARDS	TDs
1967	35	370	0
1968	*59	848	6
1969	52	658	3
CAREER	*146	1,876	9

*School records as of 1984.

1972·73·74·75

JEFF **grantz**

Any future Gamecock quarterback star must be compared to Jeff Grantz. When he lined-up behind the center, it was the beginning of a clinic on how to play that important position.

12

QUARTERBACK

12 JEFF GRANTZ

the price one must pay for becoming the starting quarterback at the University of South Carolina football team is that he will be inevitably measured against Jeff Grantz.

This means that he must have sprinter's speed; tap dancer's feet; the peripheral vision of a house fly; a coach's brain; the nerve of a sky diver; the instinct of a bat; and a throwing arm that depends more on mind than muscle. With those credentials, which Grantz used for tormenting Carolina opponents in the mid-seventies, you'd think he would be somewhere teaching young quarterbacks the trade he mastered. However, he received just enough coaching experience to convince him that it was not his cup of tea.

Although he played very little as a freshman and missed a lot of playing time during an injury-plagued junior year, he compiled a career total offense of 5,017 yards, third highest in Carolina history. And his 2,288 yards of offense in 1975 was the most productive season ever (through 1984) by a Gamecock.

Statistics never tell the entire story, of course. For instance, while he was setting an individual one-season total offense record, Grantz directed an offense that produced the first (Kevin Long) and second (Clarence Williams) thousand-yard rushers for the Gamecocks. It was the seventh time in NCAA records that the same backfield produced two thousand-yard gainers.

Jeff, who was named to the Associated Press All-America second team and was 13th in the Heisman Trophy voting after his senior year, had a taste of coaching as a graduate assistant under his head coach, Jim Carlen, in 1976 and 1977. This came after he had attended rookie camp with the Miami Dolphins and became convinced that they weren't going to cut Bob Griese, Earl Morrall, or Don Strock to make room for him.

As for coaching, Grantz explained, "I didn't have the patience. I think I did a lot of things when I was a quarterback that came natural, and it was hard for me to relate and convey certain things. It was hard for me to tell someone else how to do it—very frustrating. So, I didn't stay in it."

Jeff's degree was in Physical Education, and he had intended to get into high school coaching, but he accepted a summer job with T and T Sporting Goods in Columbia, liked the work, and stayed for three years. In 1980 he accepted a job with the Budweiser distributer in Columbia and is busily helping to spread the message that the word "light" is not complete without "Bud."

Anyone who watched Grantz play quarterback or who has heard him talk about the position would never be convinced that he would have a problem communicating his knowledge. After all, he was raised on football in Maryland, where his father, Chuck Grantz, was a coach and athletic director for 33 years.

"He taught me the right way to do things from the beginning," Jeff recalled. "I played in the Pop Warner leagues, and he would observe. After games we would sit down and talk about what I did right and what I did wrong."

However, Coach Grantz was never the beneficiary of his own son's talents on the football field.

Grantz: "Dad was head coach of the opposing team (Parksville High School) in the first high school game I ever started. We played against him for three years, and we beat 'em fifty-six to fourteen my sophomore year. I remember looking across the field and kinda feeling sorry for him, because he was running back and forth trying to get his troops together.

"We had a much better caliber of football in my county. They (Parksville) had just started football, but he wanted his teams to play good teams. He didn't want me to play at his school. You know, coaches coaching their sons, so we lived in an area where I wouldn't go to his school."

As a result of his impressive performances for Bel Air, Grantz aroused the interest of college recruiters over a wide area. He mainly considered North Carolina, Penn State, Maryland, Clemson, Tulane, and Michigan State, before committing to Carolina.

Grantz: "I played baseball, too, and I was interested in coming South, because a lot of the schools up North would play sixteen-to eighteen-game baseball schedules, whereas, in the South, teams expanded to forty or fifty games. That interested me.

"I was close to signing with North Carolina but had a trip to South Carolina left. In fact, I had told the coach at North Carolina two weeks before that, if I had to choose right now, I'd go to North Carolina. When I did make the trip here, I decided right then to get it over with and commit. One of the main reasons I became interested in South Carolina was that a high school teammate, Tom Amrein, came here on scholarship. He was a high school All-American. And Tommy was happy here.

"Bobby Richardson was the baseball coach, and that helped. The year before they didn't have a super baseball season, but they had recruited Hank Small and Earl Bass, so I knew it was a promising outlook."

Grantz was the prize recruit among 42 freshmen who reported to head coach Paul Dietzel in the fall of '72. Others who figured prominently in future Gamecock lineups included tackle E.Z. Smith, flanker Randy Chastain, tight end Jay Saldi, linebacker Garry Mott, defensive backs Henry Laws, Andy Nelson, and Zeb Shue, split end Stevie Stephens, placekicker Bobby Marino, and receiver Scott Thomas.

Grantz quarterbacked the Carolina freshman team to a 4-2-1 record and had impressive statistics. Meanwhile, the Gamecock varsity suffered through a 4-7 campaign, alternating quarterbacks Dobby Grossman and Bill Troup without great success.

Grantz was brought up to the varsity and played in a 35-3 win over Wake Forest, was used for about half the game in a 45-20 loss to Virginia Tech (and Don Strock), and, in a 7-6 setback at Clemson, he took only six snaps. During the next three years, when he was healthy, Grantz put on a clinic on how to run the veer offense, which was installed by Dietzel in the spring of 1973.

Grantz: "When I was looking at schools I didn't try to pick a school that was weak at quarterback. I basically wanted to go to the best place for me; and baseball did enter into it. At that time Bill Troup, who was a great quarterback at Virginia, had transferred here. Looking at his stats from Virginia, I really didn't think I would play.

"But the way things turned out, the line had a tough time protecting him in a dropback situation, and they went to a roll-out type thing my freshman year. When they decided to change coaches (offensive coordinator and brought in Bob Gatling from The Citadel) and those people that run the veer, I didn't go through winter workouts, because I was playing baseball.

"When they brought those guys in, and I wasn't a starter in baseball, I dropped out of baseball and went through spring football. That's how I won the starting job coming into my sophomore year. Dobby Grossman was my competition; Troup had left school and gone into pro ball.

"In seventy-three I started the first game against Georgia Tech (in Columbia). We beat Georgia Tech, and we weren't supposed to. Not that I didn't have confidence that we could, but it was a big thrill for me; because when I was growing up, Georgia Tech was always a big football school. The first college game you ever start—against a team in that tradition—it was an exciting win (41-28).

"The first decent run I ever had was in that game—it turned out to be a busted play. I might have turned the wrong way, and I turned upfield, and there was no one around. Think I ran about forty yards, before Randy Rhino caught me from behind. I think I threw two touchdown passes and ran for one or two. But the thing that really stands out in my mind is that, when they were getting ready to make a comeback toward the end of the game, Mel Baxley intercepted a pass in the end zone and ran it a hundred yards the other way. It was a big turnaround.

"Another time, after they scored, we had a kickoff return, where we handed the ball to someone running up the middle, and he'd pitch it to a guy going around the end. We did that, and Henry Laws ran it back fifty or sixty yards (actually 76) to put us in scoring position."

That performance by Jeff was impressive enough to earn Back of the Week honors from *Sports Illustrated*, a brilliant start for the season.

Grantz was asked to do a self-analysis of his role as a quarterback:

"I think my strongest point physically was that I had good speed. I was about a four-five to four-six forty. I had quick feet, and I had good peripheral vision. I had good acceleration—it might have been deceptive. Four-six isn't all that fast, although, for quarterbacks, that's supposed to be pretty good. Acceleration and the ability to cut back. I did a good job when I ran, I felt, like cutting back against the grain; as far as knowing where people were, and how to follow the blockers.

"I didn't throw the ball very well—I didn't have a strong arm. I didn't throw a pretty pass, but I knew when to throw it and who to throw it to. Basically, reading defenses, I think, was the strongest point I had, especially my senior year (1975). I threw for a lot of yardage with not the best arm or prettiest pass in the world. But knowing to throw the ball on time, when the receiver was making his break; and knowing who to throw to; knowing when to get rid of the ball—throw it out of bounds; or tuck it away and run.

"Bob Gatling needs to take a lot of the credit for my success as a quarterback. He taught so well the knowledge of the veer offense and learning to read defenses. He's the one that really made me, as far as reading defenses.

"My senior year, every play inside the twenty was called at the line of scrimmage, because defenses begin to adjust and do different things, when you get close and get ready to score. They blitz a lot more—they'll run safeties through—do a lot of things in the line to try to mess you up.

"That week before, I would see every defense I was going to face in practice, and we'd go over that. If they were going to come with a stunt from the right side, something on the left side's gonna be open. Whenever they do one thing, there's gonna be a weakness created somewhere else. And I'd see that during practice. He was a good enough coach, that I would know and could go to the line of scrimmage and call the play right there. I think we scored touchdowns about eighty per cent of the time inside the twenty. Not just score, but score touchdowns.

"I was taught that the most important thing, before I'd ever get into the huddle, was make sure I knew what I was going to do. And, even if I didn't know what I was doing, I'd act like I did—at least express confidence over the play that I was gonna call. If I go into the huddle unsure of myself, then your offensive linemen, receivers, and backs don't have confidence in the play either. Whereas, even if it was a bad play, I'd try to make it sound as if it were gonna work, so that they would feel confident that it was.

"Breaking the huddle. I'd let every one get up to the ball, get set, before I'd ever get under the center, so I could stand up there and look over the defense, before I'd call any signals. Many times in the veer, you've got so many different options, that we'd call two plays in the huddle; and when I'd get under center, I'd call whichever play it was gonna be. Sometimes on pass plays I'd have signals out to my receivers, because in Williams-Brice Stadium it was so loud that they couldn't hear what I was saying.

"So, I'd either grab my face mask or mouthpiece or whatever— the signals would be pre-set before the game. Say I'd go to the ear flap of my helmet, it would mean he was gonna run a take-off pattern. If I went to my face mask, he was gonna run a curl pattern.

Grantz prepares to release one of 12 passes he completed in a 56-20 rout of Clemson in 1975.

And, if I went to my chin strap, he was gonna run an out-pattern, let's say.

"The linemen have to do a lot of thinking. They don't know what play is going to be called, until we get to the line of scrimmage. And they're already set. Once they hear what the play is, they've got to know who to block.

"Maybe six times a game, the play would be changed completely. Defenses can always take something away, but there's always a weakness in a defense. So, we pretty much tried to keep an open mind and go where that weakness was. Through practice and Coach Gatlin showing us all these options during the week, it was very seldom that I would go up to the line of scrimmage and not have already seen what that defense was going to do.

"One that stands out in my mind—and I liked doing this more than anything—was in the North Carolina State game in my sophomore year. In the second half—and I couldn't do much physically on my ankle (injured), but I could read the defense—they were having a rover blitz on the right side. So, on the left side, automatically, the tackle stays wider, and the safety will roll over the top to cover wherever that strong safety's coming from. So, what I did was change the play at the line of scrimmage, and went to the veer on the left side, and handed the ball off to Jay Lynn (Hodgin). Since the tackle was so wide, the linebacker could be cut off, and he ran like forty yards for a touchdown.

"I like to do that more than throw a long touchdown pass, because I feel like I've mentally defeated the defense.

"I think play selection is as important as execution, especially inside the twenty, when that defense starts doing a lot of different things. I think fifty per cent of it would probably be play selection, especially inside the twenty, when the defense is trying to compensate here and there and catch you off guard. The right play with average execution is as good as the wrong play with super execution."

One of the more dramatic demonstrations of Grantz's football perception happened in the 1975 game against Clemson, which had beaten the Gamecocks three of the four previous years. Carolina held a 28-6 lead and was in possession at the Clemson 41, as time was running out in the second quarter.

Grantz: "There were seven seconds to go in the half, and there was time for one play. We had been beating their secondary with a post pattern most of the day, and we called time out. I guess we were on about the fifty, and I went over to Coach (Jim) Carlen and told him, 'If they can give me a little bit of time, we can fake that post pattern and run Phil (Logan) to the corner. I think we'd have a chance.'

"They said, 'Let's go with it.'

"I got back to the huddle and asked the guys to give me an extra second, so I could make a pump fake, because I thought we had a chance to score. Of course, they did, and Philip broke so wide open, it was the toughest pass I ever had to throw, because the wider open they are—the only thing you can do is look bad. He ended up having to wait for the ball a second, but got into the end zone. That pretty much iced the game—put us ahead, thirty-five to seven at the half."

Late in the fourth quarter Grantz passed to Stevie Stephens for a touchdown that brought a bitter post-game accusation from

Clemson coach Red Parker that the Gamecocks had unnecessarily "run up the score."

Grantz: "If he had looked at it logically, we had the ball inside the five-yard line earlier and had a fifteen-yard penalty. It ended up fourth down and goal at the twenty. So, if you bring Bobby Marino in and kick a field goal, which is a sure three points, is that running up the score? Or should a team, fourth and goal at the twenty, be able to keep another team from throwing a touchdown pass? Actually, fourth and goal at the twenty, chances of your throwing a touchdown pass aren't very good, if they've got any kind of secondary at all. I threw a terrible pass, and Stevie just made a heck of a catch in the end zone."

In that game Grantz had directed the most productive offense in Carolina's history, as the Gamecocks ran up 30 first downs and 616 yards running and passing. The 56 points were the most ever scored by a team in the Carolina-Clemson series.

Grantz: "We did some things to them with some motion that we hadn't used all year. We put one of our halfbacks in motion and brought out an extra receiver, and their secondary couldn't adjust to it.

"They had never seen it, and, before they knew it, we had four touchdown passes, in addition to running the veer as well as we did, and the great job our offensive line did. I think it really caught 'em by surprise. I threw five touchdown passes on that one little motion play. Bob Gatling came up with this the week before the game. We worked and worked on it, and it got us five touchdowns."

Another great example of scouting and pre-game strategy was instrumental in Grantz establishing a school record of 260 yards rushing against Ohio University in his sophomore season of 1973.

Grantz: "The main reason I ran for so many yards? Well, there are several ways, of course, you can defend the option. This particular team would put their tackle on the dive back; and take their defensive end and run him to the pitch back; and take their free safety and run him to the quarterback.

"So, what I would do is, when the defensive end would run to the pitch back, I would cut up the field and back behind their free safety, and he just kept over-running me all day long. Our offensive guards did a great job of keeping the linebackers out of the play. When I could cut back behind their free safety, I could get fifteen, twenty, thirty yards all day long.

"The longest run I had in that game was a kickoff return. I

Jeff Grantz helped make 12 a distinguished number for Carolina.

would be in the middle, and the deep back would catch the ball, and I would turn my back to the defense. He would hand me the ball, and then the pitch back would run around, and we would pitch the ball. We had already shown the one up the middle—the one against Georgia Tech, where we pitched it.

"In this one I was supposed to fake the pitch and bootleg it around the other way, myself. The thing about it was, when Randy Chastain was handing the ball to me, someone came through and hit both of us, and knocked Randy down. For some reason I didn't fall down, and when I turned around there was a big open lane up the lefthand side. I just tucked the ball and ran—made it to the end zone."

For his sensational game in a 38-22 romp, Grantz was named the Back of the Week by the Associated Press, and it allowed him to end his college football career with a most unusual—if not unique—statistic. For kickoff returns Grantz is credited with O (that's zero) returns for 85 yards and a touchdown! Statistically, on a kickoff return the player who first handles the ball is credited with a return and the amount of yardage he makes. If he laterals or hands the ball to someone else, that player is not credited with a return but receives credit for any yardage gained.

That just happened to be the only kickoff Grantz ran with during his varsity years.

Grantz describes the single most significant play of his four seasons as a Gamecock quarterback: "We had gone ahead of Mississippi (at Oxford) twenty-eight to nothing, and they came back and threw a two-point conversion with a minute and fifty seconds left, to go ahead, twenty-nine to twenty-eight. We got the ball on our own seventeen, and—into the wind—I threw three or four completions, and we were on the twenty-eight yard line. I threw a touchdown pass to Philip Logan—he ran a down and out and up pattern, and we scored to win the game with twenty seconds to go. That one was called in the huddle. Most of the others were at the line of scrimmage, because we were running out of time."

Grantz led the Gamecocks in another miracle comeback two weeks later against North Carolina State at Raleigh, leading a touchdown drive and passing to tight end Brian Nemeth for a two-point conversion to put Carolina ahead, 21-20, with 1:29 showing on the clock. However, the Gamecock defense couldn't contain the Wolfpack in a 65-yard game-winning march.

During his sophomore season, when he was THE quarterback,

Grantz was responsible for play selection, a duty he requested some relief from in his junior season.

Grantz: "I asked him (Dietzel) if he'd take some of the pressure off and call some of the plays, because, I was not in the game all of the time. Ron Bass was a sophomore, and they started alternating Ron and me my junior year. I'd play two series, and Ron would play two series. So, really, when you get two quarterbacks in there, to keep the continuity, I felt it would be better if they'd call the plays from the sidelines.

"We were basically the same. I might have had a little bit quicker feet. Ron had good speed and a better arm. When Ron got his knee hurt, that hurt his mobility. Other than that, he was an excellent quarterback."

Jeff was one of many Carolina football players in the 24 years, 1960 to 1983, who had to play for one coach in his final season and another during his first. He was a junior in 1974, when Dietzel resigned, and played for Carlen his senior season.

Grantz: "Our sophomore year we weren't supposed to do that well, but my junior year we were supposed to have a good season, but things didn't work out so well. I did play baseball the entire summer, and I don't feel that I was as well prepared to play football that season as I was my sophomore year.

"As a consequence I didn't have a very good first three games. We were splitting time. I was playing some, and Ron was playing some. I didn't particularly like that, because I felt like, if I was going into the game and screwed-up somehow—threw an interception or didn't move the ball for the first two series—that Ron was going to come in. He, in turn, felt the same way. As far as knowing you were gonna play the whole game—if you did make a mistake— you still were gonna be in there, instead of worrying about it.

"What happened is we lost our first five games, which was very frustrating, after you come off a seven-four season. Coach Dietzel resigned after the Duke game (second of the season), and I felt almost responsible, because I had very bad games the first and second games.

"I was close to Coach Dietzel—he was an inspiration to me. I thought he was an excellent coach and that he handled situations well. He was a great organizer, a super athletic director, and maybe he had just too much to do. He was always helping here and there. But I thought he was fair.

"The success in nineteen seventy-three—then losing several games in a row. We had a lot of young people playing that year (1974), and South Carolina wasn't used to a lot of success, as it was."

A knee injury suffered against Mississippi limited Grantz during the final five games of his junior year, and he underwent knee surgery during the winter. Meanwhile, Carolina hired Carlen, who had built a winning program at Texas Tech, to succeed Dietzel as head coach.

Grantz: "I met Coach Carlen at a team meeting when he was hired in January. Of course, I was playing baseball at the time. The first thing he did was take any suggestions any of the players had of how to improve the program. What we liked and didn't like about things. Then, after the meeting, I didn't see him, because I was playing baseball.

"Well, basically, the offense was going to be the same. We were going to run the veer, and Bob Gatling was still going to be here. So, there was no problem with that. But I did have to prove to him (Carlen) that I could start. I remember a couple of comments he made while I was playing baseball: 'The only thing I know about Jeff is that he can turn a double play. I don't know what he can do on a football field.'

"When fall came I started as second team quarterback, because Ron went through spring football. After the first scrimmage Ron hurt his knee, so, from then on, there was no choice. I never actually had to take the starting job away from Ron.

"Coach Carlen's organization was about the same as Dietzel's. Practice was well organized, well thought-out. Coach Carlen was a little more lenient. Coach Dietzel had some rules, like we had to have our beds made and rooms inspected. Coach Carlen didn't have that, but curfews were basically the same.

"We weren't allowed to go into bars during the season, with Coach Dietzel or Coach Carlen. They felt that, if we were seen in a bar, and we lost a game, people would make comments that the reason we lost was because they were in a bar.

"We weren't allowed to have women in the dormitories with Coach Dietzel. Coach Carlen gave us some privileges; at certain times women could come to The Roost.

"Coach Carlen was a straightforward, tell it like it is, whether it bothered people or not. Coach Dietzel was a little more . . . well, he made things sound a lot better to everybody than they actually were. Carlen, if something was bad, would tell you it was bad. Sometimes, depending on the individual, it wouldn't be the right way to go.

"He was very blunt, point blank, whereas Dietzel was a little bit more undercover, so to speak. They both emphasized the Fellowship of Christian Athletes, and Coach Richardson, a little moreso.

"Edward Young, pastor of the First Baptist Church, was active (under Dietzel) with the football team. He'd be there and say something to us before the games—give us a pep talk. Not a lot of religious. We'd pray, not that we'd win, but that people wouldn't get hurt. That type of thing.

"The night before a game Coach Dietzel used to take us on this thing we called 'a walk.' We'd see a movie, then he'd take us for a walk, and he would talk and tell some story, and relate it to the football game. Or tell us about letters he would get, and try to motivate us in those ways.

"Coach Carlen, more or less, left it up to the seniors. We had a real close group of seniors my last year. He'd let us take control of the motivational type things, and we'd take turns. He'd let the seniors talk, and the coaches would leave.

"I didn't say anything until before the Clemson game—just that it was my last game, and I wanted to go out winning. 'I'd never said too much all year, as far as getting people up for a game. I feel like everybody ought to be able to get up, but this is very important to me and the other seniors. Let's give the best effort we've ever given.'

"I would do mine on the field during the game. If somebody missed a block, 'Come on, you can't miss those blocks.' You know, do it then. After all, the quarterback is the leader on the field, when the game is going on.

"The leadership role was easier as a senior. As a sophomore, the people I played with made it easy—helped me with it a lot. Marty Woolbright, Darrell Austin—these guys that were seniors and had been around a long time. If I would get upset, they'd help me—pretty much motivate the others."

Although he was from Maryland, Grantz warmed-up to the Carolina-Clemson rivalry even before he decided where he was going to college.

Grantz: "I was recruited at the Carolina-Clemson game (1971). I knew I wasn't going to Clemson, and South Carolina was

Jeff and Jill were married in 1978.

Jeff and daughter Katie, who was 2¹/₂ years old in 1985.

favored to win, but Clemson ended-up winning. This was going to be my last trip (Columbia), and I was really pulling for Carolina to win, so the people would be in a good mood after the game. So, it really kinda ticked me off when Clemson won . . . and some of the comments you'd hear from the players. And I found out real fast when I went up there my freshman year, when it was raining and miserable, and we lost, seven to six."

That wasn't a contender for the bitterest collegiate defeat suffered by Grantz, however, as he assigns that distinction to the Duke game of 1974. Dietzel resigned, as of the end of the season, immediately following the game.

Grantz: "I hadn't played well, and I felt personally responsible. I had a long talk with my dad after the game. We walked around the field, and he enlightened me.

"Dad was a coach and athletic director for thirty-three years, and he saw ninety per cent of my games at Carolina. His high school games were on Friday afternoon, and then he would get home and drive to Fayetteville (N.C.) and spend the night. He'd drive to Columbia the next morning and get up Sunday morning and drive back home. I don't see how he did it."

Jeff's senior year of 1975, and his only season under Carlen, pushed football enthusiasm to a new high at Carolina, and home attendance soared to a new record average of 49,497 per game. The 7-4 record for the season attracted a bid to the Tangerine Bowl in Orlando, Florida, where the Gamecocks lost to Miami of Ohio, 20-7. The caliber of Miami teams of that era is pointed out by the fact that they defeated Georgia and Florida in the two previous Tangerine Bowls.

The record-setting offensive performance by Grantz and thousand-plus rushing yardage seasons for Long and Williams made the headlines. However, Grantz gave much credit to an efficient offensive line.

Grantz: "Brad Kline and E.Z. Smith were two of the smartest offensive linemen I ever played with; they worked together so well. They were on the right side. On the left side were Steve Courson and Jerome Provence, and they were two of the strongest. Mike McCabe was the center, and he was the most improved lineman in two years I've ever seen; he was also intelligent.

"Our offensive line pretty much combined intelligence and strength.

"Garry Mott was one of the hardest hitting linebackers we've ever had. And John Dantonio and David Prezioso—those two guys were as intensive defensive players as we've ever had.

"Russ Manzari (defensive end) was probably the most amazing, because of his height. He was only five-eight, and he didn't look like he could get the job done, but he was an excellent football player.

"Of course, Bill Currier, who's still playing pro ball (Houston Oilers and New York Giants). He was consistently impressive; he wouldn't make huge, big plays; but he was always consistent."

Grantz was especially impressed by Hodgin, a running back who finished his varsity career at Carolina in 1974 with a career total of 2,478 rushing yards, fourth highest in the school's history, as of 1984.

Grantz: "I thought Jay Lynn was one of the smartest, best all-around running backs I've ever seen. He would throw a lot of half-back passes. I'd come out on the option and pitch to him, and he would throw halfback option passes. I believe he completed about seventy-five or eighty per cent and threw for six or eight touchdowns in two years."

In 1973 Hodgin completed ten of 14 for 242 yards and three touchdowns, and in 1974, was nine of 15 for 190 yards and a touchdown.

Grantz: "I don't know why he didn't get a chance to play pro ball. Speed? He ran about a four-seven forty. But, with that, I've never seen him caught from behind. He ran a kickoff ninety-three yards for a touchdown against Houston (1973), and they supposedly had six or seven guys who ran four-fours; but none of them caught him.

"He set a new rushing record in the Blue-Gray game and got the MVP award. With his versatility, he could run away from people, and he could run through people. He had a strong upper body; he could throw the option pass; he could catch the ball; and he was a good blocker.

"Philip Logan and Scott Thomas were the ones I threw to the most. What we did was run a lot of double receivers and put the flanker almost in a slot—then the wide receiver to the outside. Logan was the wideout, but we really threw to a lot of receivers. Look at the receptions they had—I think Logan caught the most—but even our tight ends caught a lot of balls. We had two; Jay Saldi and Brian Nemeth did some alternating."

Following his great senior season Jeff went on an all-expenses vacation to California, Hawaii, and Japan, playing in the East-West game at San Francisco, the Hula Bowl in Honolulu, and the Japan Bowl in Tokyo.

Grantz: "The thing I remember most about the Japan Bowl was the fans. Instead of cheering, like they do here, when something good happened, they went, 'Ahhhhhhhhhhhh!' Instead of screaming and yelling. They filled Olympic Stadium, about sixty-five thousand."

The Miami Dolphins drafted Grantz in the 17th (last) round, which didn't place him in the most enviable position.

Grantz: "That hurt me, because they had Earl Morrall, Bob Griese and Don Strock. So, they were pretty much set at quarterback. I went to rookie camp and ran a little bit as wide receiver, but didn't like it. I didn't enjoy the whole aspect of pro football. It was so much of a business atmosphere. People were worried about how much the guy next to them was making. And I was the only unsigned player in the rookie camp. I had an opportunity to come back here, and I was graduate assistant to Carlen for two years."

His enthusiasm for Carolina football hasn't been dampened by ten years of inactivity.

Grantz: "I think that Coach Dietzel improved the program. And I think that Coach Carlen improved the program.

"I think we're going to be better as the years go by, because we've got the facilities, the fan support, and the coaching staff that can recruit. That's the name of the game—and being able to coach 'em. We've got that.

"The town, the fans, the support. And I point that out to the guys (prospects) that come in—the opportunity they have after they play. Because the people are into the overall concept of the game of football, moreso than when I came here, which was amazing to me at the time. And it has grown since.

"I've expressed an interest in helping (with prospects), and I've met several recruits and talked to them. I talked to Todd Ellis (All-America high school quarterback from Greensboro, N.C.), but that was not because they asked me to. I took it upon myself to go over and meet him."

Ellis signed a grant-in-aid to attend Carolina and was scheduled to be on the 1985 squad. He is the most highly-publicized quarterback ever signed by the Gamecocks and apparently had a bright future ahead of him.

If he does reach that predicted stardom, there will still be the unpredictable and the uncertainties to be faced. However, when excellence is achieved, there is one reaction that is sure to come. Fans will wonder how he stacks-up against Jeff Grantz.

You know, the guy from the Old Line State with sprinter's speed; tap dancer's feet; the peripheral vision of a house fly; a coach's brain; the nerve of a sky diver; the instinct of a bat; and a throwing arm that depended more on mind than muscle.

And, you might add to that, the spirit of a Gamecock!

Charting Jeff Grantz

YEAR	PASSING				RUSHING				PUNTING	
	NO.	COMP.	YDS.	TDs	NO.	YDS.	AVE.	TDs	NO.	AVE.
1972	23	10	119	1	10	35	3.5	1	26	41.3
1973	121	62	864	6	158	806	5.1	9	—	—
1974	95	39	642	3	96	263	2.7	4	26	38.8
1975	216	120	1,815	16	141	473	3.4	12	43	40.2
	455	231	3,440	26	405	1,577	3.8	26	95	40.1

Total offense: 5,017 yards

School records held, as of 1984:

Most total yards in a season: 2,288 (1975)

Highest average yards per game: 19017 (1975)

Most rushing yardage in a single game: 260 vs. Ohio (1973)

Most touchdown passes in a season: 16 (1975)

Most touchdown passes in a game: 5 (vs. Clemson, (1975)) (Tie with Tommy Suggs)

Team co-captain (with Garry Mott)—1975

Steve Wadiak Award for Most Valuable Player—1973 and 1975.

KEVIN **long**

32

RUNNING BACK

He was Carolina's first thousand-yard running back. Kevin Long made it big in college and the NFL, although his high school coach placed him at offensive guard, and his college coach tried to make him a linebacker.

13 KEVIN LONG

Kevin Long expressed an interesting ambition, especially for a football player whose high school coach insisted that he should be an offensive guard, and the college coaching staff that recruited him judged that his best chance to get playing time would be at linebacker. Keep in mind that Long's persistence was the only thing that enabled him to become a running back, the University of South Carolina's first to gain over a thousand yards in a season, and the seventh in the history of the National Collegiate Athletic Association to be a part of a backfield that produced two thousand-yard rushers in the same season.

In 1975 Long and his friend, Clarence Williams, accomplished the aforementioned yardage fete, which was even more impressive when you remember that quarterback Jeff Grantz—in the same backfield—set a school total offense record that was still intact at the end of the 1984 season.

"I'd like to mention a goal I'm shooting for," Long pronounced in a soft Palmetto State accent that survived five seasons with the New York Jets of the National Football League. Long was relaxing in his townhouse in Tempe, Arizona, where he, his wife, Frankie, and three young daughters awaited the opening of the 1985 season for the Arizona Outlaws of the United States Football League, less than a week away. This was a team that was transplanted from Chicago (The Blitz) to Arizona after the 1983 season, and Kevin found himself in the more relaxed atmosphere of that part of the country.

"You know, I gained a thousand yards with Clarence Williams in college, and the last two seasons Tim Spencer and I gained a thousand together. That's the first time it's ever been done in professional football. So, I've got another guy I'm playing with this year, and I'm hoping we can both get a thousand. Might be the type of thing that can go in the 'Guiness Book of World Records'!"

The new back of which Long speaks is Ernest Anderson, who led the NCAA in rushing in 1982 while at Oklahoma State, so, perhaps, another tandem thousand-yard season is quite realistic. Kevin's 1,010 yards, 4.5 average, and 15 touchdowns in 1984 would indicate that he has well endured eight years of pro football. Eight years that have seen a number of capable running backs retire from active duty for various reasons.

The Arizona Outlaws, as Long's team is now called, converting from Wranglers because of merger with another team, entered the 1985 season (spring) amidst predictions that the two-year-old USFL would never make it. Long isn't certain that it's an important factor in his future plans.

Long: "Here I am thirty years old, which isn't really old, but in terms of a running back, this is my eighth year. I came in the league with some great ones, and I've outlasted a whole lot of them. So, you get to a point where you don't want to burn yourself out. I'll have to see how the season goes.

"I've accomplished some of the things I've wanted to accomplish. In fact I've gone beyond things I've expected to happen. I've been able to make a decent living, and I've been fortunate enough to save some money and make some investments. Quite naturally, I'm not one of your Heisman Trophy winners or high draft picks, so I've had to budget and save along the way. I'll still have to work for a living—I'm not financially secure for life."

Kevin's success as a football player has no doubt been a very pleasant surprise for his head coach at Clinton High School, Keith Richardson, and his first college coach, Paul Dietzel, both of whom positioned him differently. However, in fairness to both, if he had put his mind to it, Long would no doubt have become a fine offensive guard or linebacker.

The late 1960's and early 1970's found Southern states wrestling with the problem of integrating schools, and the general atmosphere was one that turned normally routine problems into major crises. South Carolina college football teams had not yet begun to benefit from the wealth of talent that had been unavailable from the previously segregated schools.

For example, in 1970 all 50 players pictured in the Carolina football brochure were white, although Jackie Brown, who had come to school on a part baseball scholarship, was listed on the roster. But he had not been assigned a jersey number at that point.

Long recalls his personal journey through this period:

"I played for old Bell High School (in Clinton) my first two years. That was before integration had taken place. We didn't have access to the YMCA League or Pop Warner Football then. So, if you were large enough in the eighth grade, you went over and tried out for the team. I made the team and played my eighth and ninth grade years; I was an offensive lineman.

"In 1970 the schools merged, so I went over and met Keith Richardson, the head coach over there (Clinton High School). I made the team and played offensive guard for him. I was six-one and weighed about one-seventy-five at that point.

"I always wanted to be a running back, and I was one of the fastest guys on the team, so Coach Richardson and I had a dispute. He didn't want to take me off the line and put me in the backfield, so I didn't play my junior year. I just played basketball and track, so I ended up being the most valuable in track. I ran the hundred, two-twenty, high-jumped, and threw the discus. That convinced him (Richardson) he should give me a shot in the backfield, and he did my senior year. And I've been playing running back ever since.

"I weighed two hundred and four pounds and was one of the largest backs in the state that year. We won the state championship, and that was one thing that attracted Carolina to me. I had offers from them and the Naval Academy. I had feelers from other schools, but actual contact from only Carolina and the Naval Academy. Navy? I never could figure that one out. I was always a decent student in school, you know, around a B average; I wasn't an A student. But I did graduate in the upper half of my class. They (Navy) said I could fill a need that they had up there.

"Coach Jerry Stovall and Dick Weldon were my contacts with Carolina. My family didn't want me to go off to Annapolis and be gone with a five-year naval obligation. Coach Stovall and Weldon were very persistent. They called me, they wrote me. I had a part time job at a trailor factory. So, one day I was riding a forklift, and here this car comes on the parking lot, and they (Stovall and Weldon) get out of the car and say, 'We want you. Today's the first day you can sign. Here's the letter of intent.'

"So, I said, 'Sounds good to me.'

"I had met coach (Paul) Dietzel once when I went down to visit. There was a big group he talked to, and I was just a face in the crowd.

"That was the last year they could give out unlimited scholar-ships, and I think they brought in ninety something (65 were listed on the 1973 USC freshman roster) athletes. We had a lot of people fall by the wayside. (Only 24 seniors were listed on the 1976 roster.) Guys got frustrated at not playing, or whatever. Quit altogether or became full-time students. And, then, injuries took their toll.

"The interesting thing about it, you know, Carolina was a tough school to go to athletic-wise. They had some of the toughest drills you'll find anywhere. The toughest part about the Carolina football program was not so much the season. It was the off-season workout when we really lost a lot of people. They would run you, you know, we'd run the stadium steps. Now that I look back on it, I believe that was their way of weeding out the weak ones. You know, that would make room for them to sign more people the next year. We always lost a lot of people during that particular period.

"When I first came in I had problems, 'cause even though they recruited me, they didn't recruit me as a running back. They recruited me as a linebacker. I had trouble from the start with the linebacker coach, a guy named Bill Clay. I just had problems adjust-ing to his style . . . a lot of hard-nose stuff, fundamental type things. A lot of excessive conditioning.

"I went in and discussed it with coach Dietzel, and he told me the situation. Said that with Jay Lynn Hodgin, Andy LeHeup, Randy Spinks, Randy Chastain, and Tommy Amrein, 'there's just no way you can ever expect to break in the starting lineup.' So, he said, 'You'd be like number twelve on the depth chart, if you play running back.'

"I really had a shot at being at least third string linebacker, coming into camp. But I just felt out of place playing that position, so I took my chances and wound up playing on the 'hunk' squad. That's the team that ran the other team's plays against the first string defense.

"So, I did that for really a year and a half and really never expected to play. I was just content to go to school, get an education—just being there. That was another thing, it was a tough adjustment. The year I came in, although they had sixty-five peo-ple, they brought in only six blacks, including myself. And prior to that there were only eight or nine there. So, there weren't more than fifteen or sixteen of us there."

One of the freshmen entering with Long was Clarence Williams, who later teamed with Long as first unit running backs, but whom Long had never seen prior to enrolling at Carolina.

Long: "We had a guy named Bill Cregar, who was the starting linebacker, and he and a bunch of guys—must have been about thirty—they would all roam around the halls at night and hassle the freshmen. So, I came in one night from Burger King, you know, not expecting anything, and here this group of people turn the corner and say, 'Hey, that's one of those freshmen, let's get him!'

"And they started chasin' me through the halls, and I ran up the stairs, and I had French fries and hamburgers flyin' everywhere. And they stopped and picked those up and ate 'em. And I said, 'My gosh, where can I go?' So, I just started knockin' on someone's door, and the door opened, and it was Clarence Williams and Mike Tisdale (freshman from Kingstree).

"The first time I ever met them they saved me from this mob. I don't know what they were planning to do to me. Like I say, I was black, and my first experience, I was going to a predominantly white school, and here's this mob of white guys chasin' me. It was really frightening for me.

"We (Williams) became best of friends. As a matter of fact, Clarence is married and has three children, and I'm married and have three children. And we've been in constant contact with each other ever since we left school. Through the pros."

Williams was a running back for the San Diego Chargers from 1977 through 1981, and for the Washington Redskins in 1982.

Long: "Clarence is now living in Moncks Corner, since he retired from football. He was on the injured reserve with the Redskins in 1983, when they won the Super Bowl. So, he finished out his career up there. But he was able to get his Super Bowl ring, and I was really happy for him."

In the 1974 football brochure Long was listed at left halfback, along with returning lettermen Hodgin, Casper Carter, and Chastain, while Amrein, LeHeup, and Williams were the right halfbacks. In 1973 Long had played in one varsity game, carrying the ball twice, while Williams never made it off the bench, although both did well for the Jayvees during a seven-game season. However, this made little impression on the varsity staff, at least not enough to figure Long and Williams in their offensive plans.

Long: "The ironic thing about it was, the whole time I was down there running on the 'card' team, I was really developing my skills, because I was going against the first team defense every day.

Then, I ran a four-five forty, so, you know, I had pretty good speed. And the guys would be mad with me, 'cause I'd break a tackle and run for sixty or seventy yards in practice. I made a lot of enemies, but it made me better, for some reason.

"And going into my sophomore year I went to talk to Coach Dietzel one day after practice and told him I was really frustrated, 'cause I thought I was just as good as some of the guys they had up there starting. And I really wanted a shot. He said there was just no way he was gonna bring me up, so I threatened to quit the team. It's something between him and me that nobody else knew about, but a few of my close friends. And he told me he thought I had a lot of talent and just to be patient, and my turn would come.

"I think that year we had a losing season, and we were zero and five at one point. He (Dietzel) decided to give me a shot. He brought me up and put me in the backfield with Jay Lynn Hodgin, and we went down and played Ole Miss at Oxford. And I played real well that day. Jay had over a hundred yards rushing, and I had over a hundred yards rushing, also (17 carries for 109 yards)."

Following a 20-14 loss to Duke in Williams-Brice Stadium in the second game of the season, Dietzel had announced that he would give up his coaching duties following the 1974 season. After inserting Long into the lineup in the sixth game, Carolina won four of their final six games to finish 4-7 for the year.

In those six games Long gained 490 yards rushing for a 6.0 average, getting 96 in a 31-23 victory over North Carolina. Still, as Jim Carlen succeeded Dietzel as head football coach, and the 1975 season opener neared, Long was still listed behind senior Tom Amrein, a high school teammate of quarterback Jeff Grantz. Grantz, who had missed spring drills in order to play on the baseball team, was also listed behind Ron Bass in the pre-season depth chart.

Long: "Coach Carlen came in, so I returned that year expecting to start, and I faced the problem of Tommy Amrein. He was a senior. At the time we had a coach, Bob Gatling; he was a great guy, and I always had a lot of respect for Coach Gatling. But he wanted to put Amrein in there, I guess, because he was a senior. I hadn't played much, so Amrein was the starter up till the first game of the season.

"We played Georgia Tech, and at one point they put me in the game, and I had a couple of good runs. And, so, Coach Gatling pulled me out of the game. And Coach Carlen walked over to him

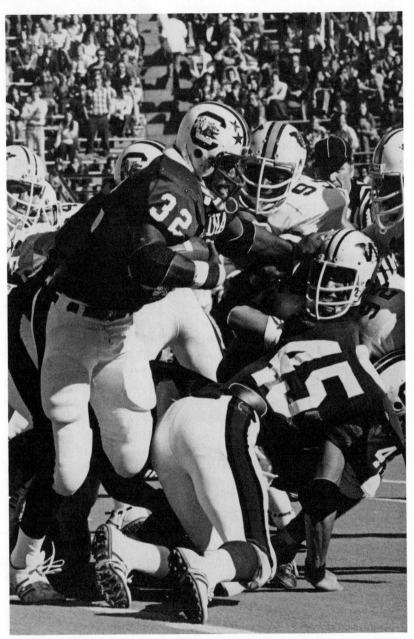

Long follows a block by tight end Brian Nemeth (45) in a 37-26 victory over Wake Forest in 1975.

and said, 'Hey, don't take this guy out of the game any more, unless I say so.' From that point on I was startin' ever since.

"I always thought that coach Dietzel was a very good coach. He was a very organized person and a pretty good motivater, and most of the players would probably say the same thing. I don't think his staff selection was the greatest. We had these coaches—I don't know if they were personal friends of his and needed a job, or what. But most of the guys seemed to have more problems with the assistant coaches. We never did have a problem with Coach Dietzel. We had a lot of people to transfer to other schools. A lot of guys who were All America, and things of this nature, to come there, and some of the recruiters had promised them that they'd play when they got to Carolina, and it just wasn't the case. So, we had a lot of problems with that.

"When Coach Dietzel resigned it was sort of a mixed reaction. Quite naturally, most of the seniors were more emotionally involved than a lot of us younger guys. I think most of the players felt, at that point, that we needed a change. Because it got to the point that the conditioning drills were more of the form of punishment than for conditioning. I guess it was the frustration of losing, and all the things that were happening to Coach Dietzel with the media and the fans. At that point I think most of the players thought it was time for a change.

"One of the characteristics of Carolina while I was there was, we always had an excellent offensive line. When I was there we put points on the board, but, for some reason, we just didn't do well on defense. I don't know if they couldn't recruit the quality players, or it was the coaching."

Hodgin, a senior who moved in behind Steve Wadiak among all-time career rushers at Carolina with 2,478 yards, was among the teammates that made lasting impressions on Kevin.

Long: "I remember when we played Appalachian State (1974) all the quarterbacks were hurt, and Jay had to play quarterback. That was sort of a fun game, 'cause we had all these running backs in the backfield. I kinda remember that game, because we all had to reach down inside and play harder, because we didn't have one of our regular leaders in there. Although, the guys really looked up to Jay Lynn and thought he did an outstanding job. He was always one of my favorite players; just thought he was a tough, aggressive guy, and he was always nice to us, even though we were underclassmen.

"I can't understand why he didn't get any pro offers. Maybe his speed had something to do with it. He was quick, and I know he had the ability. (Hodgin played in the Blue-Gray game in Montgomery, Ala., and set a new rushing record for the game.) Maybe it was because of the other running backs available.

"I always thought I could have gone higher in the draft myself, but I came out a year when Tony Dorsett (Pittsburgh) came out, and Ricky Bell (Southern Cal), and David Sims from Georgia Tech. You had a lot of quality backs come out that year."

Midway through his varsity experience, Long was dealing with a new head coach and new staff, but there were many familiar faces on the football squad, including his friend, Clarence Williams and four others who made it in the NFL—tight end Jay Saldi (Dallas, Chicago), offensive guard Steve Courson (Pittsburgh), defensive back Bill Currier (Houston, New England, and New York Giants), and punter Max Runager (Philadelphia and San Francisco).

Long: "Jay (Saldi) and I were good friends. Jay was one of those guys, you know, he was a New Yorker, and he was really cool with all of us black guys. He got along with everybody well, and it really caught us all by surprise when he got drafted by Dallas, 'cause Jay never really played that much. They moved him around a great deal. We knew he had the talent, but he was the type of guy that would do his job and went about his business. He didn't like the situation he was in—he was always talking about that. I guess he was such a long way from home, and he was there to go to school, so he made the best of it. When he went to Dallas, we were all happy for him.

"The year they went to the Super Bowl, I remember he came back to Columbia, and he was showing me his ring, and we rode around for hours, talking about how great it was playing professional football. Talking to him got me turned on about becoming a professional myself."

As did so many Carolina football players during the period from 1960 to 1984, Long had a first-hand opportunity to compare one Gamecock head coach with another, having finished out the Dietzel regime and begun the Carlen era.

Long: "Well, it was like a night-and-day situation. Coach Dietzel smiled all the time and was really the nice guy. He always projected the nice guy image and let the staff do the hard things he wanted done.

"Whereas Carlen was totally opposite. He was the type of person that was straightforward. He was firm. He would tell you what he wanted done, and if you didn't get it done, you weren't gonna be there. And I think a lot of the players learned to appreciate that type of approach. He always told us the best twenty-two players were gonna be on the field. If you wanted to be one of them you gotta produce.

"I took that for what it was worth, and I never really had any problem with it, after he told us that. I was a quiet person, did my job, and didn't cause any trouble. So, I never got close to any of the head coaches.

"In the nineteen-seventy-five season we were excited, because it was a new coach, and we were winning. The whole atmosphere was so much more pleasant. You had the feeling of winning and with people you could really believe in. So, I really enjoyed that year. It was one of the best years of my life. I'll always remember it, and I played with some great people, like Clarence and Jeff, both totally unselfish people.

"Guys like Jerome Provence and Steve Courson. We played well together, like a family, one big unit. Everybody was happy for the other guy's success. I think that was one thing we had that year that some of the other teams didn't have going for them. One big family of unselfish people."

The Carolina-Clemson game of that year, played in Columbia, was a spectacular occasion for the Gamecocks, as they demolished the Tigers, 56-20, after holding a 35-6 lead at halftime. Grantz passed for five touchdowns while rolling up 280 yards of total offense, while Williams rushed for 160 yards to join Long as a thousand-yard gainer.

Long: "We had a lot of incentive on offense. I had just gone over the thousand-yard mark the week before (against Wake Forest), and the type of team we had, just one big family, all the guys wanted Clarence—he needed a hundred and forty or hundred and fifty yards—to go over the thousand-yard mark. So our total concentration was to win the game, first of all, and to get Clarence his thousand yards.

"So, the whole day the linemen were just yellin' and screamin' every time he carried the ball. You know, 'Run as hard as you can, we're gonna block for you,' and the same thing with Jeff and myself. It was the right combination of helping him get his thousand yards, and we knew we had the better team that year, and it just made the right combination. It was just our day to win big."

The "Jeff Grantz" fan club had a wide membership, but there was none more enthusiastic about him than Kevin Long.

Long: "Jeff was the type of guy, first of all, he was an unselfish player. Then he was a leader; everyone rallied around Jeff. He had so much talent, he really made it easy for Clarence and me. We ran the triple-option offense, and it was really hard to defend against us. Clarence ran a four-point-four forty, and I ran a four-point-five. Jeff ran something like four-point-five. Jeff's the type of guy, he'd hold onto the ball to the very last second. A lot of people don't realize he took a great deal of punishment before he'd pitch the ball off to Clarence or me. You didn't find too many quarterbacks that would take that kind of punishment."

Kevin had never given much thought to the Carolina-Clemson game before enrolling at the University. "The situation I grew up in, we'd always hear about South Carolina State. We watched games on TV, and we used to watch Jackie Brown, that's how I was interested in Carolina-Clemson.

"I never really knew, until I went to college and saw all the things they got involved in. I went up there (Clemson) my senior year, and they were really out for blood. Everything I had heard a Carolina-Clemson game up there would be like. As far as the fans throwin' chickens and stuff at us on the sidelines and yellin' obscenities at us. It was very distracting. I can see why they've won a lot of games up there. The toughest places I've played are there and between the hedges at Georgia. They're by far two of the toughest places to play college football."

Another famous "tough place to play" is Baton Rouge, Louisiana, where the Gamecocks lost a 24-6 decision to LSU in 1975. However, Long's 128 yards rushing proved to be the bright spot in an otherwise sub-par offensive showing for Carolina.

"I never will forget. The amazing thing about it, you hear an awful lot about how deafening the noise is down there. But you could hear a pin drop in that stadium until they scored and went ahead near the end of the half. You couldn't hear anything from then on."

A record of seven wins and four losses during the regular season was good enough to earn Carolina a bid to play Miami of Ohio in the Tangerine Bowl in Orlando, Florida. It was the third bowl game in the school's history, and 10,000 excited fans followed the team to Florida.

Long: "We were very excited—we had a winning season. The fans were happy, and we felt at that point we were the best team in Carolina history. Going to a bowl was a real highlight for us.

"We went down there, and Miami had the better team. They had some excellent players. I remember Rob Carpenter (running back), who's playing with the Giants now, and Sherman Smith, their quarterback, went on to play running back with the Seahawks. He's the first guy I ever saw who could throw with both hands. Roll to the right, throw with the right hand. Roll to the left, throw with the left hand.

"Every team while I was there wanted to win the magic eight games, and we always came up short, to win more games than any Carolina team."

For his season's efforts, Long had 1,133 yards, averaging six per carry, and received some honors, including Honorable Mention on the Associated Press All-America team and first team All-South Independent. The latter included such teams as Miami (Fla.), Virginia Tech, Florida State, Southern Mississippi, Tulane, and Memphis state, among others. That would be Long's peak, as the 1976 season proved to be frustrating for Carolina, which won five of its first seven games, then dropped three of the last four for a 6-5 record.

Long: "It wasn't a very good year for me. I was coming off a big junior year, and they bring in a guy named Steve Dorsey from Maryland. I was really looking forward to coming back and having a great year, and I had my eye on turning professional and going high in the NFL draft. For some reason, I don't know if Coach Carlen or whoever recruited him (Dorsey) had made a promise that he was gonna play, but it was one of those situations where we ended up splitting time. So, I always felt that it might have hurt me personally. Similar things were happening with the team, and we didn't do well at all that year. We had a winning season, but with the talent we had, we didn't win as many games as we could have won."

Still, there was one game in that season that offered Kevin a once-in-a-lifetime thrill, as Carolina met Notre Dame in Columbia, with the President of the United States, Gerald Ford, looking on.

Long: "I'll always remember that. I was selected co-captain for that game, and Russ Manzari (defensive end) and I got the honor of presenting the school colors to President Ford. That was the biggest thrill of my life. First of all, playing against the Fighting Irish; as a kid I thought, 'Maybe one day I'll go to Notre Dame or Southern

Kevin Long with a trimmed-down look with the New York Jets.

Cal, or one of those powerhouse schools.' But that didn't happen, so it worked out that the Good Lord gave me a chance to play against one of those teams.

"We gave President Ford a Gamecock cap and a blanket with the state seal, and about everything from Carolina that you could get on there representing the school and the state. He just smiled and shook our hands.

"It (the game) was very good from a morale standpoint. That was probably the most physical game in college that I ever played in. They had two 'all-world' defensive ends—Willie Fry on one side and a guy named Ross Browner on the other. And a strong safety named Rufus Bradley—as a matter of fact, I played with him this year and we still talk about that game. We felt that they won the scoreboard, but we should have won the game."

The quarterback for the 1976 Gamecocks was Ron Bass, a junior from Camp Springs Maryland, who had an injury-plagued career at Carolina, but he, like Grantz, had an admirer in Kevin Long.

Long: "If Ron had stayed healthy, he might have done spectacular things—he might even have been a little better than Jeff. I don't want to take anything away from Jeff. We played North Carolina one year (31-23 victory in 1974) and Ron had something like forty carries for something like 260 yards (actually 39 carries for 211 yards). I know he made *Sports Illustrated* (Back-of-the-Week) that week. So, you know he was an excellent athlete."

One thing that Long was not an admirer of was the artificial turf that Paul Dietzel had ceremoniously installed in Williams-Brice Stadium in 1971.

Long: "Coach Carlen wasn't much different from Dietzel in terms of conditioning. It probably wore us down as the season went on, because we did do a lot of hitting and contact stuff, plus playing on that artificial surface. I was really glad to see that they took artificial surface out of there and replaced it with grass (in 1984).

"I always felt that wore the team down, as the season went along. We lost a lot of guys to knee injuries, as a result of their legs catching on the turf. It was really hard to stay healthy, due to the fact we had to play on the hard surface. When Dietzel was there we practiced on it a lot more than we did for Carlen. We practiced on the grass field over by the Roundhouse.

"From a running back and receiving standpoint, it was great for quickness. You're probably a tenth of a second faster on artificial surface than you'd be on grass. From a standpoint of your body falling on it and people tackling you, I always felt grass was a better cushion to fall on."

As for the receivers, Long recalled, "Phil Logan—he was the type of guy who was a clutch player, and I always thought he was pro material. (Logan ranked second among all-time career leaders at Carolina in 1984 with 105 catches for 2,063 yards and 15 touchdowns.) I can't understand why he didn't get an offer to turn professional. I knew he and coach Carlen had some problems, and that might have entered the picture; I don't know. Phil was sort of a quiet guy."

"Seemed like Zion McKinney could have been a great athlete, too. (McKinney was tied for 8th among Carolina career receivers in 1984, with 68 catches for 963 yards and six touchdowns.) I don't know that they used him to the full extent that they could have. I remember playing against Zion in high school (Pickens). We beat them, but Zion was one of our primary concerns. All you read about was Zion being a one-man team.

Long poses with wife Frankie and two of his three daughters.

"So, I was really expecting him to be one of those blue chip athletes coming in and doing a lot of things. He played really good while he was in there, but I just always thought they didn't get the most of his potential."

Another one of the surviving members of the 1973 freshman crop was Bill Currier, a defensive back from Glen Burnie, Maryland.

Long: "Bill and I became good friends, and I still see Bill. He was like our team leader. I've seen Bill play with more nagging injuries that any other human being. He'd always lineup and be out there when game time came. He was a tremendous, hard-nosed athlete.

"Rick Sanford (another defensive back on the 1976 squad) is the type of guy who was always deceiving. I really never thought that he was as good as Bill. He went on and had some good seasons and got drafted really high by the New England Patriots. So, I guess he proved himself to everybody. I was tackled one time by Rick (in the NFL) on the goal line; he stopped me from scoring.

"When we played Houston, we had some tough games with Bill. He'd always come up and hit you real hard, and we'd kinda laugh and say things to each other on the way back to the huddle."

Pro draft day, 1977, was a nervous experience for Long, as he hung around a telephone that seemed to be out of order.

Long: "Quite naturally, I got a lot of feelers from just about every team. I think the top teams that were really interested were Green Bay—they had a guy come by and time me in the forty—New Orleans and Kansas City. And I really thought I was going to Kansas City. In the third round they took a guy named Ted McKnight (Minnesota-Duluth), and I was drafted in the seventh round by the New York Jets the second day. I was really worried, because, if you don't go the first day, you're just thrown into the crowd the next day.

"About five o'clock the next day the phone rang, and It was the secretary from the Jets, and she said, 'Hello, this is the New York Jets calling. We just drafted you in the seventh round, and here's Walt Michaels, your head coach.'

"He came on the phone and congratulated me for being picked by them and told me he was looking forward to working with me. And from that point on they started giving me flight arrangements and when I was supposed to report.

"I was just excited about being drafted by the pros, period. That was one of my childhood dreams, even if they had taken me as a free agent. Just the opportunity to play pro football, to me, ranked up there with getting my degree from college. All those things sorta fell in line for me. And the most interesting thing about it, my first couple of years there, Darrell Austin, who was the offensive center for us my freshman year, was up there. So, I had a person I was familiar with, and who could tell me things, and kinda made the transition from college to pro a little more comfortable.

"My competition at running back was Clark Gaines. I remember I played against him at Wake (Forest) his senior year. The thing was, I made the team at tailback when I went up there, and my first year up I started the last four games. And that was a big thrill for me, because my first game was against the Oakland Raiders, and they still had Jack Tatum, and John Matuszak, and all those household names you hear about as a kid. It was really a thrill for me to start my professional career against a team of that caliber.

"What happened was, the next year, Gaines hurt the arch in his foot—it was in pre-season—so I asked the coach could I switch over to fullback to help out. And that turned out to be my natural position. I went on that year to gain almost a thousand yards—like 954 yards and ten touchdowns. So, the following year Clark was healthy and came back, so we always had an uncomfortable situation about who should be the starter. It was back 'n forth, back 'n forth. Eventually, I didn't get to start and play much at all from that point.

Kevin Long was the first Gamecock to break the 1,000-yard barrier.

"I was traded to Chicago in pre-season of eighty-two for a sixth round draft choice. So, I went in there, and that was the year Mike Ditka was head coach, and they put me on the fourth team behind Walter Payton, of all people. You know, it was going to be nearly impossible to compete with Walter Payton. So, they ended up releasing me in the second pre-season game.

"I was out of football for four months of nineteen eighty-three, and I was doing some undercover detective work at Richway Department Store. That was the year of the recession, and it was really tough finding a job that year. I had to resign myself to staying with my family and making the best of it. I had gotten my degree from Carolina, so I was still thinking about going into coaching or teaching. I never got certified to teach, so that's one of the things I would have to go back for.

"I had planned to do that, and one day the phone rang, and it was a guy named Joe Herring, who was linebacker coach for the Jets when I played for them. He was now working for George Allen (Chicago Blitz), and he was telling me they were gonna form a new league—the United States Football League, and would I be interested in playing for George Allen? So, I told him I'd have to think about it, and the following day George Allen called me himself. During the time I was talking to him I was having all those flashbacks of him with the Redskins and the over-the-hill gang and all. The guy is really a legend—never had a losing season. All those things started to become important to me, so I said, 'Sure, I'll come up and give it a shot.' He assured me I'd be the starting fullback, and he was true to his word. I never had any competition for the job or anything. I came in, he gave me a playbook, I practiced with the team, and I went on and gained a thousand yards with Tim Spencer that year.

"Our owner, Ted Dietrich, sold the team and bought the Arizona franchise, so they transferred us to Phoenix, and we were the Arizona Wranglers last year."

As Long and the Arizona Outlaws, as they are now called, following a merger with another USFL team, prepared to move into another season, sports experts predicted doom for the new league. Attendance had been limited, and, thus far, no franchise-saving network television contract had been negotiated.

Long is hopeful, however, remarking, "We went to the championship game last year, and that created some excitement around here. So, we think this is going to be a good year. We don't have many household names. Doug Williams (former Tampa Bay quarterback who played college ball at Grambling) is here. This is a budget-minded team. They aren't really going after the Doug Fluties (1984 Heisman Trophy winner who signed a multi-million-dollar contract with the USFL New Jersey Generals)."

As for the future, Kevin will take it one year at a time, re-evaluating his situation at the end of the season. Then, possibly, he will set some new goals to pursue. He has quietly achieved many of the objectives that he thought were only pipe-dreams during his boyhood days in Clinton.

He left his mark while wearing Carolina's Number 32, which was displayed with distinction by another great running back, Kent Hagood, during the exciting 1984 season. Long was in the stands to watch the new Number 32 and his teammates perform so well, as the football program reached new heights under coach Joe Morrison.

The old Number 32 obviously has faded into the shadows of Williams-Brice Stadium.

Long: "I met coach Morrison and the athletic director on one occasion. And they were both gentlemen, but, I guess, I've been away so long. . . .

"All the young guys coming in (USFL) now, you can tell how much more aware people are of Carolina football. So, the program has finally caught up with everybody else."

However, don't overlook the contributions of people like Kevin Long, who created a new excitement among Carolina fans, who flocked to home games in record-breaking numbers in 1975 and boosted the Gamecock Club treasury to new highs. And Long, himself, did his share by setting a new standard for running backs, surpassing even the legendary Steve Wadiak.

But Kevin doesn't seem to care for the limelight, choosing to seek personal satisfaction in meeting the challenges that have come his way. He has met some doubters along the way, and he hasn't emerged as a household name, even in Carolina households.

Through it all, however, things have worked out pretty well for this aging thirty-year-old, because, whenever opportunity presented itself, he was able to take advantage of it, because one most important person always believed in him.

"Quite naturally," as he would say, that individual was Kevin Long.

CHARTING KEVIN LONG

YEAR	NO.	RUSHING YARDS	AVE.	TDs
1973	2	3	1.5	0
1974	81	490	6.1	3
1975	190	*1,133	6.0	4
1976	174	746	4.3	8
	447	**2,372	5.3	15

*Third highest for Carolina, as of 1984. Had five 100-yard-plus games.
**Fifth highest for Carolina, as of 1984.

GEORGE **rogers**

The life of Carolina's Heisman Trophy winner has been an obstacle course. However, George Rogers is still on his feet and running hard into a new career with the Washington Redskins.

38

RUNNING BACK

14 GEORGE ROGERS

thus far, the life of George Rogers has been an obstacle course, and it is a tribute to his indomitable spirit that he is still on his feet and running hard.

On Good Friday of 1985 he could have been any young father whose wife had gone to the beauty parlor and left him to baby sit. In his lap was George Washington Rogers, III, born on Christmas Day, contently suckling a bottle held by his daddy. A big screen television set-up displayed a syndicated program, as Rogers patiently supervised the surroundings. Playing around the yard was little Brandon, who wore a black New Orleans Saints jersey, dominated by a white 38, the numerals worn by his father during a distinguished football career at the University of South Carolina and New Orleans of the NFL.

Enroute to his easy chair in the den of his ranch style home in suburban Columbia, Rogers had experienced mountains and valleys. The peaks were receiving the Heisman Trophy as America's best college football player in 1980, and the NFL Rookie-of-the-Year award in 1981. He became the first player to lead the NCAA and NFL in rushing in consecutive seasons.

Rogers called his son into the house, "Hey, Brandon, tell the man who you're gonna play for."

"Gamecocks," was the instant reply.

Would Rogers, whose famous "38" was retired by the University after his senior season, try to get his jersey out of retirement, if his son should play for Carolina?

"No way, man! Let him make his own number. He's not gonna be any running back, either. He's gonna be a big ol' lineman."

George has a special place in his heart for "big ol' linemen," who were constantly receiving his praise for clearing the path for his national rushing title in 1980, when he was the Heisman recipient. When he looks at Brandon, perhaps he can see something of himself when he was a growing boy in Atlanta, Georgia, where he began a distinguished football career in a most unimpressive fashion.

Rogers: "I tell you, I just went out for football because all my peers did. I didn't know nothin', nothin' about the game. Not one single thing. I just went out there because all the guys I knew—this was about the fourth or fifth grade—went out there. Little League.

"I went out there—this was a real game. My mama had bought my stuff—little equipment and stuff. I went out there—I was in the backfield—and I was always faster than everybody—taller and faster. And the quarterback looked at me in the huddle, and he said, 'I'm gonna pitch back to you, and you go right.' Something like that.

"'Pitch it to me and go right? What are you talkin' about?'

"Then he said, 'Break,' and we broke the huddle and got set. He threw the ball to me, and it looked like my line just fell down. It looked like all eleven of 'em came straight toward me. I threw the ball back to the quarterback, and they just wiped me out. I got up off the ground, and I was all dizzy and stuff, because I didn't know they were supposed to hit me like that.

"The coach took me out, and I went to the sideline like, 'What's happening?'

"The next game, my brother was going with me. I had learned. I went to practice that next week and learned. But the coach thought I still didn't know what I was doing. I took my brother to the game, and we got to the game, and the coach wouldn't let me play. I just started cryin', and cryin', and cryin'. Somebody on the sideline said, 'What's wrong with that little boy?'

"One of my teammates said, 'He's cryin', because the coach won't let him play, 'cause he don't know how to play.'

"I said, 'I do know how to play. I do know how to play.'

"I was cryin' so loud, the coach came over there and put his hand over my mouth to stop me from hollerin'. He said, 'I'm gonna put you in; I'm gonna put you in right now. And he did the same play. You know what I did? I ran a touchdown. He pitched it, and I took off down the sideline.

"And I still remember this, plain as day. I ran—I didn't know where the end zone was—so I just kept running till there was no more grass left. Then my own teammates came down and started jumpin' on my back.

"I said, 'What they doin'?'

"They were sayin', 'Way to go. Way to go.'

"I said, 'Way to go? What they talkin' about?' And I realized that I had scored a touchdown. Ever since that day I found out what you're supposed to do—that's when I started playing.

"After all that glorious time I had, I had quit. My mom didn't have any money to pay for insurance for me. So, I quit, and I started playin' hooky from school. Aaaah maan, I was like into everything, and my mom couldn't do anything with me. With me or none of the rest of my brothers and sisters.

"So, I told my mom to let me go stay in Duluth. You know, I was living in Atlanta then. I had been roamin' the streets—hardly goin' to school. I was tellin' my mom I didn't like it, because when I went to school the guys would pick at me, because I wasn't dressed good, you know. It was just messed up. We weren't dirty, but we used to wear the same clothes every day, and I just got tired of gettin' picked at all the time.

"I was getting older, and I didn't have a girl friend. But everytime I'd go to Duluth, I was in the country, and I was about the cleanest one there. Everybody there was primarily dressed the same way. I told her, 'You just gotta let me go.' If she hadn't let me go to Duluth, I wouldn't have been in school none, because I just couldn't take it up there.

"So, I went to Duluth and started playin' football again. But it was different now. I got bigger guys, and they were hittin' harder.

"Let me tell you about the first game I played in. They kicked off, and they kicked it down toward my side. So, the ball went in the end zone, and I started joggin' off the field. I thought, if it goes in the end zone, you ain't got to mess with it.

"This other guy said, 'Get the ball! Get the ball!' And he ran back toward it.

"I'm joggin' off the field. The ball's in the end zone, so I haven't got to get it. The other guy picked it up, and we got the ball on about the two-yard line.

"So, Coach (Cecil) Morris, like, 'What in the world are you doin'?'

"'I ain't done nothin'.'

"He said, 'Get over there and sit down.'

"One of the guys said, 'Why didn't you pick up the ball?'

"I said, 'It was in the end zone.'

"He said, 'It was in the end zone, but you've got to get it. You've got to down it.'

"I found that out. Coach Morris put me in the game, and we were playin' against this school that's supposed to be so good. The first play, I fumbled. They handed me the ball, and I was real, real scared.

"I went over on the sideline, and—wooooweeeeee!—you talk about somebody gettin' killed, now. He really jacked me up.

"The next week, I was out there in practice, and I was tippin'—you know—tip toein', and they hit me, and I fell on the ground.

"And here comes Coach Morris. He's about six-five. He's standin' over me. He picked me up off the ground and just shook me, like what are you doin', who do you think you are? You don't want to play no football.

"He just started shakin' me, and I started cryin' and cryin'. Boy, that made a football player out of me that day, because when he started shakin' me, I was so mad, I just started runnin' over everybody. I was just killin' everybody in sight. I didn't care. I was, like, cryin'.

"Then after practice, he told me, 'Son, I knew you could do it. From now on, if you ever, ever tiptoe on me again, you're through playing football for me.'

"I was cryin' right then, because it hurt me for him to do me like that, then call me and talk good to me afterwards. But Coach Morris, he put me on my P's and Q's. He made me play football, and, after that day, I was playin' football. You should have seen me in the next game. I was fightin' for a touchdown, and I finally scored."

Once the end zone was located by Rogers, he became a frequent visitor there, and his high school career at Duluth, just a few miles north of Atlanta, was sensational. When he was a senior he became the object of a most competitive recruiting battle, and time proved that the hundred-plus schools that were trying to enroll Rogers clearly saw his potential. Rogers decided to cast his lot with Carolina coach Jim Carlen, and this began a very close relationship.

Rogers: "I tell you what, when I met Coach Carlen, the thing that impressed me most about him was that he was a straightforward guy. He told you what he thought and what he believed in. When I was getting recruited, all the head coaches were sayin', if you come here, we'll do this for you. Make sure your mom and dad and everybody gets to the games and all.

"Coach Carlen was totally different. He was more like, 'You can come here—we're gonna give you a scholarship, and that's it. We're not gonna make you any kind of special player, other than the rest of the guys that's out there.'

"That's what got me to come to Carolina more than anything. Carlen was straight-up, and he looked me in the eyes and told me, 'Son, we aren't gonna give you anything but a scholarship.'

"I really do believe that's why I went to Carolina, 'cause Carlen was the only coach that didn't offer me anything.

"If Bill Battle had been at Tennessee, I was going to Tennessee. But he got fired that year. Georgia Tech. Georgia. The reason I didn't go to Georgia is, they were going to the Sugar Bowl, and they really didn't act like they were interested in me.

"Bear Bryant—the reason I didn't go to Alabama is, they had a big conference. He didn't talk to one player, one-on-one. When he talked to the recruits, he talked to everybody at one time—their families and everything. I didn't like that. You didn't get anything out of it. He was basically talking to everybody and saying the same thing to everybody. He was going to meet the President that day, so he didn't have much time for us, anyway.

"I had offers from everywhere—I can't remember all of them.

"I tell you what—Carolina had Kevin Long and Clarence Williams leaving—two senior running backs, starting. So, I had a better chance of playing. That's what I was thinking—I wanted to play right off, not wait so long. And with Kevin and Clarence gone, I thought I could play.

"Coach Carlen came to my high school, and he was sittin' out in the principal's office. I ain't never gonna forget that. He looked me straight in the eyes and said, 'Son, I know these other teams'—it's like he already knew what everybody's been sayin' to me—'they're telling you that they can get your mom different things.'

"Basically, what the other colleges were saying was, 'We'll take care of you real good. Just sign with us.'

"Coach Carlen said, 'Son, we can't offer you anything but a scholarship.'

"People don't believe that, but that is the reason why I signed.

"I felt like, when I came here, that there'd be a little time where I'd have to play jayvee, but I didn't. When I came to Carolina, I was full of enthusiasm. I was anxious to play, because it was my first time away from the country. It was a new atmosphere. The

George Rogers cuts behind Steve Dorsey (34) for yardage against Wake Forest in 1980.

guys on the team seemed to like each other pretty good. We didn't have anybody that was acting depressed, or anything like that.

"I was running fullback—me and (Steve) Dorsey. We were running the veer mostly. Johnny Wright (running-back in Rogers' freshman class) got hurt, and we went to the I. They were thinking about putting me at tailback, anyhow. I told 'em it didn't make any difference which position I played, as long as I'm carryin' the ball.

"Johnny didn't like that. He didn't want to play fullback, which is a hard job. You have to go out there and block all the time. Steve Dorsey was the best blocker. Maaannn, I tell you what, he cleaned those corners out. All I had to do was get to it—that helped a whole lot.

"At tailback things happen a lot slower than at fullback. At fullback you've got to have quick feet—you gotta hit the hole. It's usually gonna be right up the middle, anyway. Tailback, you go laterally a whole lot. You go outside, cuttin' and stuff like that.

"The difference for me was, at tailback, I could see my holes a lot clearer. At fullback, if it ain't there, it ain't there, and you gotta make some yards out of that. Basically, you're blocking at fullback.

"I think, basically, what you look for out of the tailback slot is where your linemen are gonna be. The more you run the same play, the better you're gonna get at it. The same thing doesn't happen twice on the same play—you have to have a different way of goin' at it.

"When I first played tailback in the North Carolina game (opener of 1979 at Chapel Hill), I got killed. Running right into the people. The defenders weren't even comin' at me. I was, like, runnin' into them. You can see on the film where I was lookin' like I was lookin' for the people to hit, instead of them comin' to me.

"Coach (Bob) Brown—he was my backfield coach—told me, 'Son, you've got to avoid some of these guys. You've got to keep runnin' outside—don't keep cuttin' back all the time. Go different ways sometime—turn the corner.

"I was, like, eight-hole at eight-hole, 'cause I had been at fullback. The more I ran it in practice, the better I got at it—and better and better. You know, pretty soon I adjusted to it. I was pretty fast for a fullback, and being at tailback made it that much better.

"They basically tried to coach us in blocking. When you're an instinct runner—not sayin' that I am—when I was comin' out of high school, I used to run the ball all the time. I could always run, but I never was good at blocking. That was always my worst asset—blocking. But I try to block, which I can do a hundred times better now than when I was in college. I never did block much in college.

"I think Coach Carlen—what they helped me with the most—was putting me at tailback and telling me not to run into the defenders, like I was during that first game. I got better and better at running the ball, as the season went on."

Rogers improved at running the ball, all right. Just like Jack's beanstalk got taller, and the sky was the limit. The first two games of 1979, while George was feeling his way into the tailback position, were not failures, by any means. Not even while he was running toward defenders, instead of away from them. He gained 97 yards in that 28-0 loss to North Carolina and added 93 in a 24-7 win over Western Michigan.

Those contests preceded one of the longest streaks of 100-yard-plus rushing games in collegiate history, as Rogers never failed to surpass the century mark in his final 22 games for the Gamecocks.

During 1979 and 1980, Rogers led Carolina to 16 victories against only six defeats in regular-season games. Both seasons were capped with bowl bids—the Hall of Fame Bowl against Missouri in 1979, and the Gator Bowl opposite Pittsburgh the following year.

Finishing his junior year as runner-up to Heisman Trophy winner Charles White of Southern Cal for the NCAA rushing title (1,681 yards), Rogers became the first Carolina player in history to be named to the Associated Press All-America first team. Especially satisfying to Rogers was a 152-yard performance in a 27-20 victory over Georgia at Athens, the second straight win and 100-plus game against his home-state university. Another highlight was the longest touchdown run of Rogers' career, an 80-yarder against Florida State at Tallahassee.

Although Rogers had done well at fullback during his freshman and sophomore seasons, the unfortunate injury to Wright just prior to the 1979 season opener and the subsequent shift of Rogers to tailback finally enabled him to display his true talent. Rogers had set a Carolina freshman rushing record of 623 yards and followed with a 1,006-yard total in his second year.

The stage was set for Rogers to become a legitimate Heisman contender in 1980, although for a player from a lesser football school to win the honor, it would require a truly sensational season. That, it was. First, Carolina had a showcase schedule, which allowed Rogers to be seen in California against Southern Cal and against Michigan in Ann Arbor. Later he would face national champion Georgia before a national television audience. Rogers gained 141 yards and scored a touchdown in a 23-13 loss to the Trojans, then followed with 142 yards and a score in a big 17-14 upset over ultimate Big Ten and Rose Bowl champion Michigan.

Carolina lost the battle "between the hedges" in Athens, Georgia, by a narrow 13-10 margin, but Rogers was personally impressive with a 168 yards.

From mid-season through Monday, December 1, there was much media speculation, as usual, as to the probable recipient of football's most coveted honor. Rogers was in the middle of the speculation, as were Hugh Green, defensive end for Pittsburgh, and Mark Herrmann, Purdue quarterback. Some guessed that Georgia's Herschel Walker might become the first player to win it as a freshman.

Rogers remained very much low key through it all, rejecting accolades and shifting attention to the role played by his offensive line in clearing the path for his runs. Shortly before the Heisman

On Dec. 16, 1980 Rogers appeared with the Associated Press All-America team on the Bob Hope Special on NBC-TV.

voting took place, Rogers, Green, and Herrmann appeared on one of the national TV network morning shows, and each player was asked to comment on his chances for the Heisman Trophy. Green explained that he felt that time had come for a defensive player to win the award, especially since a lineman hadn't won it since Notre Dame end Leon Hart in 1949.

When the question was passed to Rogers, he responded with an answer that qualified for a PhD in public relations. He replied that he agreed with Green that it would be nice for a lineman to win it, and he uttered no words in his own behalf. Nobody could argue that Rogers' modesty was for real.

Although Carolina was upset by Clemson in the final scheduled game, Rogers had another great effort, picking up 168 yards, bringing his season's total to 1,781 yards, tops in the nation, and moving his career total (not including bowls) to 4,958, fourth best in NCAA history.

On Sunday, November 30, Rogers was flown to New York City, where the Heisman winner was to be announced the next day, but it was also reported that the two other leading candidates (Green and Walker) were also to be present. The latter was merely a decoy, as only George was invited, and the announcement came at the Downtown Athletic Club on Monday. Again, Rogers accepted the honor typically, sharing credit with all his teammates.

That evening, when Rogers arrived at Metropolitan Airport in Columbia, 10,000 well-wishers were on hand to cheer him. However, Carlen, who was highly protective of his superstar, led Rogers through the mob and to a waiting bus, which sped away without allowing many of the fans even a fleeting glimpse of their hero.

Rogers: "Coach Carlen was like my daddy. You know, my daddy's been in prison, and I never looked up to nobody, other than my real daddy, like I did Coach Carlen. Coach Carlen was a guy that I really admired. He kept me straight, I'll tell you that.

"Anytime I did something wrong—like when I didn't go to class. Going to school wasn't one of my favorite things, even though I had to do it to keep my grades up. But Coach Carlen made me get up at six o'clock—he didn't have to do it but one time. I didn't want that no more. He told me, if I didn't go to class and get those grades, I was goin' home, and, 'Ain't nobody gonna be disappointed but you and me.'

"And that was good enough. He said some more things, I ain't gonna say. But Coach Carlen was like a dad. There ain't a guy that

I give more respect than Coach Carlen. He really helped me along the way.

"He kept the press off me, and he kept a lot of people from buggin' me all the time—especially during the Heisman Trophy year. I stayed around the press aaalll the time. They aaalllways wanted to talk to me. I never could have any free time, and I really wasn't liking it.

"You can't act like you're real mad, but I was under a lot of pressure. I didn't like talkin' to the press all the time. I was more of a fun guy. I liked to be just like the other guys—I didn't want to get all the write-ups, and all the credit, and all that. I didn't want to be the center of attention, 'cause I liked to have a lot of fun, and I didn't want anybody takin' that away from me.

"My teammates—the thing was—they thought I was crazy. They thought I should love to get all that publicity and credit. But they knew what kind of guy I was. There were so many times when I told Coach Carlen I didn't want to talk. He told me, 'You have to, son.'

"It was killin' me one time. When I was at the roost, I was gettin' calls aaalll the time. I was sick of talkin' about football. It seemed like that's all anybody wanted to talk about.

"You'll never know how much he (Carlen) did. When they wanted to talk to me, he'd get all of 'em together, and all of them talked to me at one time. When they'd get through, he said, 'No more.'

"That saved me a lot of time to go talk to my parents after the games and stuff. 'Cause they were crowdin' me.

"I'll tell you the worst thing about it was that, when I got out of school, I realized all that pamperin' (protection, guidance) I was gettin'. I needed it when I got in the NFL.

"To make a point, when I got in the NFL, I had never done drugs. When I got up there with the guys that I started hangin' around with and associating with, they led me astray. Well, I did it. Because I should never have started that in the first place, because that wasn't what kind of person I was.

"But after you get on your own and start realizing how much money you've got—and especially me. Because I never knew how much free time I had, until I started gettin' involved with drugs. And that's the worst thing I ever did.

"'Cause when all that stuff happened to me, I stayed in the hospital three months. I didn't even go outside. I was so depressed

Rogers led the NFL in rushing, set a new rookie record, and was named Rookie-of-the-Year with the New Orleans Saints in 1981.

and so heartbroken from me being George Rogers and the Heisman Trophy winner. I just couldn't face-up to a lot of people.

"They were eatin' me up. I must have gained ninety pounds after that happened, 'cause I didn't workout; I didn't run; I didn't do nuthin', man. I was just totally depressed. Depressed so much that all my enthusiasm for football had left me. I tell you, man, that's behind me now.

"But I didn't have to go to any rehabilitation center. I had to let the team know that I wasn't hooked on drugs, which I wasn't. But I had so much free time, and people was comin' around me so fast, I didn't know. I just didn't know. I was a victim of circumstances—that's the way I look at it.

"Now that it's over with, I just thank God that I didn't have to let Brandon and them right there (motioning to his children) see me do all that. Now I've got a family, and it's workin' out right. I got three kids—three real good kids. Now, I've got something to do with my money, instead of throwin' it away.

"At that time, Coach Carlen, again, said, 'Babe, hey, I'm on your side. I'm you friend.'

"Right at that time I didn't think I had no friends, besides my girl friend (wife, Lynn). She's the one that really stuck by me. In the beginning, she didn't know I was doin' it. I was just hiding it from everybody, except the guys I was doin' it with.

"I believe, if I'd never gone to New Orleans or had some of the teammates I had, I'd have never started in the first place. I'd never seen nuthin' like that, before I went there. I'm a man, though, and I had my own mind, and, if I didn't want to do it, I didn't have to. I did do it, and it cost me. It didn't cost anybody else.

"I think I'm a stronger person now. I would never—you couldn't even pour none of that stuff on me anymore. And, if I'd see you with it, I'd tell on you. They won't even come around me no more with it. 'Cause that's something I should have never done, and didn't realize it, till I got caught.

"I walked away, and, thank God, I can hold my head up and do some of the things I used to do. You don't have to do drugs to have friends. This can happen to anybody—it just didn't happen to me. There are a lot of NFL teams that get rookies that come in, and the veterans influence 'em, and they go right to drugs.

"I didn't think I had to go along to be accepted. I thought, since I had all the money . . . Aaaahhh maaannn, you didn't want to know me then. I can't elaborate on some of the things that went on. I was totally out of my control at one time.

"If it hadn't been for Lynn and having babies . . . if it hadn't been for her, I don't think I'd have made it. She's my home girl—she's from Duluth. We dated a little bit when I was in high school, and broke up, and went back together. I said, 'If I'm gonna spend my money anymore, I'm gonna spend it on her.'

"I've got George the third, born on Christmas Day. And that's Brandon, and I've got my little girl, Lashaun."

Rogers' Heisman Trophy season had been followed with his selection as the first player in the NFL draft, going to the New Orleans Saints, who had only one victory against 15 defeats in 1980. George had a sensational rookie season, leading the NFL rushers with 1,674 yards, a new record for rookies, receiving Rookie-of-the-Year honors, and playing in the prestigious Pro Bowl in Honolulu.

With the offense centered around Rogers, the Saints won four games in 1981, and optimism surrounded the future of the team under Coach Bum Phillips. In the strike-shortened 1982 season, Rogers' yardage dropped to 535, but he was back up to 1,144 in 1983, in spite of missing three games and part of a fourth with a leg injury. The Saints finished 8-8 and barely missed a playoff berth.

In 1984 Rogers was whole again, but his role in the Saints offense had diminished, and he was called on to run mostly on first down, when the entire world knew what was going to happen. Later in the season, Phillips made a trade that brought another former Heisman Trophy winner, Earl Campbell, to the Saints. Phillips had previously coached Campbell at Houston. The New Orleans coach then alternated Campbell and Rogers, and neither approached the effectiveness of their past efforts. It was not a happy situation for either.

However, Rogers looks back on his productive college career and forward to, perhaps, a more satisfactory role with another NFL team.

Rogers: "I think Bum really got mad because I did those drugs that time. That's what I think—I don't care what anybody else thinks. He knows I'm not doin' it now, but I don't think he got over the first time.

"I don't want to play for him no more. I want to play for a new team this year, hopefully. I am, anyway. I've gotta be in a trade, 'cause I don't want to play for him no more. They're gonna have to trade me, or pay me for just sittin' around. I ain't gonna share no time, because I haven't got long, and I can't make the Pro Bowl that way.

"I'd love to play for the Washington Redskins and Joe Gibbes. Or Seattle or Miami. But I want to play for the Washington Redskins. I don't want to tell him (Phillips), because I think he already knows; because of the way I've been saying it in the paper and stuff. I ain't said, 'Bum, I don't wanta play for you no more. I ain't said that. But he's gotta know I don't wanta play there.

"Ed's (Ed Holler, Rogers' attorney) already told him I wanta get traded, and these are the teams I wanta get traded to."

On April 26, exactly three weeks after Rogers made the above remarks, the Washington Redskins held a press conference to announce the acquisition of Rogers from the Saints in exchange for their No. 1 pick in the NFL draft. As a practical matter, the Saints were receiving the 24th overall pick in the draft, and they gave up Rogers, plus their fifth-, 10th, and 11th-round choices in the draft.

This placed Rogers with a club that had played in two of the past three Super Bowls and whose top running back, John Riggins, was 36 years old, bothered with back problems, and contemplating retirement. Rogers could now look to the future with optimism and ambition, as he accepted a brand new Redskins football jersey with a number that assured him of retaining his beloved "38."

Rogers: "I want to play long enough to accomplish some of the things I've always wanted to, like two thousand yards. I can get two thousand yards, if I play. I wanted to do it before (Curtis) Dickerson (Rams) did it, but Bum really messed me up. He didn't give me the ball at all—I averaged thirteen carries per game." (Rogers averaged 24 carries as a rookie.)

Looking back over a college career, obviously a back who achieved as much as Rogers did could reflect on many highlights.

Rogers: "I particularly remember the N.C. State game my senior year. (Carolina won, 30-10, and Rogers ran for 193 yards and three touchdowns.) I tell you what, I hit some people that game. I separated one guy's shoulder and hurt about three of 'em on one play. I've forgotten what it was, but I hit this one guy—BOOM—man, he bounced off, and I kept goin' forward. I fell down, but nobody tackled me. I slipped on the turf.

"I was north and south, If I could make a move on you I did, but I didn't have too many moves, unless I was in an open field."

A more painful experience came against Georgia, when, in the fourth quarter, Carolina had moved inside the Bulldog 20, mostly on Rogers' determined runs. Removed from the game, because he was slightly "shaken up" on a sweep, Rogers was sent back in and fumbled on the next play, Georgia recovering.

Rogers: "I tell you what I remember most—the fumble. And Coach Carlen didn't blame it on me, and it should have been on me. He took up for me. My hand was bleeding and stuff, but, if you play football, you're going to get cuts and stuff. Everybody was tryin' to say that I was hurt, but I wasn't. I'm tellin' you I wasn't. I just fumbled. Why? 'Cause I got hit—the guy just knocked the ball out of my hands.

"I was depressed for that whole week. We had to play another game (The Citadel), and they called me from upstairs to ask me what's wrong with me; because I still hadn't gotten over the fumble from the Georgia game.

"We were playin' Citadel. Stump Mitchell? I said, 'Here we go again. If it ain't Herschel (Walker), it's Stump. Every week—somebody. (Mitchell finished third in the nation in rushing, behind Rogers and Marcus Allen of Southern Cal.)

"All of a sudden, Coach Brown said, 'Look, you're gonna have to forget about that game in Georgia.'

"I was tryin' to forget about it, but that game stuck with me the whole week, because I had fumbled; and, if I hadn't fumbled, we'd have tied it or we would have beaten 'em. I couldn't take it."

In what George described as his depressed state of mind, he gained 179 yards and scored two touchdowns, leading Carolina to a comfortable, 45-24, win.

Although it was obvious that opposing defenses were geared to stop him, as Carolina's offense was described as "Rogers right, Rogers left, and Rogers up the middle," the Gamecock star recalled few cases of unusually severe physical or verbal treatment.

Rogers: "I never got much comment out of anybody since I've been playing football. We played Oklahoma State (1979-SC 23, OSU 16), and a defensive back started talkin' that noise to me, and I told him I was gonna get him. And I got him, too.

"I smacked him—you can get a defensive back. Now, you can't get those linemen as much as those defensive backs. They usually try to steal you all the time—wait till somebody stands you up, and then come in and try to hit you.

"But, man, we were goin' one-on-one in that situation, and I hit him and went down his back with my face mask. When I hit him, he ducked, so I went ahead and ran my helmet down his back."

George refused to join in speculation that, with a more prominent passing attack, his road would have been easier.

Rogers: "I would say that Garry (Harper) wasn't tall enough to play quarterback, but, to me, he was pretty good. He could throw, but he was just throwin' what they gave him to throw at. Just told him to throw out, and out, and out. We never did send somebody deep, except that one play against Wake Forest. (62-yard TD pass from Harper to Horace Smith with 57 seconds left to win. 39-38).

"Like (Mike) Hold is doin' (USC quarterback in 1984). We didn't have none of that. If we had him—boy, boy, boy—we'd have been real good!

"Our linemen were more for a running team—George Schechterly, Fred David (senior in 1979), Steve Gettel, Mark Austin, Chuck Slaughter, Willie Scott, and Ben Cornett. You talk about a line—those boys came off the ball. They were makin' me look good, and they were gettin' all the injuries.

"They were always callin' me 'smiley.' Made me sick when they said that. But they took up for me. Plenty of times they were hittin' me late, and my linemen would come over there and try to fight. They said, 'Stay off George!'

"It wasn't like I was doin' it, that's why it was OUR Heisman Trophy, instead of mine. I loved playin' with those guys, and they liked playin' with me, too. I asked Coach Carlen if I could take 'em to the Heisman dinner, but he said he couldn't take all of 'em. He said all the seniors can go, and all of 'em went. Coach Carlen was a good guy, I'm tellin' you.

"We rode on Governor Riley's plane, and I really liked that. We had a real good time. Everybody else was ridin' on a little private plane, and we had the governor's jet! I had my mama and my aunt (Otella Rogers of Duluth), and I had a real good time.

"I tell you what, we had a good time when we were playin' here, but we didn't have more fun than those guys now (1984). Those guys are having a real good time—that's what makes them a better team than when we were playin'.

"Some of the things they're doin' now, you couldn't have paid one of us to do. They hit somebody, and they jump up 'n down. We couldn't do that. Coach Carlen didn't allow you to do none of that, you know. He thought that was hot doggin'. Back then, it was. Now, everybody's doin' it. You know, when you make a tackle, you jump up. Tony Guyton (1984 junior tackle)—I've heard how he runs around the grass before the game. That emotionally fires your team up. That helps.

"Coach (Joe) Morrison is a real, real good coach. I've gotten to know almost his whole coaching staff, like Coach (Tom) Gadd and Coach (Keith) Kephart. I like Kephart, he's a real nice guy and a

Rogers gestures to the Heisman Trophy, as he addresses the Carolina student body. (Photo courtesy of the The State, Columbia)

smart strength coach, too. They've got some people down there that know their stuff. When I was there, we had some good people, too.

"But the facilities at Carolina now are three hundred times better than when I was there. They've got the new dressing room, and the new weight room. They're gonna get better players, because of the facilities.

"Yeh, I've been asked to contact prospects. I do it, because I want Carolina to do good. That gives me my braggin' rights when I'm in the NFL. I bragged on 'em so hard this past year. When they were nine and O—aaahhh maaannn—you should have seen me. I said, 'We're gonna be number one!'

"And they went up there and let Navy beat 'em. And these guys shot that stuff right back to me, 'cause I had been braggin' on 'em all year.

"I won more beer than I lost. I usually would be losin' a whole lot of 'em the last two years. But, this year, I got it all back. Especially when they were playin' Florida State. Everybody thought Florida State was gonna beat 'em, and I was right in my hotel room watchin'. Wasn't that a show?!" (Carolina won, 38-27, in a nationally televised game.)

Rogers was much impressed with the Gamecocks, especially running backs Kent Hagood and Thomas Dendy. When Hagood was a freshman he was hailed as "the next George Rogers," and he had shown flashes of brilliance before suffering a broken leg against North Carolina State and missing the Gamecocks' final three games, including the upset to Navy.

Looking ahead to the future, when his earning potential will likely decline, Rogers has a good agent—Jack Mills of Denver—and a financial consultant—Don Bailey (Former Carolina defensive back, 1968-70) of E.F. Hutton in Charleston, South Carolina.

Rogers: "Don is doin' a real good job. I'm into the timberwoods, oil, apartments in Los Angeles, and condominiums out there. I just started gettin' money about a year ago. I had it in there about four years, and I'm sayin', 'Gollee, what about my investments?'

"He said, 'George, it takes two or three years before they even get started. I'll be pretty well off when I get through playin'. Football's not everything.

"I think I could do a good job coachin'. If I got into coachin', you know where I want to coach? Carolina. I wouldn't go any farther than that. I'd beg Coach Morrison for a job! Hopefully, he'll still be there."

Adversity hasn't been lacking in the 26 years that George Rogers has been on this earth, but it hasn't deprived him of that wide grin, which was his trademark during the quest for the Heisman Trophy. He still has that ability to laugh aloud when he laments the bad times, as well as when he remembers the happy ones.

You would think that a young man who emerged from a background that promised nothing into a situation that brought national acclaim might be content to rest his case. The fifth grader who couldn't afford the insurance premium to play little league football, now discusses six-figure investments and financial security. And the home he bought in Atlanta for his mother.

The green kid who didn't know where the end zone was found it more often than any player in 93 years of football at the University of South Carolina. That nervous tenth-grader who tip-toed up to the line in Duluth, Georgia, became bold enough to defy the leading defenses of college and professional football enroute to winning rushing championships in both, along with the most prestigious awards they could offer.

Rogers reflects the added maturity that new experiences, new challenges, successes, and failures bring to a person.

"I wouldn't trade my years with Coach Carlen or with the University for anything in the world," Rogers said, philosophically. "What would I change? Probably my attitude toward going to school. I could have learned a whole lot more than I did learn.

"Still, I wouldn't trade my four years of college for anything. Nobody can take those years away, either."

Yet burning inside of Rogers seems to be the same desire to achieve that enabled him to accomplish what only a special few football players have achieved. There are still goals to be attained, and, behind that fun-loving exterior of George Rogers lies an unwavering determination.

Rogers contributed more to the Carolina football program than just the highest honor in its history—the Heisman Trophy. He brought a new, more positive atmosphere, to the program, and a new level of national identification.

It was more than coincidence that, following Rogers' run to glory, the following names were among the freshman recruits:

Emory Bacon, Bill Barnhill, Bill Bradshaw, Chris Corley, Tony Guyton, Kent Hagood, Ira Hillary, Earl Johnson, Quinton Lewis, Skip Minton, James Seawright, Harry South, James Sumpter, Chris Wade, Frank Wright, Tom Garner, Hinton Tayloe, and others. These were the freshmen who became the senior base for the Gamecocks' fabulous 1984 season. The excitement created by Rogers enhanced Carolina's attractiveness to talented high school prospects.

There's no doubt that Rogers' presence enabled the University to sell-out every home game (in 1980) for the first time in its history, and the Gamecock Club experienced the largest increase (28%) ever in its receipts, which grew from $1.504 million in 1980 to $1.928 million in 1981.

Thus, George Rogers has earned a unique position in Carolina football, comparable to Red Grange at Illinois, Charlie Justice at North Carolina, and Tony Dorsett at Pittsburgh. Regardless of how many great ones pull garnet or black jerseys over their heads in future years, none could ever replace the unique position created by the powerful tailback who wore number 38 with such class.

Nobody can name the second person who flew solo across the Atlantic Ocean, but everybody remembers Charles Lindbergh.

By the same token what Carolina devotee can ever forget George Washington Rogers, the likeable young man who extended the horizons of the school's football program and provided that long missing ingredient—an authentic legend.

George Rogers' Run to Glory

OPPONENT	NO.	YARDS	TDS
1977			
Georgia Tech	12	36	0
Appalachian St.	9	40	0
Miami (O)	6	46	1
Georgia	9	30	0
E. Carolina	17	78	1
Duke	15	68	1
Mississippi	7	50	0
North Carolina	21	87	0
N.C. State	10	53	0
Wake Forest	22	97	0
Clemson	5	15	0
Hawaii	10	23	0
	143	623	3

Rogers happily displays his Washington Redskins jersey at the announcement of his trade from the Saints on April 27, 1985. (AP Photo)

1978			
Furman	12	53	2
Kentucky	16	63	0
Duke	23	150	1
Georgia	29	128	1
Georgia Tech	21	148	0
Ohio	9	33	0
Mississippi	(Injured and did not play)		
North Carolina	2	3	0
N.C. State	14	68	0
Wake Forest	27	237	2
Clemson	21	123	0
	174	1,006	6

1979			
North Carolina	23	97	0
Western Michigan	19	93	0
Duke	28	161	2
Georgia	28	152	0
Oklahoma State	35	165	2
Mississippi	27	158	1
Notre Dame	30	113	0
N.C. State	30	217	1
Florida State	21	186	1
Wake Forest	18	104	1
Clemson	27	102	0
Missouri	25	133	0
	311	1,681	8
1980			
Pacific	13	153	2
Wichita State	10	108	2
Southern Cal	26	141	1
Michigan	36	142	1
N.C. State	26	193	3
Duke	36	224	1
Cincinnati	22	128	0
Georgia	35	168	0
The Citadel	27	179	2
Wake Forest	38	177	2
Clemson	28	168	0
Pittsburgh	27	113	0
	324	1,894	14
CAREER TOTALS	954	5,204	33

(All USC records, as of 1984)

Honors Acquired by Rogers

1979—All-America: Associated Press, first team; National Editorial Alliance (NEA), first team; United Press International, second team; American Football Coaches, second team; Football News, second team.

1980—Heisman Trophy Winner

College Football Player-of-the-Year, ABC-Television Sports. All-American first team: Associated Press; United Press International; National Editorial Alliance; American Football Coaches; Football News; The Sporting News; Walter Camp Foundation; Football Writers of America.

1981—National Football League Rookie-of-the-Year

All-Pro Team, NFL

Selected for the Pro Bowl

Set new rushing record for NFL rookies

RUSHING RECORD WITH
NEW ORLEANS SAINTS

	NO.	YARDS	AVE.	TDS
1981	378	1,674*	4.4	13*
1982	122	535	4.4	3
1983	256	1,144	4.5	5
1984	239	914	3.8	2
TOTAL	995*	4,267*	4.3	23

*Saints Record

Rogers also set a new Saints record of 206 yards rushing for a single game against St. Louis in 1983. Rogers had rushed for over 100 yards in 16 games, through 1984, also a Saints record.

WILLIE **Scott**

47

TIGHT END

The shadow of the Heisman Trophy winner was turned into a spotlight by Willie Scott. The National Football League selected him as the nation's number one tight end, and Carolina coaches recognized him as the ultimate team player.

15 WILLIE SCOTT

On that crisp morning of December 11, 1980, Willie Scott found himself in high cotton. Seated comfortably aboard a Lear jet, as it zoomed above the towns and farmlands of South Carolina, he exchanged idle chatter with Governor Richard Riley. Most of the talk centered around football, and their destination was New York City.

Three of Scott's teammates were also passengers—George Schechterly, Steve Gettel, and Ben Cornett. They were the senior starters in the offensive line for the University of South Carolina football team, and their main occupation during the fall had been clearing the path for the nation's leading rusher and Heisman Trophy winner, George Rogers.

The four Gamecock linemen had been excused from practicing for the Gator Bowl game against Pittsburgh on this special day, and they were to attend the Heisman Trophy Award Ceremonies at the Downtown Athletic Club. They boarded the state-owned jet, along with the Governor and his two children, and headed north.

"It was a thrill seeing one of our players up on the podium with all those great ones," Scott recalled with pride. "Garrett, O.J., a lot of good ones."

In accepting the award, Rogers asked the four Gamecock linemen to stand up and take a bow, stating, "This trophy should really be awarded to my team instead of me."

"After the banquet," Scott related, "we picked up George, and he went back with us. Coach Carlen and everybody in the world got on the other plane . . . President Holderman and his wife, ex-Governor McNair . . . everybody went to the Heisman banquet."

If Rogers was any prouder or happier over the Heisman award than Scott, it wasn't evident. This makes a strong statement about the general make-up and attitude of this big guy from Newberry, South Carolina, whose career at tight end paralleled that of Rogers as a running back.

If anybody on the team could have had a temptation toward resentment over the avalanche of publicity received by Rogers, it would have been Willie Scott. In the absence of Rogers, Scott would have been the obvious choice for All-America build-up, because there wasn't a better player in the country at his position. The National Football League expressed that when the Kansas City Chiefs made him their first-round draft pick and the 14th player to be chosen in 1981. Rogers had been the number one choice, but Scott was the only tight end picked in that round.

It doesn't require a lengthy conversation with Scott to understand why he received Carolina's George Terry Best Attitude Award for the offense in 1980.

Scott: "I'm a hyper person—I'm always doing something. That was just my outlook. A lot of people would tell me I was gettin' the short end, because George was gettin' all the publicity. I said, 'We're all in this thing together, so let's just work it out.'

"You've gotta complement each other. The offensive line wanted to do great, because we knew George was back there, and when he gets publicity, we get publicity. And George knew we were doing our best to get those guys out of the way, so he could get on down the court. So, he's gonna run his best, too.

"Like a wide receiver; if he knows the quarterback is gonna throw it in the right place, he's gonna do his best to get there. If a running back knows the hole is gonna be there, he'll get there. If we know the back's gonna get there, we'll get there—we're gonna make the hole.

"I guess you could say I was a rah, rah, but a pat on the back never hurt anybody. In nineteen-eighty the seniors were the team leaders. Like Steve Gettel and George Schechterly, who was really not that much of a talker. But when George said something, you knew he meant it.

"George Rogers never said anything but, 'Let's go. Gimme the ball. I'm ready to go. Y'all give it to me; I'll be there.'

"It was a great time. George (Rogers) would say, 'Way to go, fellas—couldn't get there without you. Let's keep it going.'

"I'd say, 'Let's do it again.'

"He'd run over somebody, help 'em up. Then he'd come back and say, 'Let's get him again next time!'"

Therefore, during Rogers' quest for the Heisman, Scott became a part of college football's number one escort service. His primary duty became blocking for the Gamecocks' potent running attack, especially after a disappointing opening game loss to North Carolina in 1979.

Scott: "We lost to North Carolina, twenty-eight to nothing, and we had been picked by *Sports Illustrated* as one of the top teams in the nation. That's a heck of a way to start off.

"They were trying to mess with Coach Carlen about being both athletic director and head coach. He pulled us to the side and said, 'Men, hey, I'm gonna be here. If I leave, they better stack my money nice and neat in a Brinks truck, and I'll be gone. But y'all just play ball, and I'll worry about the press and the school being on my back and all that. You guy's just play—you just play.'

"And when the man comes up to you and says, 'Don't worry about all this stuff that's ramroddin' you from the side; y'all just do your part . . .'

"That's what it's all about!

"Ben Cornett and I shuffled in plays the first three games. Then, Coach Carlen pulled us in at halftime and said, 'We're going to two tight ends. It might not look good, but it's effective.' We played that way the last two years.

"They used to call us 'the twins.' Look at our backgrounds a little bit. We're both from South Carolina. Both play tight end. Both came to the University. Ben's also an Episcopalian. Only thing that's different is Ben's sort of the quiet type, and I'm the talkative type. And he was white, and I was black.

"My junior year I had made a big turnaround, as far as strength is concerned. Ken Shipp (who served as offensive coach under Marvin Bass at Carolina in 1963) was a good friend of Coach Carlen; he was coaching at Houston. He came down here, and Coach Shipp told me—I think it was my sophomore year when he was helping us out a little—'Son, you can play ball, if you get stronger. Start getting on those weights, and two years from now you'll be a first round draft pick.'

"I thought he was just joking. That was a turnaround period in my life, because I finally realized that this weight lifting was going to help me out.

"Me and DeWayne Chivers lived together, and that's all we did—eat, sleep, and lift weights. That's all we did, and it turned out pretty good. I raised my bench press seventy-five pounds over the summer. I moved it up to three hundred and twenty-five pounds, and that's not too bad.

Willie Scott dives on a Gamecock fumble to his team's first touchdown in a 30-10 win over North Carolina State in 1980. (Photo courtesy of The State, Columbia)

"When I came to Carolina, the first thing I had to work on was blocking. My pass catching was always halfway decent. Being big, in high school all I had to do was lean on people, and they'd move out of the way. Then, when you come to college, you've got other athletes who are just as good as you. You've got to do something besides trying to muscle 'em out the way.

"Working with Jerry Sullivan (receivers coach), I got to be pretty good at blocking. I usually had to block the defensive end that was standing over me; occasionally had to go down and hit a linebacker; and occasionally had to double team a defensive tackle. Going against (John) Dantonio every day and working with Coach Sullivan, all we did was work on hook blocking and drive blocking. Drive blocking is taking a man straight on, trying to get him out the way—running a play right behind me. Hook blocking is when I want to get to his outside and keep him pinned in, so we can pitch the ball to the outside.

275

"Which is actually what we did my sophomore and junior years. Whenever Johnny got hurt we put George back there at tailback, but even before that, all we did was pitch left and right, especially when we got into that two tight end offense.

"When you've got an awesome running back like George Rogers in the backfield and Johnny Wright, who was my roommate for a year—these guys make a whole lot of things happen for you. When people started realizing he was coming this way, they were trying to jump to the outside; and, in that case, I'd just keep on pushing him, and George or Johnny would cut back. That would be history, if everybody else did their job.

"When people know it's coming at 'em, they're gonna be ready, for it puts them in bad position and can put them out of place. A lot of times that happened. They run out there, and there's a big gap between them and the tackle, because they don't think together. Whichever side it went to, the end was the key block. If we took him out, he (runner) cut it back in; if we pinned him off, he took it around the outside.

"When you get an exceptional running back, you don't have to do a whole lot. All it takes is one or two good shots to get him in the wrong position, if he's cutting right, he's gone. Sometimes all good blocking is getting in the right position and shielding him off—and he's history then."

Now, don't get the idea that Scott did nothing but collide with defensive ends and linebackers, paving the way for running backs, because he was the pass-catchingest tight end ever to play for Carolina. During the 1980 season, while Rogers was leading the nation in rushing, Scott led the Gamecocks in receiving, with 34 catches and 469 yards. His career total of 70 catches was fourth (as of 1985) among all Carolina receivers, and they were good for 896 yards and seven touchdowns.

If you had to pick one reception that stood out above all others, you couldn't find one that was more significant than a catch against Clemson in the final game of 1979. It turned out to be a key play in gaining the Gamecocks their first eight-win season ever and a bid to play in the Hall-of-Fame Bowl at Birmingham, Alabama. The situation in Williams-Brice Stadium was 2:39 left in the half, with Carolina in possession at the SC 29 on a third down play.

Scott: "It was a delay pass. I was blocking on the left side, and I laid back for three counts, then I stepped over the middle, turned around, caught the ball (from quarterback Garry Harper) and ran. I caught it right on the hash and took it down the sideline for about sixty yards. Eddie Geathers (cornerback) caught me from behind (at the nine-yard line).

"Coach Carlen˙said, 'I didn't know he could run that fast.' People said I wasn't s'pose to get that far. I'm one of those players that doesn't do things for statistics, but get the ball in my hands, and then we can run."

Scott's catch and run set-up a Harper-to-Cornett TD pass with four seconds left in the half, putting the Gamecocks up, 13-6, and they held on to win the game, 13-9. That gave Carolina a final 8-4 record, if you include a loss to Missouri in the Hall of Fame Bowl.

The following season (1980), at Clemson, Scott was involved in another key play, which backfired in Clemson's favor. With the Gamecocks and Tigers tied at 3-all in the third quarter, Carolina had the ball at the Clemson 16, when Harper threw a sideline pass toward Scott, only to watch Willie Underwood of the Tigers intercept and run it back to the Gamecock 24-yard line. Clemson scored to take the lead, and, moments later, widened it, when Underwood intercepted another Harper pass—this one intended for Cornett—to score and put the game out of reach.

Scott: "We were supposed to go up there and just wear Clemson out. We beat 'em everywhere except on the scoreboard. Those two passes were identical. The same guy (Underwood)—he became a hero for that. He was playing for Eddie Geathers, who got hurt the week before. He (Underwood) really never played that much. And he wound up being the hero of the whole week.

"It was like a little outlet pass, that's when I'm out at the sideline. It's supposed to be thrown out of bounds, where nobody can catch it, except the receiver. The guy was in the right place at the right time. When you've got a fresh player in there, sometimes he's guessing. An experienced player wouldn't have been there; this guy was taking chances. If I had taken two steps when I saw him coming, it would have been a touchdown the other way. Sometimes that's how you set-up a player who comes in.

"George (Rogers) caught him on the twenty-four—but we were on the ten. So, he ran about sixty yards. I remember Coach Carlen talking about that—all the running ability that George had. He ran him down. He turned around from a full start, took off and caught him. That says a lot for a guy that all he does is run the ball—to turn around and make a touchdown-saving tackle."

This led to the subject of Garry Harper, who quarterbacked

the Gamecocks through two eight-win seasons in 1979 and 1980, including big victories over Georgia at Athens, Michigan at Ann Arbor, and Clemson.

Scott: "Some people try to say Garry wasn't a good quarterback. Regardless, he was the best thing we had and exactly what we needed. And it worked; that's the name of the game. He did exactly what he knew how to do, and he did it well.

"He pitched it out, and he threw occasionally, and it went where it was supposed to. Garry was an exceptional athlete. He didn't even play football until he was, like, a senior in high school. So, this must be a pretty smart person who can pick up on something like that, and keep it going."

As of 1984, Harper was Carolina's third ranking passer in career completions (225) and yards (2,971), and ranked sixth in total offense (3,137 yards).

Ironically, one of Scott's finest games was not at all good for the Gamecocks, as they fell to Pittsburgh, 37-9, in the 1980 Gator Bowl. Pittsburgh, which was ranked fourth in the nation, featured defensive end Hugh Green, who was runner-up to Rogers in the Heisman Trophy voting.

Scott: "A lot of people say that game raised my awareness level, as far as the coaches (NFL) were concerned, quite a bit. There were two or three plays that made the difference in that whole game.

"One was right before halftime, when a guy interfered with me in the end zone. Everybody complained, but the referee didn't call it. The guy hit me on my foot, but you can't change the call. That would have been a touchdown and made it thirteen to ten.

"Right before the half, I got to the one-foot line. That was a little swing pass; I bounced off the guy and ran it on down. (Last play of the half.)

"Hugh Green was supposed to be one of the best, and I kinda kept him under control." (Green was involved in only five tackles in the game.)

The close relationship between runner and blocker—Rogers and Scott—didn't end on the football field.

Scott: "We were all tight—we had to be tight. George and I were pretty good friends. He lived right around the hall. We came in (to USC) together, and we had to grow together as a team and as individuals. We used to ride down to Atlanta on occasions, because

Heisman Trophy winner George Rogers (38) cuts behind a block by Willie Scott (47) enroute to a touchdown against The Citadel in 1980. (Photo courtesy of The State, Columbia)

that's where he was from, and he got to be pretty good friends with my sister (student at Spellman College).

"I didn't see the George Rogers saga (TV special on Rogers). I do remember where I took him when he told me to take him home up at Duluth (15 miles north of Atlanta). It was quite a different background from mine. But what you see on the outside still may not have anything to do with on the inside—the love and affection, and the people that are behind you. Money can't buy happiness, and money can't buy support. It can't buy the tenderness in someone's heart for a child.

"I see George every now and then. He works out in the after-noon early, and I usually get there a little later."

Although Carlen developed a public reputation for abruptness and often saying the wrong thing at the wrong time, he came across as a genuine person to Scott and his teammates.

Scott: "I liked his coaching style. Some people say I have a biased opinion, because I never had any controversy, as far as play-ing, and all that. I liked him, because he was straight up. I like to know where a man stands.

"Coach Carlen, he'd tell us, 'You know, I love all of y'all. I might not like some of you, but I love all of you. I'm gonna take care of you.'

"And, where I was concerned, that's what he did.

"We were all in this together, and we were winning. You have all kind of problems when you go five-five-one and five-seven—he's playing favorites, and all that. But when you're winning, people pop you on the back, and say, 'Let's keep going. Save a little bit for me. Both those years Dewayne Chivers was playing behind Ben Cornett and me, and all he could say was, 'Way to go, Willie. Way to go, Ben. Save some of Hugh Green for me—I want some of him.'

"Coach Carlen didn't say too much, but when he said some-thing, you knew it was said. If he came down out of the tower, you knew there was something going on—something heavy.

"For instance, getting ready for the Gator Bowl, Coach Carlen had a speaking engagement. He left with the coaches that we were supposed to be out (at practice) like an hour. Coach Carlen came back, and we were on the field. He said, 'I thought I said one hour.' We'd been out there about an hour and fifteen minutes. 'Get in!' And that was it.

"Coach Carlen was not a believer in long, drawn out practices. He was more of a quality man. An hour and fifteen minutes was long enough. Spend your time well and go. That's what we did.

"In 1979, except for George Schechterly, who had transferred from Penn State, Carlen had recruited all the players. He would say, 'Now I've got all the players I recruited; I know what you're made of; I think I know what you can do; I know what your capabilities are. Let's see you do it. Period.'"

Carlen had recruited Scott from Newberry High School, and it turned out to be one of the prize catches of his five freshman groups.

Scott: "Coming into high school, I had all the skills, because my dad (Willie Scott, Sr.) was a high school coach. When I was in the seventh and eighth grades I practiced with him and did everything they did, except the contact. When I got to high school it was kinda automatic—I went on and played. My freshman year, my father stopped coaching and moved up to assistant principal."

Scott had an active four years at Newberry High School, playing football and basketball and participating in the triple jump, long jump, high jump, and 440-yard relay for the track team. When young Scott grew to 6 feet, 5 inches and 227 pounds as a senior, quite a few college football coaches became interested in seeing that he obtained a higher education.

Scott: "My dad said, 'You're going to get your education, even if you have to stop playing ball. I don't want to see you go to the school where you can get in; I want you to go to the school where you want to go. I want you to have the choice of where you want to go to school.

"Coming out of high school, I told the people out of state to leave me along. I got a letter from Notre Dame; the Naval Academy wanted me to come play basketball; and I had an opportunity to go to West Point.

"I decided to save my father some money, so I narrowed it down to Carolina and Clemson. Every other weekend I was at one of the two. Living halfway between, I never took sides; never gave it a second thought.

"I had people from Carolina and Clemson at my door all the time. Coach (Red) Parker was at Clemson, but right at the Shrine Bowl (in which Scott played defensive end), that's when Parker got fired, and (Charlie) Pell took over.

"One of the ironic things—I graduated in nineteen seventy-seven—if you look back, you'll find that, nineteen seventy-seven through nineteen eighty-one, the University of South Carolina was the only place in the state, besides P.C., to have the same coach all four years. I had Carlen the whole four years.

"The deciding factor in my going to Carolina was that the first person I talked to when I came to the University was the academic adviser, Coach Harold White. Coach White and my father were in the same fraternity, and, right then, my daddy was like, 'I'm going to know exactly what you're doing in classes.'

"When I went to Clemson they were talking school, but they were talking football first. I just decided I'd better go to Carolina.

"Coach Carlen said, 'Son, you know I want you to come to school here. We haven't offered you anything. All I can offer you is a chance to play and an opportunity to build a program.'

"And that's what it's all about. I love being in a program that's on the upswing. When I came to the University they'd never won eight games in the history of the school. The first two years it was a struggle, but my junior year we go eight-three—best they'd ever had in the history of the school. And turn around and do it the second time and get the Heisman Trophy, something they said couldn't be done.

"We raised the level of awareness, and this year (1984) these boys turn around and win ten games. Now the level is raised a little bit higher. They've got to keep it going."

Scott was instrumental in attracting to Carolina one of the key performers on that 1984 team—tight end Chris Corley, who was a much sought-after player for Irmo High School near Columbia.

Scott: "Corley almost went to Ohio State. Coach (Dale) Evans came to me and said, 'Willie, I need you to talk to Chris. Chris is talking about going to Ohio State.

"I said, 'Chris, I want to talk to you a few minutes.' I said, 'Hey, you want to go to Ohio State. That's fine. You can go up there, be on another Rose Bowl team. And you'll be just another Rose Bowl team, no big deal. Here, you're ten miles from home, so your folks can see you play. You get to come to a school where they're still building. And you also get a good education. You can go to Ohio State—that's fine. But if you come to the University, and you find out I lied to you about something at the University, I'll pay for anywhere you want to go to school anywhere in the country.'

"I said, 'Hope to see you here. If I see you at Ohio State, that's fine. But I hope you come to Carolina.' And I walked out.

"I don't know if that made him decide, but he came, and he's graduating this year, and he'll have possible playing time in the NFL."

Scott is becoming an increasing authority on NFL tight ends from his vantage point with the Kansas City Chiefs, who had watched him perform impressively during the Gamecocks' 8-3 season, including an impressive victory over Michigan's Rose Bowl champions, a three-point loss to ultimate national champion Georgia, and a good showing at Southern Cal, although the Gamecocks lost by a 23-13 score.

Scott: "My senior year was supposed to be the big year of tight ends. Myself, Marvin Harvey of Southern Mississippi, Dave Young (Purdue), who made All-America—they were talking about three going in the first round. When all the smoke cleared, there was only one in the first round, and that was myself. They look at the guy's abilities, what he's done, and they also look at the person—the kind of person that he is, and if he's willing to work; willing to do the job; and not too hard to coach. They look at all these things.

"When I was there (Kansas City) with Marv Levy, blocking was more important. Now, with (John) Mackovic, it's pass catching. We've thrown fifty times in a game.

"Three years ago I was rated as the third fastest tight end in the league. I run about a four-six forty, which isn't too bad for a tight end.

"My first year I got my finger hurt right before the first pre-season game, and I didn't play that much my first year. The second year I played a little bit and started a few games. Alternated with Al Dixon.

"The third year Mackovic traded Al, and I wound up being the starter. And, last year, I was the starter also and caught about twenty-seven passes, which isn't bad for a tight end."

Scott appeared to be a young man enjoying life to the fullest, making his home in Columbia during the off-season, and, with his

Willie Scott poses in his familiar Carolina "47."

weight now at 245 pounds, he appears almost to be wearing the BMW he drives around town. He's one of those people who never met a stranger.

He talks about his agent, Marvin Demoff of Los Angeles, as if he were a member of the family.

Scott: "He only works about four people a year. He has a criminal law practice, and he just got into it because people said, 'I like you, you're a good lawyer, and you're a pretty good friend. He handled Jack Youngblood (Rams), Ray Perkins (Giants), Dan Marino (Dolphins), and John Elway (Broncos).

"I met him through this guy who knew Alex English, and he came to see me right before the Gator Bowl. My contract in eighty-one, even though I was picked fourteenth, was like number seven. My contract is up after this season. I signed a four-year contract with an option. That means I have a four-year contract definitely. At the end of four years, they can give me more money, or they can say we wish to exercise our option, which is that I make a hundred and ten per cent of what I made the year before. Which is standard, even if I didn't sign a contract.

"Right now, I'm teaching school at Mill Creek Elementary School, where I'm a substitute teacher. I'll be at this school eight weeks. I work at the National Youth Camp at the University, going into my sixth year, and I teach swimming down there. I do a lot of public speaking. I do it, not for the money, but I do it for the interaction with the kids. They know that, and we have a good time."

Scott has teaching in his blood, because both his parents have been in education as lifelong careers, his father as coach and assistant principal, and his mother, as a teacher.

Scott: "My sister (Pamela), I consider a genius. In the next six months she'll be a doctor of neuropsychiatry. She went to Spellman and was graduated Magna Cum Laude, went to Princeton in the PhD program, and now she's working for General Mills in Ossing, New York."

Nelson, Willie's brother, chose music over football, and is a sophomore at Carolina, where he is a member of the marching band, as well as leading his own band on the side.

In his travels around the NFL, the first thing Scott does when he travels to a town is look-up any Carolina alumnus on the opposing team. He was denied watching the 1984 team, because of travel, but he points out, "When you're winning big, you don't have to keep

Scott switched to number 81 with the Kansas City Chiefs.

up. All you have to do is walk in the dressing room, and they say, 'Hey, how 'bout those Cocks!'

"People ask me what I think about (Joe) Morrison and some of the players he's getting. Some of these players he's getting now are some of the kids of people he played with when he was in school. And they really couldn't care less about Carolina, but they know that Coach Morrison is there, and he's gonna take care of their kid. Not as far as money is concerned, but they know he's gonna give 'em a fair shot.

"Like Todd Blackledge (Chiefs quarterback) said, 'I didn't know you guys had Morrison. My daddy knows Morrison, Y'all got a heck of a coach.'

"I go out and speak at his (Morrison) camp, and he says, 'We appreciate you coming out, Willie. Anything we can do for you, let me know. That's what it's all about.

"And the boys like him. I haven't heard one bad thing about him. Usually, you'll hear something about a coach, but, hey, they love him."

Scott is too busy to project his life beyond his current career, but he is quick to say that, if he gets into coaching, he would like to do it on the high school level, where he would have a chance to touch someone's life. At the same time, that is an indirect tribute to his father, who spent so many years in high school coaching and touching lives.

Tight ends are normally as overlooked as the catcher in a trapeze act, but they perform highly essential jobs. They're rarely among pass reception leaders, and they don't get to run under those long bombs that they run over and over on instant replay. When they happen to be on the team with an All-America running back, they're expected to direct traffic.

The latter is exactly what Willie Scott did most of the time during his four productive years at Carolina, although under other circumstances, he would have commanded the star status. And it is such unselfish attitudes that produce winners; and NCAA rushing champions; and Heisman award recipients.

In the case of Willie Scott, it produced an unusual individual, who could no doubt be a success in whatever he undertakes, and his options will no doubt be many down the line. For now, he's content to work at his trade of dealing with menacing linebackers in the violent world of pro football during the autumn. Yet, he's just as enthusiastic, and also effective, in helping to develop the tiny bodies and searching minds of grammar school kids during the winter.

When football professionals injected the term "tight end" into the game, they were merely indicating closeness in distance to the rest of the offensive line. However, in the case of Willie Scott, "tight end" more appropriately reflects the modern slang meaning of "tight." A true closeness with everyone with whom he comes in contact.

CHARTING WILLIE SCOTT
RECEIVING

YEAR	NO.	YDS	TDS
1977	9	132	0
1978	13	127	4
1979	14	168	1
1980	34	469	2

JAMES **seawright**

Many people attributed Carolina's great 1984 season to "Black Magic." James Seawright considered it matter of mind and heart, with a touch of mesmerism from head coach Joe Morrison.

LINEBACKER

16 JAMES SEAWRIGHT

James Seawright sat there staring at a stranger—a man he had never seen before, but the man who would run his life for the next two years. Seawright was making rapid progress toward at least tying the NCAA record for having played under the greatest number of head football coaches.

It was January 1983, and Joe Morrison was introducing himself to the University of South Carolina football team. Seawright, a rising junior linebacker, was meeting his third football coach in as many years.

Jim Carlen, who recruited Seawright, had been fired in December, 1981, and his successor, Richard Bell, had met the same fate one year later.

As Morrison talked, Seawright recalls, these thoughts were running through his head: "He seems to be a shy person, like me in a way. I wonder how long he'll be here. He used to play pro football—that's good. I remember readin' in the paper he said he travels light. I said to myself, 'I hope so. The way things are going, I hope he did travel light.'"

Seawright was experiencing a much happier January in 1985. He had been named to several All-America teams, Carolina had completed the best season in its history, and Seawright could expect a respectable showing in the National Football League draft. His philosophy is to never look back, as a way of living, but he's certainly not one to forget those who have helped him in the past.

Seawright: "I had two coaches (Carlen and Bell) that I'd give my life for—just as they did for me. But we were reaching for a way to pull this thing together."

Carlen, who succeeded Paul Dietzel as head coach in 1975, had been discharged for reasons that were never publicly stated, while Bell was released for failure to follow a directive from athletic director Bob Marcum to fire four assistant coaches. Both later received sizeable monetary settlements as a result of litigation over terms of their contracts.

Now Morrison was brought in as the new saviour of the Gamecock football program, which paled further in the shadow of super success by arch rival Clemson. Morrison had coached New Mexico to a 10-1 record in 1982, and had outstanding success at the University of Tennessee at Chattanooga prior to the New Mexico job.

His 10-1 season in his second year at Carolina, climaxed with a Gator Bowl bid, was labeled "Black Magic" by joyful Carolina fans, reflecting the all-black attire worn by Morrison as he paced the sidelines.

Seawright made a major contribution to creating the "magic," leading what was labeled a "fire ant" defense, because of what you might call "swarm tackling" practiced by this unit. Even though the football program had operated in sporadic turmoil during Seawright's freshman and sophomore years, he never allowed that to question his decision to attend the school. Nor did it deter him in his quest for personal and team excellence.

When he was attending Hillcrest High School at Simpsonville, South Carolina, he pictured himself as more of a basketball player. A broken ankle suffered during his first junior varsity game when he was a freshman did nothing to warm his enthusiasm for football.

So, he concentrated on basketball and track during his sophomore semesters, later establishing a state triple-jump record that still stood in 1985. However, there was no way Coach Andy Jones was going to allow someone of Seawright's obvious athletic ability to stay away from the football field.

Seawright: "Coach asked me to come back out my junior year and take one more chance. He felt that I had the ability to play. He tried me on offense, but I really couldn't play. Had me at tight end, and I really didn't like it, 'cause you got to listen to snaps and words and changeovers—and that was messin' my head too much.

"Then they moved me to defensive tackle, which I liked better. I had a good year and got some awards, like all-conference, and most tackles on the team. And the respect of a lot of guys over me. 'Cause when I came out they were gonna dog me and run over me, but it seems like it was vice versa!

"My senior year I played linebacker, and I had a good year. One thing I had going for me—I wasn't the big, stocky, muscle type, but I was always the quick, flexible person. Could get around. And I'd find a way to make it to the ball. I used my speed."

That speed was enough to make Seawright competitive in the sprints and broad jump, and it was track that led to his first meeting with Carlen, whose assistant coaches had been impressed by James' football potential.

Seawright: "I saw Coach Carlen my junior year. I came down here (Columbia) for the state, and during that time Coach (Dale) Evans told me that Coach Carlen wanted to talk to me. So, I went to his office, and it surprised him when I walked in. I didn't say much. Just smiled. This was somebody I had never seen, but he was a straightforward person, and he was tellin' me about coming here to play.

"He told me, 'I'm not worried about your ability, because I can tell on the film. I'm worried about your grades. You've got your two-point-two grade-point average, but we also want to build it up.

"He was the only coach who had ever said anything about building my grades up. He said then I could be anything I wanted to, and I told him I wanted to be a Criminal Justice major. Coach told me, 'You've got to have your grades, because football isn't going to carry you all your life. You've got to have something to fall back on.'

"So, I was impressed with what he was sayin', and before I left to run my event he said, 'You're a junior now. You'll be a rising senior. If you want this scholarship, it'll be waiting for you. When you're ready, let me know.'

"It was the last day before signing day before I signed. During basketball (1980-81) they kept asking me what was my decision, but they didn't pressure me. Clemson and Georgia kept on, but Clemson was the main one. I called coach Evans and told him I was ready. I was at school with my mother, they took a picture of us, and she was happy. At first she wanted me to go to Clemson."

The Bulldogs and Tigers really never had a chance, as Seawright explains: "I hated Clemson, because our high school rival was Mauldin, and they wore orange, like Clemson. So, I never could stand it. My principal was a Georgia fan—wanted us to go to Georgia. 'Goin' to Georgia, right?'

"No, I'm not plannin', unless something comes up. Some teachers wanted me to go to Clemson, so I was really in the middle, 'cause nobody talked about South Carolina.

"Georgia didn't recruit me hard at first. Like, if you come, we'll give you a scholarship. But not a lot of enthusiasm.

"I thought about Clemson. They recruited me, but they already had their superstars, like J.D. (Jeff Davis), 'the judge'. I wanted to be Seawright and go somewhere I could play. I've always given it all I have, and I didn't want to sit on the bench and lose that determination."

Although he was selected on the South Carolina 4-A all-state team, Seawright was not selected to play in the Shrine Bowl, which matches all-stars from South Carolina against a squad from North Carolina in Charlotte each year. Seawright was selected for the intra-state North-South game, but he felt that he should have been chosen for the more prestigious Shrine Bowl.

Seawright: "I felt like I was cheated. I'm not puttin' the North-South down, but it isn't the same."

Of his decision to cast his lot with the Gamecocks, Seawright recalls, "When I got here I was happy. My freshman year wasn't as good a season as I wanted, but I said what I was gonna do before I came here, and I did that year. Except for injuries."

Seawright cut his college teeth on a team that eventually won six and lost six, ranging from a 31-13 rout of North Carolina, ranked No. 3 in the nation at the time, to humbling losses to Cincinnati, at home, and Hawaii at Honolulu.

As fall practices began, Seawright had found himself competing with two sophomore linebackers who had already earned their spurs—J.D. Fuller and Mike Durrah.

Seawright: "I was on the third unit and trying to work my way up. I had respect for them (the other linebackers), because they had helped me. But, at the same time, we had an understanding that whoever outworked the other would start, and there'd be no grief or misunderstanding.

"During practices I had to learn one lesson—to always be alert. I would mess around and wasn't alert like I normally was, and Percy Reeves (senior running back from Columbia) caught me up under the chin and knocked out my two front teeth. So, that's a lesson I learned.

"They gave me all kind of names. They called me 'Jam Daddy'. I liked that better, 'cause I feel like I'm jammin' sometimes.

"Another lesson. Coach Carlen called me over one day and said, 'Seawright, you run like a reindeer—you're a thoroughbred.

You've got all the qualities a football player needs. But one thing that holds you back is learning your plays. I'll start you, I'll play you then.'

"If you proved yourself he'd (Carlen) play you. But if he had doubts, no.

"I started takin' time out to learn what I needed to do in that defense. We played Wake Forest, Mississippi, and Duke. I played some against Mississippi and Duke. And I got in the last two minutes of the Georgia game."

At that point Carolina was 2-2, beating the Deacons, 23-6, and Duke, 17-3, while losing to Ole Miss, 20-13, and Georgia, 24-0. Then Pittsburgh, which had thrashed Carolina, 37-9, in the Gator Bowl the previous year, moved into Williams-Brice stadium for a game to be televised regionally by ABC-TV. A crowd of 57,000, capacity at the time, was stunned as quarterback Dan Marino passed for four first-half touchdowns to give the Panthers a 28-0 lead. ABC-TV "pulled the plug" and switched to "a more competitive game."

Seawright: "Against Pitt, Durrah went out, hurt his ankle on the first play, I believe. Coach Carlen called me and said, 'Seawright, get out there.' I said, 'Now?' And he said 'That's right.'

"I let myself go and just relaxed. This is my chance. I remember Coach (Richard) Bell (defensive coordinator) tellin' me, 'When opportunity comes, take it. If opportunity doesn't come, make it.'

"So that time I was tryin' to make opportunity, but it came. My chance to show what I could do. I wouldn't have a chance like that again, so I started playin' good.

"I sacked Marino one time, and we hit him on another play, and we made him mad. That's when he started pickin' us off. I give that man a great deal of respect, 'cause when he got up, the game was over. 'Cause he started pickin' us off. We came back, but the first couple of quarters, there was no way we could stop him."

Carolina rallied for 28 points in the second half to make the score more respectable, but Marino's final total of six touchdown passes in the game sealed an impressive victory.

Seawright: "Marino is the best quarterback I've played against. He's the best. No one can top him."

An impressive performance against Pittsburgh earned Seawright a starting position, and the Gamecocks ran up a string of four victories over Kentucky (28-14), Virginia (21-3), North Carolina (31-13), and N.C. State (20-12). The win over the Tar Heels, who were ranked No. 3, kindled bowl talk in Columbia, as Gordon Beck-

Seawright (45) participated in 15 tackles, as Carolina routed Pittsburgh, 45-21, in 1984.

ham's performance at quarterback showed promise of solving what had been a problem position. Beckham was named national back-of-the-week, completing 16 of 17 passes for 195 yards and connecting on 14 in a row for a new school record.

Seawright was the defensive standout, and Carolina fans were beginning to compare him with other fine linebackers who wore the Garnet and Black. But disaster struck in the N.C. State game, as Seawright injured his knees, watching the latter part of the contest from the bench, with both knees packed in ice.

He missed the entire game against Pacific, a bitter loss for Carlen, and, although he played against Clemson's ultimate national champions, he wasn't physically up to the challenge.

Seawright: "In the first and second quarter the fluid started coming back, and I couldn't move. I messed around and let (Homer) Jordan (Clemson quarterback) score a touchdown. I had him pinned in the backfield, but he made a fake on me, and my knees wouldn't let me bend back."

The Gamecocks had taken an early 7-0 lead over Clemson but lost, 29-13. Thus, within a two-game span, Carolina had dropped from a 6-3 record and bowl possibilities to 6-5, and a season-ending loss to Hawaii, 33-10, encouraged increasing criticism of Carlen. The Carolina coach had already alienated a lot of people with what they considered abruptness, and Carlen was in the midst of marital difficulties that ultimately led to divorce.

You'd never get James Seawright to relate any of this to the performance of the team.

Seawright: "When you lose you begin to ask questions. What does it take to get us where we want to go. And, at that time (after beating UNC) we had decided we were going to have a good season and go somewhere (bowl). We had a lot of problems—a lot of people not playing. Now, I feel everybody should have a chance to play; but, if you don't, don't start trouble. Because when one started griping, everybody else started griping about not enough playing time. We had a little trouble in the first three games—everybody wanting to start.

"We started winning, and everything went good. We knew we had to beat Pacific or Clemson to go to a bowl. So, we messed around and lost to Pacific."

Did a history of Carlen-coached teams starting the season strong and fading during latter games indicate a deficiency in physical conditioning or strength?

Seawright: "I think we could have been stronger physically, but I'm talking about strong at heart. Because you've got to have that determination. Some people think because you're big and you get out in front of somebody, they're gonna move. It's not like that.

"I was going against guys weighing like two-sixty, two-seventy, and two-eighty, and I was only weighin' about two-ten to two-fifteen. The coach can't make you do it. It's really up to yourself (strength training). They may think you're lifting hard, but you can always fake. We were lifting, but we didn't have all the facilities we have now. Now we have a weight room that's among the top ten in the nation.

"We got more weights to lift on different parts of your body, whereas in eighty-one we didn't have that. So, you had to work with what you had. It could have made a difference, but I don't always look at strength. I'm gonna look at the heart. A lot of people are stronger than me now, but when they go on the football field it's a different story.

"Coach Carlen was doing everything the head coach is s'pose to do. His part was fine. I look at the eighty-one season as OUR fault, and I'll tell anybody who was on the team with me, and I'll tell anybody else straight up. It never was the coaches, it was the players. Because, if the players won't go out and sacrifice, the coach can't go out there. He's tryin' to help you prepare. We wanted to win, but we didn't do the things it took to win.

"In eighty-one, if you made a tackle, you might get up and yell, but it wasn't like everybody runnin' to the ball. It's like you make a tackle, you go over to make sure he don't break loose. But this year (1984) it was at least four or five guys tryin' to get on one man.

"It was like offense and defense goin' at one another's throat. Sometimes we complained about being on the field too long, and the offense not movin' the ball. In eighty-one and eighty-two we were doin' a little running. The offense—they would run—but nothing like as hard as we (defense) were running. When a team sees one side have an advantage—and most of the time you get beat, they're gonna look at your defense as the weakest. So, it was a conflict in eighty-one and eighty-two.

"In eighty-three and eighty-four there was no conflict. We all worked together. We might run more than the offense, but they really didn't have it easy. We always lived together, and we all paid the price together. If one loses, we all lose. And at that point we started working together in the weight room, pushin' one another and cheering one another on. We came closer together as a family. You could feel it, because I remember tellin' some of the guys, 'We're gonna have a good year.' You just felt the closeness. And it happened my last year."

As it turned out, the Hawaii game was Carlen's finale as head coach, as he received a telephone call on a subsequent Saturday morning, informing him that he was no longer head coach at Carolina.

Seawright: "We thought coach Carlen would be there another year. We said, 'Okay, we messed up this year, but we'll come back and do better. We'll find a way.' Next thing we know, he was fired."

The University's first step toward finding a successor to Carlen was to hire an athletic director, and Bob Marcum, who had held the same position at Kansas, was the choice. Marcum's first priority was to select a head football coach, and he decided on Richard Bell, who had served as assistant head coach and defensive coordinator under Carlen for the previous seven years.

In effect this was an extension of the Carlen system, as six of the assistant coaches under him were retained by Bell for his staff, along with three additions.

Seawright: "Coach Bell really didn't change anything. He just continued what coach Carlen was doing.

"At that time whoever wanted to come in suited me. I wasn't worryin' about who the coach was. I was worryin' about can our team pull together and play as one. A coach can come in and help pull a team up.

"But we still had the same conflicts, 'cause everybody wanted to play. A lot of frustration. A lot of people 'at' one another. And he (Bell) never could pull it out."

One casualty of the transition was running back Kent Hagood, a freshman from Easley who had been hailed by some as "the next George Rogers." Hagood, who later cited conflicts with an assistant coach, was the team's second leading rusher in 1981 but left school after the season for "personal reasons." (He returned to Carolina when Morrison took over and had great sophomore and junior seasons.)

Bell's first two games indicated promise, as the Gamecocks avenged their 1981 loss to Pacific, 41-6, then dropped Richmond, 30-10. Losses to Duke (30-17) and Georgia (34-18) preceded a 37-10 win over Cincinnati. Carolina fans could accept losses to major opponents, but when Furman came to Columbia and upset the Game-cocks, 38-23, it was the beginning of the end for Bell. A 17-14 win over Navy was the lone bright spot in the final five games, the last of which was a 24-6 loss at Clemson.

Seawright: "Coach Bell was tryin' to find the people who were causing all the frustration. It was really hurting the team. You know, one person can spoil a team. That hurt us in the eighty-one season. But we had some guys on the team who weren't really serious about playing. But, at the same time, you give 'em a chance on the football field, and they'll make something. Most of 'em were complaining about getting a chance. That's what most were complaining about.

"A guy's first string and that's all good. He's better than me. But I'm pretty sure that, if I get a chance to play, I can prove myself and challenge him. I challenge him in practice, but I need to challenge him on the field. That's where a lot of the problems started.

"He (Bell) picked out some of the guys he thought were causing the trouble, but when you pick out some guys who cause trouble, they could also help the team. Like Richard Pryor and Eddie Murphy (comedians), when things are down they like pull you together. Sort of like, cut those two off, and it starts a little bit more frustration. At that time, like in the middle of the season, it was really not enough people playing. And they were looking at a lot of guys.

"And I agree with 'em. I know I played every game, and I know I get tired sometimes, and I want somebody comin' in. I won't lie about that part. A lot of other people should get a chance to get in there and express themselves and show what they can do. I got my chance, so why can't others get their chance? That was a problem—and a lot more stuff."

Invited to compare his first two head coaches, Carlen and Bell, Seawright displayed complete loyalty to both.

Seawright: "You really can't compare coaches. Both had contact (with) and respect for the players. And they told the truth. Both wanted to find a way to pull things together.

"Coach Carlen was the type of coach whose voice would make you come to a stop. He was the type of person that what he says, you take seriously. He wouldn't back down to you or me or anyone. No question who was boss.

"Bell, he was the type of person that, if you don't believe me, I'll show you. Coach Carlen was the type person, if you don't believe me, hit the road. Coach Bell's way was, if I can't make you, I'll break you.

"I'll give Coach Bell credit. He told us they wanted to get rid of some of the coaches on the staff, and he's not gonna get rid of them. If it comes down to his losing his job—which he did—that he would lose his job first, before he'd do something he felt wasn't right. As a coach, that's why I had so much respect for him.

"He was the type of person that, when it came to his coaches, he would lose his job—something he cared about a lot—for his friends. He was really a Gamecock fan, as well as a coach. You can't ask for a better coach than that.

"I don't think he had a long enough chance. To come in one year. Every coach has a different way of how he wants a game plan. You've got to give him more than one year. He had to recruit. 'Cause when you change head coaches, guys we had coming to play for Carolina switched over to a dozen different schools. They (Bell staff) spent a lot of time on the road, tryin' to get players back.

"I'll never say nothin' bad about either one (Carlen and Bell)."

The 1982 season, from Seawright's standpoint, was further complicated by his knee problems, which caused him to miss the Pacific, Duke, and Clemson games and limited his activity in others.

Seawright: "I played the whole season injured. They didn't know what caused my knee to swell up till the eighty-three season. I went into the hospital for two weeks after the Florida State game. I heard Navy and Clemson on the radio. Still I felt that we were getting things together at the end of the season."

The question of how much progress—or lack of—the Gamecocks had made in Bell's first and only season was strictly academic. Within two months Seawright and returning members of the squad were face to face with another head coach, Joe Morrison, who had played 14 years with the New York Giants before becoming a college coach at UT-Chattanooga in 1973. He was a head coach without one day's experience as an assistant.

Seawright: "Coach Morrison had a way in his voice that hypnotizes you. When you sit there and listen to him talk his voice is not like a shout. It's soft and calm. You don't hear no cuss words. You don't hear no screamin'. Just calm. 'Well, men, it's time to go on the field, and you've practiced hard, and you had a good practice. You know, yourself, you had a good practice. There should be no doubt in your mind how you should play the game. Like you practiced. So, you should win this game.'

"And it's like you're hypnotized in your head. You go out on the field and, 'We're s'pose to win this game. We should not lose this game.' And you go out and you just play.

"You come in at halftime, and he'd tell you what you're doing wrong. But he'd never scream at you. And you'd go back out there, and you'd try to make that adjustment. He was the type of person that he'd tell you straight out. He was, 'You don't like my way, it's the highway.'

"Like a lot of guys, they break curfew, and he had 'em rollin' down the hill (near athletic dormitories) with coach Morrison out there blowin' the whistle. He was no rose, but it was like, 'You're men, and I'm gonna treat you like men. We'll do men things, and you know you'll make decisions you're gonna live with. You got a problem, come to me. I'll talk to you, and we'll try to find a solution.'

"I never had a problem. I'm the type of person, when I have a problem I sit in my room, or ride around, or walk. And while people are thinking I'm lookin' at TV, I'm thinkin' inside my head."

When Morrison's staff began spring practice they moved Seawright from inside linebacker to outside, where he had played as a freshman. It was a position that Seawright preferred, and it would reduce the number of confrontations with huge interior offensive linemen, thus relieving his problem knees of some impact.

Spring practice was also a revelation to the squad in that it brought a new meaning to the word "conditioning."

Seawright: "They must have looked at some film, or somebody gave some inside information. Because when Coach (Tom) Gadd (defensive coordinator/outside linebackers) came, we started running. We ain't never run that much. We was like in the army. You run till you can't run. Thirty minutes of running. 'I don't care how you run; I'm not gonna beg you or plead with you. I'm not gonna feel sorry for you. You're gonna do what it takes.' And that's what we did.

"He gave guys like Frank (Wright) hell. If you weighed over 265 pounds, you were fat—a fat "Fire Ant" (nickname attached to the Carolina defensive unit midway of the 1983 season). And you ran, and you were on a diet. And, if you couldn't lose it that way, you'd lose it by running afterward (practice was over). By that time everyone was losin', because we ran so much.

"Coach Gadd's idea was to have a small defense, but strong and quick. And his concept—he wasn't lookin' for any fat tackles. No fat linebackers. He was lookin' for guys who had some weight, if they could run with their weight. 'Okay, if not, you fat fire ants, you lose it.'

"And you don't question him. Some tried it till they found out they lose. 'Cause he can put you through a drill that'll lay you out in five minutes. After the workout you go through, you might not live through it. Sometimes I was tired, but I never let him know how tired I was. I was getting to the point I was gettin' in shape, and it was taking longer to get tired.

"All coaches are different. In eighty-one we had coach (Tom) New. He could tell you some stuff and make you do some stuff you wouldn't believe. You had other coaches that didn't believe in all that cruelty to a human. They believe it's up to you how far you want to go in life.

"Sometimes in practice we'd be hittin', and you get your head hurt. Coach (Bill) Michael (inside linebackers coach under Morrison) would say, 'You didn't even hit hard enough to even go out with Dolly Parton's sister,' or sumpin'. They were all different, but they were comedians. (The Morrison staff.)

"Coach Mike (Bender, offensive line) liked to hit a lot. He'd want to see you knock one another out, if possible.

"Coach (Jim) Washburn (defensive line) was more like tryin' to get Frank and them being the 'Road Warriors,' so they'd look like they're gonna tear the building down, if somebody even smiled at you.

"And coach (Tom) McMahon (defensive secondary) was the type of person that he'd make the cornerbacks look like 'Le Demon,' in a way. He had a quick temper, like if you didn't do something right. And he'd want to make them go against guys two-sixty and two-thirty and stick their face in their neck and knock 'em out, knowin' there's a good sixty or seventy pound weight difference.

"Coach Gadd was like the ruler of everything. He was like a 'Mr. T'. He was a short, funny comedian. But he could kill you in less that two or three minutes. On the field it was more serious. Off the field it was like togetherness.

"All of them have a vocabulary I've never heard. Not cussin' or anything."

The 1983 season was an orientation for both coaching staff and squad, as Morrison installed the veer offense, replacing the "I" of Carlen and Bell. Morrison's staff included five assistants who served under him at New Mexico and one holdover (Bill Michael) from Bell's group.

In 1983 Carolina faced one of the toughest schedules in the nation, including North Carolina, Georgia, Southern Cal, Notre Dame, Louisiana State, Florida State, and Clemson. During this familiarization process the Gamecocks managed a 5-6 record, including a 38-14 rout of Southern Cal, and a 31-7 romp over Navy, both before huge crowds in enlarged (74,000-plus) Williams-Brice Stadium.

The Southern Cal game legitimated the comparison of the Carolina defense to fire ants, as they swarmed over Trojan ball carriers, limiting them to 49 net yards on 41 attempts.

Seawright: "That was when we started jumpin' around. You make a hit, and you jump up and scream. Eleven guys on the team started jumpin' around. 'Cause that's one thing we believed in—everybody being around the pile. Everybody be there before the camera cuts off. You gotta be there because you want to.

"We started readin' necks and helmets, instead of going by action. We go by the linemen. Learned to read the linemen. We weren't readin' running backs. You always read the guy you're in front of, because he's gonna take you to the ball. That was a learning process, because we had to know the defensive scheme, and it takes more than one year to know it.

"So J.D. (Fuller), Rickey Hagood, and those had a rough time. We really didn't know everything we could do with that defense. J.D. and Mike (Durrah) and some of the seniors—they are the guys who threw a puzzle out there. They made it, like paper. Cut out the design, put a little covering over it, and threw it out there. And it was up to us upcoming seniors to find it and put it together. Once that puzzle's completed, we'll have a winning season.

"We came out with a five-six record, but we did some things some people didn't think we could do."

Seawright wasn't injury-free during '83, missing games against Georgia, Southern Cal, and Notre Dame, but it wasn't his knee, but an ankle that was the problem this time.

On the other side of the ball, Carolina's offensive unit improved its competence in the veer offense, with Allen Mitchell becoming *THE* quarterback, thanks to leading a second-half rally that beat Duke at Durham. Sophomores Thomas Dendy and Kent Hagood began to feel more comfortable in their assignments as running backs.

Against Navy (10th game) Carolina was confronted with Napoleon McCallum, the nation's third leading rusher but held him to 62 yards in 21 carries, as the Gamecocks won easily, 31-7. It was McCallum's worst day of the year.

Seawright: "We meant for him to have his worst day. We didn't give him anything, inside or outside. If you play a running team, try to make 'em throw. If it's a throwin' team, try to make 'em run.

"I don't think there are any gods in runners. All of them have their thing. I never put a running back down, but you're only as good as your linemen. Kent and Thomas are just as good as McCallum."

On the subject of running backs, the name of Herschel Walker, Heisman Trophy winner at Georgia in 1982, was introduced. Seawright had faced the Walker-led Bulldogs in his freshman and sophomore years.

Seawright: "I would not say that Herschel Walker is a tough runner. He won't lower his head and try to knock you off. My sophomore year we had him pinned (33 yards in the first half). He couldn't get any yards. In the second half they started sweeps, and he got outside. (Walker finished with 143 yards.)

"The only person I've played against that I feel is a tough person to try to stop is Kent Hagood. I'm not saying that because he's on the team. I'm saying it because I've got a great deal of respect for the man. 'Cause he'll lower his shoulder, and he'll try to knock you out. He doesn't try to do that dodgin' junk.

"Walker will try to get to the corner or cut inside you, but it's not like, 'You're in my way, I'm gonna knock you down.' And keep on going.

"George Rogers was like that, but I never played against him. I told him one time that I wouldn't mind tackling him one time!"

Carolina was locked in a desperate struggle in the 1984 opener against heavy underdog The Citadel in Williams-Brice Stadium. The Bulldogs led, 21-14, at halftime and kicked a score-tying field goal in the fourth quarter, but Quinton Lewis connected to split end Chris Wade on a 40-yard halfback option pass with 1:02 left on the clock to give the Gamecocks a shaky victory. Fans left unimpressed and with little anticipation of what would take place during the rest of the campaign.

Seawright: "I knew at halftime we would win. Coach Morrison said, 'I know it's your first game, and everybody's a little nervous. This is not how you practiced. Let's get back out and play like we're s'pose to. Offense, let's get some points on the board. Defense, let's get back out there and stop 'em.'

"After The Citadel we said. 'That's one down, let's chalk-up another one. I never think negative—don't look back. Except to look at film to see how we played.

"Duke? We knew coach Bell (he became defensive coordinator at Duke when he left South Carolina) was at Duke, and we had respect for coach Bell. But we didn't want coach Bell, with all this law suit and stuff, to come in and win. We had to win that one.

"I felt good inside, because I was back to where I was used to playing. Every guy I went against was a challenge. I'd say, 'You got fifty or sixty pounds more than me. Let's see what you can do with it.' (Seawright had been returned to the inside linebacker position for his senior season.)

"You make more tackles—you're in on everything. Outside you had to do too much sittin' back, and I wanted to go in and make something happen. I'm hoping, if I go pro . . . inside. I can play well against any offense, if I do the things that coach Gadd and coach Michael taught me.

"I've learned something from every coach, and that's gotten me this far."

The term "this far" included some exciting victories in 1984, as Carolina won its first nine games, including The Citadel, Duke (21-0), Georgia (17-10), Kansas State (49-17), Pittsburgh (45-21), Notre Dame (36-32), East Carolina (42-20), N.C. State (35-29), and Florida State (38-26). Seawright insists that one victory doesn't mean any more than another, and no loss hurts more than any other.

Seawright: "Notre Dame? Beating them didn't mean a thing. I was just glad we beat 'em at—what's that thing—the dome? You don't have to be Notre Dame to come out there and be somebody. You could be a Gamecock!

"N.C. State? I hate the sound of that wolf—that made us mad. Everytime they score they play a little howl—a record or something- and we just can't stand it.

"Florida State? That's the one game I thought we'd have trouble. It was like a surprise for me. In the first quarter I got hit on the knee, and I was out I sat on the sidelines and watched Bryant Gilliard's four interceptions. Willie McIntee (defensive end), Otis Morris (cornerback), Harry South (defensive end), and Shaun Sadler (defensive back) also got hurt. But we'd been playing a lot of players, and we didn't feel like the pressure was on us that much. You like the pressure, but you know a fresh guy is better than a tired guy, and you can go out there and give everything you got. And, if you're tired, somebody's coming in to relieve you. That way your mind is clear, and you're thinking clearly and ready to give a hundred per cent. Freshmen, sophomores, juniors comin' in. They knew what they were doing.

"I forgot all about TV (the game was televised nationally by ABC-TV), because I had to pull down my pants to get my leg wrapped!"

During the nine-game win streak South Carolina had moved steadily through the national rankings and, after the impressive showing against the Seminoles was rated No. 2 behind unbeaten Brigham Young in both the Associated Press and United Press International polls. Carolina fans were already discussing which major bowl they would prefer—Orange, Sugar, or Cotton.

Gamecock supporters were also buying anything black they could get their hands on, as Morrison's black coaching attire inspired the trend, which had now been described as "Black Magic." Seawright was at a loss to define "Black Magic," but he and his close friend, Frank Wright, agreed that it was probably the fans, who fanatically supported the Gamecocks wherever they played. It was the crowd that injected that extra measure of enthusiasm into the players, which prompted visiting teams to begin describing Williams-Brice Stadium as one of the tougher places to play.

Unfortunately Carolina's tenth game, which had been scheduled in Columbia, was switched to Navy's home field at Annapolis, Maryland, so that the Gamecocks wouldn't have too many home games. Still there were as many South Carolinians among the 27,000 fans in Navy-Marine Corps Stadium as there were Midshipmen supporters.

Whether playing in Columbia would have made any difference will never be known, but the game ended Carolina's streak, 38-21, and the bowl picture was dramatically changed. While the Carolina-Navy game was in progress ABC-TV commentator Beano Cook reported during halftime of a nationally-televised game that Carolina and Orange Bowl officials had already reached an agreement for the Gamecocks to play in Miami, regardless of how the Gamecocks fared at Navy or Clemson.

Of course, NCAA policies forbade any such agreement prior to November 10, so Orange Bowl officials reacted with a denial, although ABC-TV had based their story on "inside sources."

Regardless, there was a lot of bowl talk in the air prior to the Navy game. One of the missing ingredients in the Gamecock defense that Saturday afternoon was Seawright, who had wanted to play but was held out to avoid risking aggravation of the injury received in the Florida State game.

Seawright: "The press people I talked to asked me about the bowl situation. I said, 'I don't want to know, 'cause I've got nothing to do with it. I'm here to get an education and play football.' Suddenly it hit me, 'We're behind.' We didn't have that fire. We came out in the second half and said, 'Let's work that magic again' But we didn't. Lots of fans were talkin' about the Orange Bowl and Clemson, but that didn't have any effect. Navy just came out and played."

One of the wands in Carolina's magic was the throwing arm of quarterback Mike Hold, who watched Allen Mitchell start the first ten games but came off the bench to initiate some spectacular plays throughout the season. A 62-yard pass to Ira Hillary set-up the winning TD against Georgia, and a 43-yarder to Eric Poole on the last play of the first half gave Carolina an insurmountable lead over Kansas State. Scoring passes of 31 and 33 yards to Chris Wade put the Pittsburgh game out of reach, and Hold's 33-yard run in the fourth quarter provided the margin over Notre Dame. A 71-yard strike moved Carolina ahead to stay against East Carolina, and a 61-yard scoring toss to Chris Corley put the Gamecocks ahead of N.C. State for the first time in the fourth quarter. Hold's 44-yard pass to Hillary at the Florida State two set-up a TD that gave the Gamecocks a 17-7 halftime lead.

In the final game of the season against arch rival Clemson, Hold had a 36-yard pass to Wade and several key runs in an 84-yard drive that gave Carolina the winning margin (22-21), with only 54 seconds remaining on the clock.

Seawright insisted that the Clemson game meant no more to him than any of the others, in spite of growing up near the Tiger campus, and the fact that the Gamecocks hadn't beaten Clemson during his college career.

Seawright: "I wanted to go out winning and beat the teams (Georgia, Pittsburgh, Notre Dame, Florida State) that had beaten me, a least once in my life. And I did.

"When we were behind twenty-one to seven at the half we got back to the dressing room, and coach Morrison talked to us. Then we split-up into groups to find out what we were doing wrong on defense and what we needed to do. Had to help the right linebacker out some. He was getting too many reads. Quit missin' tackles, keep the quarterback inside. And HIT. That's what we did. I had fun. We'd go in the huddle, and I'd say, 'All right, Frank (Wright), I'm lookin' at you. One more time, let's go.'

"Clemson was talkin' junk, but the referees was tellin' us to quit talkin'. One guy hit me, and I made a tackle, and I said, 'I'm gonna be on you all night long.' Then I said to myself, 'Wait a minute, I'm in Clemson now.' So I just hit, and don't say nuthin'. But that don't bother me none. In the game of football it's all in the mind, and I was playing like I wanted to. And, to get a person talkin' junk, he forgets what he's s'pose to do. And he starts makin' mistakes. Like any other sport, it's a MIND game."

So, in spite of the victory over a Clemson team that had been the consensus pick to win the national championship in pre-season polls, Carolina had to settle for a bid to the Gator Bowl to play Oklahoma State on December 28. The Orange Bowl bid went to Washington (10-1), a team that had never been scouted by bowl officials.

Seawright: "When a ten-one team like ours goes to the Gator Bowl, something's wrong. That had some effect on our team—I had some questions myself. However, I don't think it hurt my playing (in the Gator Bowl).

"Even if we had ended up eleven-one, we still wouldn't have been champions, 'cause we were in Jacksonville. We didn't play in the number one bowl. Next year we'll be back, and it won't be any Gator Bowl. Orange Bowl or Cotton Bowl. The James Seawrights, Wrights, Gilliards, Corleys and all the seniors—we may be gone—but our spirits will still be there."

The Gator Bowl was almost Black Magic, but not quite. This time it was Oklahoma State that sustained a long time-running-out drive to down the Gamecocks, 21-14, after Carolina had rallied to take a 14-13 lead in the second half. It was definitely not a case of the Gamecocks being unprepared or unmotivated, as the school had never won a bowl game in five previous efforts.

Seawright: "He (Morrison) wanted to make you comfortable; he wanted you to enjoy it. But his main thought—you could look in his eyes—WIN! We gonna win. We're gonna practice hard, and we're gonna win. Practice sessions were hard, and we went out and played hard, and it came down to the final seconds. They (Oklahoma State)

James Seawright (45) participates in sacking Clemson quarterback Mike Eppley in 22-21 victory in 1984. (Photo courtesy of The State, Columbia)

used a little of our magic. Before the game I told reporters, 'It'll come down to who wants to get dirty more, and it's gonna be in the fourth quarter.' If I'm not successful in sports, I might be a mind reader!"

You'll never detect an ounce of regret over anything during Seawright's college experience, during which he saw the worst of times and the best of times. It comes across that he takes greatest satisfaction in being a part of raising the Gamecock football program to a new and permanent high. He expresses unqualified optimism about the future of the sport at his alma mater.

Seawright: "There'll be plenty of Seawrights. Plenty of guys with Frank's (Wright) potential. There'll be plenty of guys with Corley's hands and Bryant Gilliard's feet. We've had them through the years, but we just couldn't find the puzzle. Black Magic? I don't know, ask the coach. I do know what Carolina pride is. Guys who'll go out on a limb and give everything they've got on every play.

"If you believe in yourself . . . When I came here they were teasing me about being little, but I've never backed down. You can do anything, if you put your mind to it. Every game I've played, I've not been satisfied. Haven't been satisfied with how I played. I think I could have given it a little bit more.

"I've gotten my goals where I can see them in sight, but I can never reach them. I may come close, but I never get my hands on it."

Seawright has "gotten his hands on" a lot of achievements that millions of young boys would consider enough for a lifetime. He was named to several All-America first teams, including the Associated Press, which carried with it an appearance on the Bob Hope Christmas Special on NBC-TV. He also played in the Senior Bowl at Mobile, Alabama, where the cream of the college football talent officially turn professional.

Teammate Del Wilkes, offensive guard, joined him on the AP All-America, making it the first time two players from Carolina had been named in the same season. In fact, George Rogers was SC's only previous first team choice by AP.

Ask James to name people who have helped him along the way, and he'll hand you a long list, but there's no doubt who would be at the top.

Seawright: "My mother. She was like a father and mother to me when she got a divorce when I was a freshman in high school. She was always doing stuff for me when I needed it, and now I feel it's my time. I can never pay her back in the time that she'll be living. But to go out and do the stuff I want to do for her, so she can sorta relax, that's my life. She came to every home game since I started and even wanted to go to the Senior Bowl, but I told her, 'No.'"

There would be a number of coaches, head and assistant, on Seawright's list, along with a family that he describes as extremely close. He recalls a day in 1982, when his first college coach, Carlen, visited him in the hospital and told him, "You're the number one linebacker I've ever seen and ever coached." And Seawright replied, "Coach, I've seen some great coaches, and you were one of them."

James Seawright looked to the future with nothing but confidence, aspiring to play in the pros, but adding, "I want to do more with my life than play football." Down the road is a possible career somewhere in the field of criminal justice.

What kind of a professional player will James Seawright be?

Seawright: "He's going to be himself—crazy, wild, and anytime a challenge comes to him, he's gonna take it. I don't care where they put me. I'm not worried about lettin' anybody down, because the only person I can let down is myself."

Seawright was somewhat disappointed that it wasn't until the 11th round of the NFL draft on May 1 that he was picked by the Buffalo Bills, and his record of injuries during his college career might have been the reason he didn't go higher. His consensus All-America teammate, Del Wilkes, fared even worse, being completely ignored in the draft and facing a free agent entry into the NFL.

However, professional careers are made on the field, and pro history is full of cases when high draft choices failed and late-round or free agent players made it big. Both Seawright and Wilkes had fought uphill battles before, and both had made it to the top.

Three other Gamecock seniors were chosen in the draft, including wide receiver Ira Hillary, 8th round to Kansas City; tackle Frank Wright, 9th round to the New York Giants; and defensive back Earl Johnson, 9th round to New Orleans.

The year 1984 will go down in the University of South Carolina's football history as something special, because that was the year in which so many good things happened to so many people who had suffered so much in the way of disappointment. Joe Morrison was the "magician" that brought the ingredients together, making such a season attainable, but the dictionary describes magic as "any mysterious, seemingly inexplicable, or extraordinary power or influence."

Perhaps it would have happened, even if James Seawright had never dressed-out in garnet jersey number forty-five, because, as he insists, there were "Seawrights" in the past and there'll be more in the future.

However, if any one player represented the embodiment of the talent, spirit, and strength of purpose which Morrison brought into focus to produce the magic season, it would be James Seawright, a young man who was hypnotized into realizing the full potential of his body, mind, and—most convincingly—his heart.